# THE ROCK AND THE SAND

is a fascinating account of Catholic
missionary work in north-western
Australia – and of the dedicated men
and women whose work was
sometimes inspired, sometimes blind,
but whose sole aim was to convert
the Aborigines to Christianity.

Also by Mary Durack

KINGS IN GRASS CASTLES

and published by Corgi Books

Mary Durack

# The Rock and
the Sand

**CORGI BOOKS**
A DIVISION OF TRANSWORLD PUBLISHERS LTD

# THE ROCK AND THE SAND

A CORGI BOOK 0 552 11054 X

Originally published in Great Britain
by Constable & Co. Ltd.

PRINTING HISTORY
Constable Edition published 1969
Corgi Edition published 1971
Corgi Edition published 1979
Reprinted 1985

This book is set in 10-11 Times

Corgi Books are published by Transworld Publishers Ltd.,
Century House, 61–63 Uxbridge Road,
Ealing, London, W5 5SA
Made and Printed in Australia by
The Dominion Press–Hedges & Bell, Victoria

*To the memory of*
*Father Ernest Ailred Worms, S.A.C.*
*Missionary, anthropologist*
*and dedicated interpreter of*
*the Aboriginal point of view*

# CONTENTS

# ILLUSTRATIONS

Bishop Matthew Gibney in 1887
(*Battye Library, Perth*)
Father Duncan McNab, pioneer missionary
Aboriginal elder of Western Kimberley
Aboriginal dancer with headdress
Group of West Kimberley coastal Aborigines
West Kimberley coastal Aborigines with a catch of
dugongs or sea-cows
Dampierland Aborigines on a raft
Broome, about 1900 (*Battye Library, Perth*)
Foreshore quarters for Broome pearling crews
(*Battye Library, Perth*)
Second church in Broome
First church at Beagle Bay mission
(*Battye Library, Perth*)
Mrs. Daisy Bates in 1901
(*Battye Library, Perth*)
Pallottine missionary Father William Drostë in 1923
Mother Antonio O'Brien, about 1920
Church at Beagle Bay mission
(*West Australian Newspapers Ltd.*)
Father Ernest A. Worms
(*West Australian Newspapers Ltd.*)
Father Francis Huegel
One of the compensations of a missionary's life
Pope Pius XII receiving from Bishop Otto Raible a
copy of the anthropological works of Father Worms
The brothers Remigius and Gabriel Balgalai
(*West Australian Newspapers Ltd.*)

# FOREWORD

The Most Reverend John Jobst, D.D., S.A.C.
Lord Bishop of Broome
Broome
Western Australia

My Lord Bishop,
    Here at last is the story of your missions that grew from a
series of illustrated articles written in 1961. You will no
doubt recall how research for this minor task revealed that
not only the record of missionary endeavour in Kimberley
but much of the unwritten history of the district, with its
pearling and pastoral industries, lay in the quickly deteriorating records of the mission centres and the memories of
their ageing people. It was material that would clearly be
lost if an immediate attempt were not made to assemble it,
to follow up the clues it provided and to distil fact from
legend by relating spoken and documentary evidence; and
so, with your trusting co-operation, this work was begun.
    The task proved more formidable and far-reaching than I
had imagined, as the fortunes of these remote mission outposts were closely linked with those of Western Australia as
a whole and also with overseas events that led to successive
religious bodies from France, Germany and Italy entering
the field. The work has involved the study of hundreds of
church and departmental records, files and reports, books,
theses and newspaper articles, as well as interviews with
government officials, missionaries, anthropologists, poli-
ticians, pastoralists, pearlers and Kimberley residents of
various colours in other walks of life – some in favour, some
critical and some politely dubious of missionary work.

11

Many notebooks have been filled with data gathered from mission-educated people scattered through the State or resident at Beagle Bay and Lombadina. Because of the native tendency to give the story thought most likely to please, this information was usually taken at group interviews in which the people corrected or checked each other until satisfied that the account was as near the truth as possible. Even seemingly irrelevant details obtained in this way provided clues to episodes that would otherwise have been lost and that I was later able to follow up through obscure records. One such instance was the natives' frequent reference to a 'poor old Father Mac-a-nab' which set me on the trail of the almost forgotten Scottish missionary who preceded the French Trappist monks to the Dampierland area.

The completion of my project has been so long delayed that you may almost have forgotten my undertaking it and might wish, on reading the result of my labours, that I had been less persevering. I can only say that I have tried to present as balanced a picture as possible from the material at my disposal and to keep in mind the quotation from Cicero's *De Oratore* used by Pope Leo XIII when throwing open the Vatican Archives for historical research: 'The first law of history is to dread uttering falsehood, the next, not to fear stating the truth; lastly, that the historian's writing should be open to no suspicion of partiality or of animosity.'

To be free from any bias is of course all but impossible. A commitment to Christianity is a bias to begin with but I did not set out to produce an apology either for Christian missions in general or Catholic missions in particular. It was my aim rather to give as honest an account as possible of the circumstances in which missionary work was undertaken and continued in north-western Australia, the people to whom it was directed and those who espoused or opposed the task. I have tried to show the effects of different personalities, methods, attitudes and outside events on these isolated fields of activity and to trace recent changes of

12

public opinion that promise a brighter era for the full-blood and part Aborigines of Australia.

It would be misleading to suggest, however, that I was in no way personally involved in my subject. The Kimberley district is the 'spirit country' of my earliest memories and its Aborigines claimed my affections long before I reached any understanding of their situation as a race. Some of the missionaries associated with this book I have known almost from childhood. Others I have come to know and to venerate over the years, the more so since my research has revealed the steadfastness of their purpose and its overall results.

My work on this chronicle would have been greatly limited but for the wholehearted assistance of the Perth Diocesan Archivist the Reverend Father John Senan Moynihan, formerly editor of the Dublin literary magazine *The Capuchin Annual*. Father Moynihan not only furnished me with all the relevant material from the central archives but joined me in my quest for the more elusive characters concerned, read the text with a critical eye for historical and ecclesiastical detail and was an unfailing source of ready reference and warm encouragement throughout.

For detailed information concerning the French religious who left the imprint of their charity and their agricultural skill on that arid land, I am indebted to the generous help of the Cistercian historian the Reverend Father Joseph O'Dea, who obtained records from the monastery of Sept Fons from which the monks came. I would like to mention also the great assistance and co-operation I have been given at all times by the Battye Archives, Perth, the Nedlands Public Library, the University Library Crawley, and also to West Australian Newspapers Ltd., for help in obtaining photographs. I am deeply grateful too for the help and advice of G. C. Bolton, professor of history at the University of Western Australia, to my brother Kim Durack, who checked the text with scholarly care a few weeks before his death in

May 1968, and to the unfailing patience and efficiency of Marjorie Rees who typed the ms. in at least three drafts.

To the St. John of God nuns, dispersed among the centres from Broome, and Derby to Balgo Hills on the desert frontier, I owe a special debt for notes and information painstakingly supplied and for the trust and friendship, not to mention the cups of tea that have so often revived my flagging spirits. Thinking of the cheerful kindness emanating from the oldest to the youngest of your widely scattered communities and of all the help and hospitality the missions have extended me from the time of my old friend Bishop Raible, I would like to have been able to include in this generally rather sombre story more of the lighter side of mission life and of the experiences I enjoyed when collecting material. I have happy memories of the expeditions your Lordship shared with me, including the search for Father McNab's base on Disaster Bay and our interesting encounter on Cygnet Bay with the old Aboriginal who had accompanied Father Nicholas Emo to the Benedictine mission on Drysdale River in 1908.

With so many deserving of special thanks and appreciation it may be wondered why I should dedicate the book especially to Father Ernest Worms. This I have done because he was the first to impress on me the importance of studying and appreciating the Aboriginal in the context of his own culture. I knew Father Worms from the time of his arrival in Kimberley in the late 1920s and followed his anthropological articles with the keenest interest from that time on. His penetrating and respectful approach to every aspect of Aboriginal life moved me deeply and was largely instrumental in convincing me that I should persevere with this checkered history. We corresponded fairly frequently after he left the Kimberleys and discussed from its inception the book he planned to call *The Religion of the Australian Aborigines*. I saw him for the last time in Sydney in 1962 when he had just completed this great work which he knew would be his last.

The few years since his death have shown an amazing

change of attitude towards the people he loved so much and whose culture and point of view he strove always to interpret. The small band of idealists who worked so long alone for the welfare of the native people have not today, for all their difficulties, to contend with as strong a cross-current of public and official apathy as previously, for which reason I am able to conclude this narrative on an unexpectedly optimistic note.

The extent to which past missionary work has benefited the Aborigines will be differently assessed according to the reader's own criteria. One who sees progress in purely material terms may find little to have justified the continuance of these establishments in the face of such terrific odds. Those who seek evidence of the wholehearted conversion of the Aborigines and their satisfactory integration into the white man's social system may also find reason to doubt. Be that as it may, it seems clear to me at the conclusion of my task that the work of the missionaries, sometimes inspired, sometimes blind, was the only evidence the Aborigines had of anything in the nature of consistent altruism within an otherwise ruthless and self-seeking economy. It provided a ray of hope in the prevailing gloom of their predicament. It was for many their only means of survival and their sole reason for regeneration.

With thanks for your trust in placing before me the documentary evidence of the years I send you at last what I have made of it. If it can contribute anything to an understanding of the cause to which your Lordship has brought so much initiative, courage to experiment and breadth of vision I shall be more than gratified.

Warmest greetings
MARY DURACK

June 1968

*The Rock and the Sand*

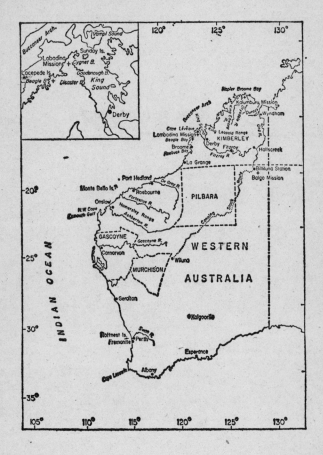

Time without time was the dreaming and of the dreaming was the land and the life that was one with the land. And the people of the land were kindred of all that was made and had right neither of birth nor of might but of the law. And the creator spirits had union with the children of the dreaming outside the domain of the flesh and kept new the law that was the source and strength of life.

# CHAPTER ONE

THE people of the dream watched the people of the clock come out of the sea and strike their flagstaff firmly into the sand. They assumed that these pale-skinned mariners were the spirits of their ancestors returned from the islands of the dead and that they would act in accordance with ancient intertribal etiquette. When gifts were exchanged on the beach the only curious sign had been the eagerness of the newcomers to retrieve the ticking timepieces that the natives had found a diverting novelty, but this breach was forgiven as being an understandable lapse of memory.

Tht strangers, for their part, secure in the certain values of expanding empire, had no doubt that the simple but apparently intelligent primitives would soon appreciate the blessings of civilization and gladly abandon their godless and feckless ways for those of a superior culture.

Both people were mistaken, for the clock was not a toy but a way of life, as the dreaming was a way of life, the one defining time by an arrow, the other in terms of heavenly bodies and seasonal change. Neither could appreciate the other's logic, but whereas the Aborigines learned to anticipate the whiteman's conduct with reasonable accuracy, they themselves were seldom, if ever, to behave as was expected.

Certain unpredictable tendencies, noted with some indulgence at the beginning of settlement, were to prove a mere prelude to the repertoire of contrariness on the programme of history. Benevolence would be found prone to result in thankless exploitation; forthright self-interest in loyal cooperation. Confidence in the natives' potential would court disillusionment; denial of their mental capacity invite surprising evidence to the contrary. Expected to flourish under improved conditions the people would lie down and die; lamented as a dying race they would unaccountably revive.[1] Encouraged into the new economy they would languish for loss of their tribal ways; given reserves they would be drawn to the amenities of civilization; withheld citizenship and social benefits, the injustice of their situation would strike at the whiteman's self-esteem, but let them be granted equality in all material respects and the whiteman would stand condemned by their spiritual deprivation and lack of incentive. Let Welfare Departments declare a policy of assimilation and the dark people would rediscover their pride of race; recognize their right to a separate identity and they would suspect a move towards segregation. Set up a Royal Commission of inquiry and it would be found that there was no longer one dark race with specific problems but a mixture of races with many different problems and in many different stages of development; attempt to grade their needs according to colour and it would appear that the degenerate near-white could be more dependent than the robust black.

In fact, what had seemed at first sight a relatively simple matter was to become one of such growing complexity over the years that the shattered tribespeople could not, had they tried, have devised a more subtle retribution. They had planned nothing of the sort, of course. They had merely reacted as human beings to the shock of impact with a race unable to concede them a point of view and in whose outlook they found neither solace nor sincerity.

Such a state of affairs is by no means unique in history, for what indigenous people was ever successfully integrated into an invading culture? It might well be claimed, however, that of all subjugated races the Aborigines were the most mysterious and hence the most misunderstood.

The impression they gave was a false one from the beginning, for despite their primitive implements, nomadic hunting economy, innocent nakedness and lack of worldly goods they were not living relics of some manlike species that preceded *homo sapiens*. They were in every way representatives of Modern Man, their religious beliefs and ceremonies integrated into a close-knit and logical sequence of transcendent elements far removed from what was taken for a primitive confusion of purely fear-inspired magic and animistic rites.

Thrown on their own resources – how many thousands of years ago, after what incredible journeys, from what far land or many lands? – ocean-locked within a country that provided no plants that might be cultivated for grain crops, no animals to be ridden or husbanded as flocks and herds, far from the trade routes of cultural exchange, they had developed a pattern of survival that becomes ever more impressive in the increasing light of scientific research. Within a system based on a highly intricate framework of social and religious laws, the continent was divided – how or at what time who can say? – into a network of some five hundred tribes, each subdivided into hordes or minor groups with distinctive traditions and modes of speech. Their languages had continued to branch and diversify through countless generation. Many differed radically and each had its distinctive and well evolved grammatical form, but in common with other races generally considered more 'advanced', the Aborigines had developed no form of writing beyond the simple 'message stick' which required the interpretation of the bearer.

The law, powerful by right of mystical authority and in some respects harsh to outside eyes, constrained its people to the limitations of the land. Its ancient convention disciplined or destroyed the rebel, the greedy and the importunate, abandoned the ailing and the weak in the interests of the fit. Attributing creative ideas or special skills to supernatural agencies, it kept its tribesmen down to size, restrained personal ambitions to prescribed outlets and channelled competitive drive into group solidarity. But, austere as the environment with which it was so closely linked, the law was rich in myth and legend, in sacred ritual and secular dance and song. A complicated kinship system

23

established the tribal relationship of its children and, more in keeping with Oriental than Christian religious concept, lnked them in mystical association with the land and all that sprang from it. But the importance of human life was never underestimated. Man was both flesh and spirit, and his life a significant progression from pre-existence, birth and death into a hereafter, not of reward and punishment but of continuity as some part of the life stream of Eternal Dreaming.

The early colonists, absorbed in their own struggle for survival, are hardly to be blamed for their ignorance of this complicated and interlocking structure of tribal life, for it was after all several generations before scientists began to understand its overall significance. On the whole Australian settlers showed no less, if no more idealism than other colonizing people. As in all similar situations the invader was the implement of history and the indigenous race its victim.

The settlement established at Swan River on the west coast in 1829, with whose outcome this history is concerned, began with the loftiest intentions towards the Aborigines This project was founded under the upright leadership of Captain James Stirling, a Scottish naval officer whose company comprised a small detachment of soldiers and a selection of British county families with their servants and agricultural labourers.

Most of these people, in retreat from the industrial upsurge at home, had sold all they possessed for a chance of finding new horizons and implanting the best traditions of the old world in this untamed land. Their settling in was simplified by the friendly welcome of the local Bibbulmun, a term meaning literally 'many breasts' and applied to a large tribal group whose territory extended from Jurien Bay in the north to Esperance in the south. A temperate region of fine forests, rivers, lakes and streams, it provided well for its children and their law of hospitality had hitherto implied no hardship.

Captain Stirling held solemn parley with the tribal leaders, embracing their people into the favoured family of

24

the British Empire and placing them under her protection. His policy, at least in its original form, was strongly influenced by the condescending though conscientious humanitarian movements of the day, the prevailing image of primitive man as Noble Savage requiring that local customs were accorded due respect. The question of tribal rights was never raised, for as the tribespeople had shown no resentment of this intrusion on their land, and there was no evidence of any cultivation or permanent settlement, it was assumed that they were footloose nomads, lacking all sense of ownership or attachment to particular areas.

It would have been difficult for the Aborigines, even had they seen the necessity, to explain that they were nomadic only within inherited boundaries. It did not, at this stage, occur to them that they could actually be driven from their land, for although intertribal issues were contested from time to time, the possession of territory had never been in dispute. Whether a native's inheritance included fertile river or coastal frontages or comprised little more than arid dunes and barren gibber plains, he could conceive of no country as being more desirable. It was the mother that had begotten and nurtured him and to which he was bound by ties of both flesh and spirit.

In the early years of the western colony invitations were extended, on the one hand, to witness church services, military parades and formal balls, and, on the other, to attend tribal corroborees and displays of skill with spear and boomerang. Gentle English ladies sipped tea with friendly elders; gifts were exchanged and the children of black and white played together with the smiling approval of all concerned.

But no amount of goodwill could reconcile the way of the dreaming with the way of the clock. Nor were the two concepts of time the only obstacle to understanding. A mutual ideal of brotherly love that promised a basis for dialogue was cancelled out by the opposing scales of value and the radically different views of men's relationship to each other and to the land.

The Bibbulmun mother of the many breasts, resistant at first, after all failed her children, yielding acre by acre to the axe and the plough, allowing the natural tribal boundaries to be defaced, the sacred waters and increase sites to be fenced off. As settlement pressed on inexorably the bewildered tribesmen sometimes struck out but their attacks were seen as treacherous and unreasonable resistance to progress rather than a rightful defence of property. There were killings, reprisals and attempts at reconciliation on both sides but the outcome was unfortunately predictable.

So rapidly did the image of the noble and amiable savage degenerate into that of the treacherous nigger that within twenty years of the foundation of the colony a Church leader, in a sincere effort to present a reasonable assessment of the situation, was moved to write to the Secretary of State for the Colonies:

... I cannot agree in opinion with those who either deny to the natives of W$^n$ Australia the enjoyment of reason or ascribe to the whole race propensities so vicious, so malignant and so treacherous as would degrade them even below the level of the brute creation. I consider the moral and intellectual character of the natives of New Holland by no means inferior to that of any other dark description of men.

I can neither admit the reasoning nor admire the humanity of those who, after taking possession of their country and depriving them of their hunting grounds where they found heretofore the Kangaroo, the Emu, and the Opossum in great abundance compell them to retire into the mountains and barren country there to drag out a miserable existence, living upon lizards, the larva of insects, and roots, describing them as [not] being capable of civilization, calling them a race of cannibals upon whom the hand of nature had set the mark of malediction, and, in order to persecute them the more, they assert publicly and wantonly that it is necessary to treat them with

26

rigour, otherwise it would be impossible to live in the country. . . .

That the natives of Western Australia behave to others according to the treatment they receive may be faithfully gathered from the best sources of information. They have not, indeed, reached that sublime height, that beautiful principle of Christian morality: 'The returning good for evil' probably because they have not the example set them by their oppressors. . . .

Alas! the wicked policy of designing men joined to the most cruel and insatiable avarice deliver up to destruction numbers of those poor children of nature who will one day rise up in judgment against those wholesale murderers and they will sooner or later feel the weight of Divine justice, which although slow in taking revenge for the innocent blood that they have spilt and which cries to Heaven for vengeance will fall one day upon their guilty heads as did the blood of Abel upon the head of Cain. . . .

I beg leave therefore to submit to Your Lordship's kind consideration the enclosed plan which after long experience and mature deliberation is considered the best adapted to the wants of the Aborigines of Western Australia . . .[2]

But when the settlement was only thirty years old it was obvious enough that the south-western tribespeople were on the way out, the majority, not as a result of violence but from contact with sicknesses against which they had no immunity and with a driving force that had changed the face and nature of the land.

By this time settlement had begun to move north of the temperate region of winter rain to which the million-square-mile colony had been hitherto restricted.[3] Here good open grazing country and coastal waters abounding in high quality pearl shell had promised rapid prosperity, but the north-west did not yield easily to settlement. Aborigines, less

27

submissive than in the south, chased and killed the precious stock, and the cyclonic rains, on which so much depended in that arid land, too often swept out to sea to menace the settlers' lifeline of coastal cargo ships. Sheep could subsist indefinitely on spinifex if wells were provided but cattle could not survive drought seasons that extended sometimes over seven years. Pioneer pastoralists, in order to withstand hard times, therefore took up spare-time pearling activities while struggling pearlers embarked on sideline grazing interests.

Since white workers were costly and hard to come by and the government had refused convict labour[4] for the north-west settlers, local Aborigines were pressed into service. Native labour, more or less abandoned in the south as lazy and unreliable, proved of great value here.[5] In this area of vast leasehold properties the people's tribal lives were not immediately threatened by the press of settlement and a reasonable compromise was possible. Native men and women took readily to the saddle, learned to control the wandering stock, helped to sink wells and to put up shacks, fences and yards. They also entered cheerfully into the dry shelling game and as they were rewarded in proportion to their take, proceeded from dredging the shallows with their nets to diving from luggers into deep water.[6] For this the women showed even more enthusiasm than their men and would dive, naked, to a depth of ten fathoms, emerging minutes later, their canvas neck bags crammed to capacity.

By 1868, ten boats operating in and around Nickol Bay had shipped away £6,000 worth of mother-of-pearl, mostly procured by native women, and soon the news went forth that there were fortunes for the taking along the north-west coast. Before long the rising price of shell and the discovery of a few big pearls attracted traders from China, Java, the Celebes and the Dutch East Indies. It was to these, for the most part unscrupulous, adventurers that the original pioneers attributed the breakdown of trust on the part of the Aborigines that flared into the spearing of a pearler at the end of 1868. This was quickly followed by the kind of reprisal that, if it taught a lesson to the tribespeople at all, it was not the one intended. More spearings followed by even harsher reprisals, merely succeeded in dispersing the people so that their labour, particularly in the pearling industry, became harder to secure. A few enterprising crew masters moving farther up the coast became skilled in the art of luring natives on to their luggers, while others, seeing the writing on the wall, began importing crews from Malaya and the Celebes.

Companies soon began running fleets of luggers attended by luxuriously equipped 'mother' schooners from which the owners supervised the operations and collected the shell to pack for market. Cossack, the port of Nickol Bay, was then the main pearling centre, but rumours of rich new beds sent schooners, luggers, sloops and junks speeding to Exmouth Gulf, Admiralty Bay, the Monte Bello Islands and the Buccaneer Archipelago, prospecting reefs and inlets as far north as La Grange and Roebuck Bay.

At the start of the summer lay-up the fleets made for the shelter of the tidal creeks where repairs went on until the end of the monsoons, but sometimes a 'blow' or 'cockeye bob' would catch them unawares. Only occasional boats and lives had been lost before the latter part of 1871 when the discovery of a rich bed tempted pearlers to gamble on a late monsoon. The first 'cockeye' of the season pounced a savage surprise – its kill, twenty-two boats and all but a handful of their crews, mostly Aboriginal. But a fatalistic attitude had grown hand in hand with the pearling industry that was by that time the most remunerative in the colony.

As the price of shell continued to increase, so did the traffic in native crews. 'Shanghaied' divers were held in labour pools on isolated islands to meet seasonal demands. Others were locked in the smothering heat of the holds when the luggers lay within swimming distance of the shore. Natives with damaged lungs, often sick with scurvy and venereal disease, were cast off to fend for themselves along the coast, and stories of cruel abuse began to spread abroad.

Pearlers denied allegations while denouncing pastoralists

for inhumanity and massacre. Pastoralists deplored the un-principled traffickings of the pearlers but upheld their own right to discipline native labour and to defend their families and stock from the increasing hostility of the bush tribes.[7]

Some declared that many aspects of native employment in the north-west were worse than in the slave States of America and urged the need for effective control. The picture presented may, as others argued, have been grossly exaggerated, but it was sadly evident that the good intentions of the early colonists had lapsed in the preoccupations of growing settlement and in the overall conclusion that the black race was doomed to extinction in any event. The once effective Aborigines Protection Society in London had come to serve little other purpose than that of passing on from overseas hit-or-miss allegations of cruelty and by 1870 every trace of the early ideal of native advancement was submerged in a half-hearted policy of protection.

Governor Weld's protests against the more blatant forms of exploitation marked him down as a crank in the eyes of the north-westers[8] and although the legislation of the 1870s, for which he was responsible, led to a tightening of control on native employment, the situation had, in many respects, gone beyond repair. The best interests of the natives, never properly studied or understood, were by this time totally obscured in a tangle of good and bad intentions, complicated human relationships and local anomalies. The women on station properties, adept in the handling of stock, would exchange the hazards of riding after sheep and cattle, which in fact they had enjoyed, for what represented to them a decline in status to the safe tedium of domestic work. Children too, cut off from the tribal pursuits of former years, no longer permitted to ride or to dive for shell but offered no alternative interests, were left to hang listlessly around the stockyards and squalid camps, a burden to their elders and themselves. Indentured Asian and Island crews that would liberate many natives from the demoralizing conditions of the pearling boats would also introduce them to alcohol and its concomitants of prostitution and disease

30

that would spread a slow corruption of body and spirit through the coastal tribes.

It was in this situation that the Aborigines were to win as staunch a friend as they had ever known or were ever likely to, in the person of a priest named Father Matthew Gibney, a man who perceived through this network of rival interests and contradictions what he saw to be a clear-cut case of right and wrong. Many years later, Paul Hasluck, in his history of the contact between black and white in Western Australia, was to write to him:

> To Bishop Gibney perhaps more than to any other single man belongs the credit of reawakening in Western Australian life a conception of Christian duty towards the natives. His position gave him greater influence than others who had the same interests at heart, and his fearless denunciations of northern events, his insistence that any human life has a value and that a Christian community has certain standards, woke a controversy that brought the claims of the native to the forefront.[9]

The simple pledge of this Irish priest to fight the cause of the Aborigines was to begin a complicated sequence of events involving political and religious issues extending far beyond Australia. In attempting the impossible he was to achieve the incredible, and in seeking an answer he was to uncover a multitude of questions, no less concerning the Aborigines than the people of many races who aimed either to exploit or to save them.

# CHAPTER TWO

## 1878 – 1883

So long as there is a traffic in human flesh between certain
gross and unscrupulous men, and so long as I consider
that the blacks are being cruelly treated under the sacred
name of justice, I shall not cease to raise my voice . . .[1]

BORN in County Cavan, Ireland, in 1835, Matthew
Gibney had come to Western Australia as a young priest in
1863. His superior was the zealous and revered Spaniard,
Father Martin Griver, who, owing to his poor command of
English, soon began to rely on Father Gibney as his spokesman. Pushed to the forefront of public life, the young Irish-
man, his activities ranging over most of the vast western
colony, became known as 'the people's priest', the 'soggarth
aroon' of the small but widely scattered Catholic flock that
still existed more or less on sufferance in an Anglican
stronghold. Fewer than half a dozen Catholic families were
of 'the gentry' that dominated the young colony, the rest
being mainly Irish working people, including emancipated
Irish convicts. A devoted friend and champion of the outcast and the poor, Father Gibney had none the less some
ability for winning influential friends, these including the
Surveyor-General (later Premier) John Forrest and the
Catholic Governor Weld. Being, however, outspoken and in
many respects uncompromising he was also to make
influential enemies.

By nature retiring and benign, the very whisper of injustice stirred in his breast the smouldering fires of ancient
wrongs and hardened the downward lines of his kindly Irish

countenance. While in the north-west in 1878 he had seen, in the town of Roebourne, native prisoners chained together by neck and ankle as they worked in the blistering heat on buildings and roads. He heard men joke of how absconders had been found dead in their chains in the dry creekbeds and of how, having the hides of animals rather than the skins of ordinary men, they were insensitive to the ordinary form of lash. He was told that some had been guilty of spearing stock, some of impertinence, disobedience or running away from their places of employment, while others had been found in the company of wrongdoers when the police closed in on them.

With sorrow the priest had witnessed the ruthless persecution of the proud and strong, the body and soul subjection of the co-operative and the weak. He saw the despised half-caste children of the lordly white and humbler Asiatic, the growing degradation and disease of natives around the townships and lay-up camps, and worst of all the vice and squalor of the pearling boats. He had seen women forced to dive even in the later stages of pregnancy, and some whose hands had been crushed with heavy tools for having clung too long between dives to the lugger sides.

Of his visit to La Grange Bay he wrote:

When the natives gathered together at nightfall, I was surprised to hear the heartrending wail that went up from the crowd. I found, on inquiry, that some of the young men, who had been forcibly detained on a pearling boat, had been drowned on making an attempt to escape from their captors. They believed that they could swim to shore, a distance of about six miles, but only one man reached it, and I had a conversation with him. For a long time I believed the story of the employers of native divers that the blacks went with them willingly, but I afterwards found such was not the case . . .[2]

Haunted by the lament of the suffering and bereaved, he had returned to the south to fight their cause against public doubts and indifference and a fairly general conviction that time and money expended on the Aborigines was so much thrown away.

As a churchman, Father Gibney thought of native welfare in terms of gradual integration under missionary guidance. His knowledge of native law was superficial enough but he had a warm appreciation of the native character and outlook, and although he saw some of their customs as incompatible with Christianity he believed their sense of spiritual values provided a firm basis on which to build.

Even then this view was by no means revolutionary, for it had been the ideal of the Spanish Dom Rosendo Salvado who in 1846 had founded a Benedictine mission at New Norcia, eighty miles north of Perth. This establishment, financed mainly from European funds and run by devoted agricultural monks, was the only one of a succession of government and church welfare schemes[3] that had shown any consistent promise and it was in this direction that Father Gibney, when campaigning for a missionary foundation in the north in 1879, had cast 'a wistful glance'.[4] In the prime of his vigorous optimism he had no doubt whatever that the Benedictine policy of training the indigenous people to farm and gradually reassume their land would ensure the healthy increase of stable and industrious full-blood families firmly implanted in the Christian way of life. On return from visits to New Norcia he extolled a flourishing community of native people, firm in faith and growing in the will to succeed, the children with scrubbed and shining faces, diligent in the pursuit of learning, destined to play a leading part in the future of their country.

The mission was then entering its period of greatest prosperity but Abbot Salvado knew from long experience that his beloved 'children of the forest' were possessed of an elusive spirit that still threatened to defeat his dream. So far, in fact, all his attempts to interest them in land husbandry in the fertile south had failed and he may well enough have been sceptical of training Aboriginal farmers in the arid north. At all events he declined the hint and he was well in his grave before the Benedictines took up their task among the formidable tribes of western Kimberley.

It was at this stage that Father Gibney made contact with a priest who had for years been fighting a forlorn battle for Aboriginal rights in Queensland and who seemed the sort of dedicated apostle needed to prepare the way for missionary work in the north-west.

The name of this now all but forgotten priest was Father Duncan McNab, his background, as a Scottish Catholic, one likely to have inclined his sympathies to a people he saw as a persecuted minority. Of scholarly bent and the devoted son of pious parents, he had entered the seminary at an early age with the hope of working in the Australian missionary field, an idea that may have been suggested by his relative Mary McKillop, foundress of the Australian Sisters of St. Joseph. The frustration, however, that was to dog him to the end of his career was already at his shoulder for, since priests were scarce in Scotland, his bishop detained him in Glasgow until he was forty-seven years old. By this time his parents were too old to leave behind and the debt incurred in bringing them with him to Victoria in 1867 obliged him to remain as parish priest in Portland until 1871.

When seeking an opening for missionary work during this time he wrote asking to be received into the Benedictine order at New Norcia,[5] but the abbot, possibly thinking his age against his settling into a Spanish community, declined his application. Relieved at last of his debt, he obtained an appointment on the Aborigines Protection Board of Queensland and began work on a native reserve on Bribie Island in Moreton Bay. He rates a mention in Tom Petrie's *Reminiscences of Early Queensland*, where, in consequence of a dispute with a native over smoking a pipe at prayers, he is said to have abandoned the islanders to their unregenerate ways. This story indicates a lack of realism and faintness of heart that other evidence belies. Indeed, many of the welfare measures he propounded read more like those of experienced social workers and anthropologists of our own day which may be the reason they were turned down *in toto*[6] by his fellow commissioners. He thereafter lost faith in their sincerity, told them what he thought of their *laissez-faire* policy, resigned from the board and went to work on a

35

reserve that had been gazetted for the Aborigines at his suggestion.

The authorities in his own Church seem to have been no more sincerely interested in his efforts or closer to understanding his problems than those in the government. Asked at a later date for a full report of his missionary experiences he wrote:

From the beginning I was told that any attempts to civilize them [the Aborigines] would be fruitless because they are said to be the lowest of the human race, incapable of forming an abstract idea and certain soon to die out. I did not think it necessary to discuss these points, knowing them to have been created by God for the same end as other men ... and that it did not so much matter that they should die out as that those now living should be saved....

When I went to Queensland ... I asked for an associate priest ... who had gone to Queensland expressly for the natives and who had three years experience of the Maoris ... but he was promised only when another priest should come to the diocese. Another and another and another came and yet he was still withheld.

I spent my first year in acquiring a knowledge of the habits and disposition of the natives, in acquiring a slight acquaintance with their language and in negotiating with members of Parliament to procure them their civil rights. When the Government acceded to my requests and empowered the Secretary for Lands to give homesteads or reserves to those whom I should persuade to support themselves by industry, I began to settle them on the land. Then I was anxiously looked for and expected by them for hundreds of miles around. I intended to continue at this for eighteen months believing that it was necessary to civilize them first and that afterwards they would willingly listen to religious instructions. I hoped to prepare for the entry of missionaries but the Bishop said I was wasting my time, forgetting the main object of my mission, that there was no fruit from my labours and that I was become a mere tool of the government.

To please him, much against my own judgment, I then commenced to teach them the truths of Christianity. Some became converts were Baptised and married . . . but subsequently, for want of necessary facilities for certain matrimonial dispensations, I found that I disturbed the consciences of the people without being able to apply a remedy. I told his Lordship that I would cease giving instructions and confine my efforts to acquiring the language till he should give me the necessary faculties. He told me he wrote for these but the Cardinal Prefect said he never got his letter.

The bigots then got up a cry in the Legislative and petitioned against grants of land for the blacks. The Secretary for Lands did not want to bring a hornets' nest about his ears and declined to exert the power given him for the benefit of the natives. . . .

I maintained myself here for the first year by means that I had earned in Victoria. For the rest of the time I subsisted by fishing and begging. . . .[7]

When malaria fever, sore eyes, lack of finance, hostility from neighbouring landholders and finally sunstroke convinced him that he must seek others to carry on, he set sail to interview Cardinal Simeoni, Prefect of the Congregation of Propaganda Fide in Rome, who advised him to try for helpers in the United States. Here his cause received some sympathy and two religious orders made half promises to assist at some future date. He returned, however, again alone, to find that public opinion had by this time led to the cancellation of the gazetted land which was later proclaimed a police reserve.

When he decided, on the invitation of Father Gibney, to come to Western Australia, he was already in his sixty-third year. Toil, sickness and frustration had left their marks on him and his appearance was then less that of a churchman than of a battered and bearded pastoral pioneer. Persistent

to the point of doggedness, a man of ability and practical
independence, he had been repeatedly forced into impractical situations in which one of less steadfast and sustaining
faith might well have lost his vocation or his sanity. What he
now lacked in physical strength he made up for in experience and zeal and it would not be his fault if his efforts were
again to fail.

On arrival at Fremantle he cheerfully accepted the
temporary post of chaplain on Rottnest Island, twelve miles
from the port – then an Aboriginal penal reserve established
by Governor Hutt over forty years before as a humane
alternative to the close confinement and chaining of prisoners on the mainland. It had been seen as a place from
which natives would graduate 'instructed in useful knowledge and trained in the habits of civilization', but instead
hundreds had died there of epidemic diseases or sheer
homesickness and none who survived had returned to their
country with any noticeable desire to imitate the whiteman's way of life. The island, today a popular holiday
resort, was at the time of Father McNab's arrival a de-
pressing place where 'gangs of exiles, ludicrously clad in
short flannel smocks, expiated in misery the error of not
changing the ancient ways for those of the white'.[8] The
priest, however, regarded his assignment as a means of gaining some knowledge of the local tribes.

He reported to the Legislative Council[9] that the 180
inmates responded well to his simple instructions in the
whiteman's law but he urged that they should, at this stage,
be tried in the light of their tribal teachings, since it was
patently both futile and unjust to punish them for reasons
that they seldom understood.

Obvious as this advice now seems, it touched an issue that
had for many years worried and confused the western
colony. In 1840, the report of Lieutenant (later Sir George)
Grey on the best means of civilizing the Aborigines had
been approved by the Colonial Office and had since formed
the basis of official policy.

I would submit [he wrote] that it is necessary from the moment the aborigines of this country are declared British subjects, they should, as far as possible, be taught that British laws are to supersede their own, so that any native who is suffering under their own customs may have the power of an appeal to those of Great Britain; or ... that all authorized persons should, in all instances, be required to protect a native from the violence of his fellows, even though they be in the execution of their own laws.[10]

Grey, writing in the era of optimism for rapid Aboriginal integration, saw this as the best way of combating the resistance to progress of the conservative tribal elders. As time went on, however, and both interest and belief in native advancement began to wane, his forthright argument lost force and local juries often returned findings of 'not guilty' or recommended mercy for ritual murders and punishments with a fervour for fair play never conspicuous in cases concerning Aborigines versus whites. By the 1880s few remembered that such rulings had been originally discouraged as implying that the violence of black against black was a less serious matter than that of white against white. Therefore, although Grey's policy operated officially for another twenty-five years, Father McNab's recommendation was favourably received.

The priest, while maintaining that Christianity should be taught with emphasis on the best aspects of Aboriginal beliefs, reiterated Hutt's intentions, that they should be taught to make fishing nets, boats, baskets, mats and clothing and trained in market gardening, the care of small flocks and herds and the management of their own affairs. He warned, however, from his experience on the Queensland reserves, that little could be done with those who had abandoned their tribal code for the worst practices of white society.

Father McNab's reports were placed before the Aboriginal Commission of 1883 and as a result two men were sent to instruct the prisoners in carpentry. The effort was half-hearted and short-lived, its failure merely adding weight to the commissioners' summing-up that 'the experience of fifty years finds us at a point as if we had never begun . . .'[11]

Father Gibney had tried meanwhile to convince the government officials of their responsibility towards the natives of the north-west, urging that since 'absolutely no compensation has been made them to the present time . . . and that moreover thousands of pounds are being annually expended not for their protection but for their detection and punishment, it cannot be considered inappropriate to ask help for them . . .'[12]

Whether or not the request was thought inappropriate its timing could hardly have been more inopportune for a Commission of that year into the condition of the Aborigines had come to the conclusion that since there was no hope of the native ever becoming more than a servant to the whiteman his education should be restricted to this end.[13] The commissioners expressed the utmost scepticism of missionary efforts and while admitting that New Norcia had attempted and done more than any other native institution they could see 'no striking evidence of its good effect (outside the institution itself) in the neighbourhood or in the colony'.[14]

It was left, therefore, to Father Gibney, backed by his bishop and a few parishioners, to raise enough money for a modest start.

An Italian priest named Father Martelli, who was to have accompanied the expedition, fell ill, so Father McNab set off on his own. This was a state of affairs with which he was by this time well acquainted but if his Queensland reverses had caused him some loss of confidence, he was now in good heart again. He had, on the whole, been well received in Perth and it seemed only reasonable to suppose that he could stake a claim, somewhere in the vast, empty colony, for the people to whom it had once belonged.

# CHAPTER THREE

## 1883 – 1887

WITH a good riding horse and five strong packs Father McNab, under the shelter of a broad 'cabbage tree' hat, set off inland from the port of Geraldton. It was an adventure after all, perhaps the grandest of his life. He was used enough to the bush and to sleeping under the stars but the people on the scattered stations extended him their hospitality and supplied rations to carry him on. It seemed natural enough that a priest should take a trip outback to visit isolated members of his flock and it was on this basis that they accepted him.

A few in whom he confided the real reason of his journey suggested possible mission sites that proved, on inspection, to be part of existing station properties. He also examined and reported, with surprisingly bushmanlike perception, on Aboriginal reserves. One in the Murchison, marked off at the request of the Anglican Bishop Parry, had not been used for missionary purposes, but he realized that it would hardly be given over for a Catholic establishment.

He reported, in reference to the policy of reserves, that 'the whole thing seems intended only for a name'.[1] Such areas, published in the *Government Gazette*, 'which the natives never see and if they did they cannot read' could be of use to the people concerned, he wrote, only if they could be pointed out and their purpose explained. As mission sites, however, these so-called 'reserves', although containing some good country, lacked river frontages or sufficient springs and pools for cultivation.

Between the Murchison and De Grey Rivers, seven hundred miles as the crow flies, the priest must have covered, in his rambling route, well over a thousand miles north and as many back again. He had been delayed by an attack of fever and lame horses but had gathered a good deal of information in the meantime. Reduced to tin tacks the situation appeared to be that all areas embracing river frontages or other good waters had been taken up by squatters or speculators and that the best chance of obtaining a mission property lay in bidding for a forfeited run of twenty to fifty thousand acres between the Ashburton and the De Grey.

Even then it would not be easy to find natives to establish themselves there, for most of those not attached to pastoral stations or pearling luggers were either serving sentences on Rottnest Island or seeking refuge from the police in inaccessible areas. The station natives, apparently seeing no prospect within the new regime of a better way of life, seemed content enough. Of the six hundred employed in the Cossack pearling fleets most had been 'recruited' from tribes between Champion Bay and King Sound and their masters had the greatest difficulty in preventing their running away in an attempt to get back to their country. Miserable though their condition might be, it was hard to convince them that one white man held their interests much above another. Nor would they be likely to settle on a mission far removed from their tribal areas.

Although down-to-earth in most respects, what Father McNab hoped to find was that desiderate of most missionaries – a people untouched by the corrupting hand of civilization through whom the Christian message might be revived in all its original dynamism. Father Gibney, in sympathy with this ideal, then suggested that he investigate the Kimberley district, an area of 120,000 square miles where settlement had only recently begun.

Father McNab, his hopes renewed, sailed north from Cossack in the S.S. *Otway* in March '84. The port of Derby he found to be a hot, ugly little trading post, hurriedly thrown together in the makeshift Australian style from bush timber and galvanized iron, its inhabitants a few business people, a contingent of police and the inevitable chain-gang of native prisoners. The priest, having urged his horses ashore through heavy tidal mud, was given a kindly welcome and the use of a cottage, but no one offered him much encouragement for a mission in that area.[2]

It was less than five years since Alexander Forrest had opened the district for pastoral occupation but already most of the good accessible country had been taken up. Cattle men were then pushing their stock overland from Queensland and the Northern Territory to holdings selected on the map, while sheep that had arrived by lugger a year before were rapidly spreading along the fertile frontages of the Fitzroy River and its tributaries.

A tour of inspection only confirmed the fact that there was no land available for a mission in the Fitzroy area, nor, from what he could gather, except for an inaccessible region north of the Leopold Ranges, anywhere between there and the Northern Territory border. Back in Derby he decided to accompany a police patrol that was leaving by boat to investigate rumours of trouble on the Dampierland peninsula where there were said to be unclaimed areas and big encampments of tribal-living Aborigines.

Already a bizarre collection of ships from stately 'mother schooners' and cutters to broken-down luggers and flat-bottomed tubs were ranging as far north as Darwin, with ever-increasing activity around this peninsula and the outlying Lacepede Islands. Roebuck Bay, where the port of Broome was soon to be proclaimed, had by this time become a popular depot or lay-up base and crews centred at Cygnet Bay were prospecting in King Sound, already known as 'The Graveyard' because of the many ships and human lives that had been claimed by its 'heavy water' and eight-knot tidal rips.[3]

Since his letters were limited to the cryptic reportage of plain facts, we do not know the priest's reaction to the colourful and torrid scene into which he was now plunged – to the harsh green of mangrove thickets extending into the milky jade of tidal seas, the glowing red and ochre of tumbling coastal cliffs against the mysterious tangle of the pindan[1] scrub. He leaves us no description of the trouble spot at Cygnet Bay to which the police had been summoned to investigate an unspecified number of violent deaths, nor of the white pearlers, Asiatic crews and Aborigines who proffered a confused babble of 'evidence' on all sides. Other reports of the period, however, show it to have been the usual story of Malays and Chinese supporting European pearlers in allegations against the Aborigines, Japanese giving evidence against Koepangers and Filipinos against Solonese and West Indians. The few Aborigines who spoke any English at all made statements of classic ambiguity. Bodies were exhumed from sandy graves in an attempt to establish foul play, but it was impossible, at that stage, to ascertain the time or manner of death. Some of the deceased were said to have been killed in drunken brawls over native women, others to have been speared by blacks either for motives of theft or from what the settlers interpreted as a primitive instinct to kill.

The pearlers, with the support of their nervous divers, alleged that the natives were hatching a plot to massacre all the whites and Asiatics on the peninsula and strongly urged a 'punitive expedition' to demonstrate who was now master in the land. The blacks admitted to a few murders in protest against the use made of their women and the holding of their young people on the Lacepede Islands to sell to pearlers down the coast. The pearlers claimed that the blacks habitually offered their women as consorts and their boys as workers for payment in tobacco and alcohol.

The police, having made a few token arrests, gave warning of the general tightening of regulations concerning the employment of Aborigines on the luggers and announced that the use of native women was now forbidden for any purpose other than as station domestics. Although it was clearly impossible for a small force stationed in Derby to police the widespread activities of the pearling fleets or to prevent the exploitation of the only women available in that wild land, a number of pearlers had already seen the advantage of taking up pastoral rights, running up timber shacks, bringing in a few head of stock and claiming that their lay-up bases were pastoral properties.[5]

In some cases legal rights had not been established by those in occupation but Father McNab knew he would get nowhere by setting up in competition for the natives with these tough freebooters of the pearling coast. A quick investigation of the King Sound side of the peninsula indicated that Goodenough Bay, a so far unoccupied site just south of Point Cunningham, might be suitable for a mission, especially if the country adjacent could be declared an Aboriginal reserve.

The police, who were for the most part of Irish Catholic descent, agreed with him, for they believed that a mission in that area could help to control a situation that was virtually beyond them. They had no wish to take more native prisoners than they could accommodate and organize into working gangs, while the punitive expeditions that were frequently urged in the north were apt to result in long, embarrassing inquiries from outside.

Father McNab found Governor Broome in Derby on his return and spoke to him of having inspected what seemed a suitable mission locality on the peninsula. He explained that he was now awaiting the arrival of an associate and that once established they would seek the assistance of some appropriate society.[6]

The governor on his return to Perth acted on having a native reserve proclaimed in the area mentioned by Father McNab but at the same time indicated to Bishop Griver, possibly due to some misunderstanding, that the priest did not appear to have selected a site or made any practical headway whatever.[7]

Father McNab's reply to a letter from the bishop informing him of this unpromising interview bespeaks something of his exasperation. After recalling the ill-health that caused him to seek others to carry on in Queensland he continued:

I told Cardinal Simeoni, Head of the Congregation in Rome, that I was not able then to do any further missionary duty among the Australian Aborigines but he insisted on my returning to give the benefit of my experience to any who might come. I also told Father Gibney I was not fit to carry on alone and understood another priest might be sent within three months. Of course none came. If anyone could be found and there was any prospect of an Order or Society coming I would continue till they came.

I have managed a boat and done many kinds of work and have experience with the natives but now have no more strength than a boy of 14 or 15 . . .[8]

In a further letter written somewhat later he continues to state what must surely have been obvious to all concerned:

Without means I do not believe a mission can be successfully opened anywhere, for a savage will only listen to a missionary as he would to a musician unless he can confer on him some tangible benefit . . .

I never desired to have the direction or management of a mission in Western Australia. I am not the originator of this scheme . . . I only agreed to co-operate, leaving the honour and merit of the enterprise to others . . .[9]

The firm promise of a helper and news of a recently launched Australia-wide appeal for funds decided him to carry on, but he waited in Derby for three months in vain. Then, weary of inaction and hoping to make at least some preparatory contact with the natives, he sailed by lugger, with his horses and a few stores, to Swan Point, at the north-most tip of the peninsula and set up a camp.

The natives thereabouts spoke no English and were less touched by civilization than any he had yet encountered. Members of the Bard tribe that occupied the northern part of the peninsula and the adjacent Sunday Island, they were well built people, their pleasant features somewhat marred, to outside eyes, by their custom of knocking out the two front teeth and the wearing of long nose bones. Their torsos and limbs were adorned with the usual raised, tribal cicatures and many of the men had fashioned their hair with the aid of mud and twine into strange, elongated headdresses. While resenting the blatant appropriation of their women they had come to accept the exchange of goods for wives as a benefit accruing from their custom of wife-lending in token of hospitality. They understood the pearlers' lust, while their other activities, however seemingly nonsensical from the native point of view, were no longer a mystery but they found the behaviour of this celibate hermit, who sought them out without apparent motive, peculiar to say the least. Since he was unarmed they probably dismissed him as a harmless eccentric but after the first encounter they avoided his camp, except when he was absent, and melted into the scrub on his approach.

He communicated with only one Aboriginal, an exceptionally tall, strong boy who had somehow acquired the curious name of 'Knife'.[10] This youth spoke a little English and seemed disposed to help him, but said he had first to complete a contract with a pearling outfit and promptly disappeared.

In letters posted from Derby the priest gave Bishop Griver and Father Gibney some account of his days. After saying his morning prayers, Office and occasionally Mass, he would spend two or three hours trailing and tending his horses, fishing, cooking his simple meals and wandering the lonely beach and scrub in search of native camps. He did not pretend to have made any promising contacts but pointed out that, under the circumstances of his lonely struggle, his mode of life 'must appear to the native more irksome and laborious than his own, so that they will not be inclined to follow his example or harken to his teaching'.[11]

Sometimes the natives thieved from the priest's supplies 'but not', he recorded thankfully, 'when I had got least, but when I had got a supply from the pearling boats. They could have taken the whole but did not and left me a supply for the time I was to remain.'[12]

He considered it prudent not to provoke ill-feeling by

locking up his stores and, believing defencelessness his best means of protection, he had no weapon of any kind. He did not fear greatly for his life but he knew that the blacks were liable to take revenge at random for the murder of a countryman.

Typical of all his letters was his scrupulous regard for the unvarnished truth even when it might have profited him better to evade or to elaborate. Pressed by Father Gibney, anxiously fighting meanwhile to gain support for his cause, to give some estimate of the numbers of natives on the peninsula, he refused almost irritably to commit himself even to a guess: 'I only tell the truth but cannot tell that till I know.'[13]

In June '85 he wrote briefly of the spearing of Captain Richardson and his mate on the beach at Cygnet Bay, just north of Cunningham Point[14]. The motive was said to have been to rob the lugger but the Chinese cook, with a spear through his leg, had quickly up-anchored and sailed to report to the police in Derby. About the same time a pearler named Kelly was murdered off Cape Londonderry by his native crew who, making off with the loot in a dinghy down four hundred miles of notoriously treacherous coast, performed an incredible feat of endurance and seamanship only to collide with the police party at Cygnet Bay.

The police force, under fire from outside for brutal tactics against defenceless natives, must at this stage have found local criticism for failure to discipline the savage hordes the harder to withstand and forthright, punitive measures were organized. Officially four natives were shot 'resisting arrest'.[15] Word of mouth accounts have it that the police rounded up all the tribespeople they could find between Cygnet Bay and Swan Point, pushed aside the women and children and shot at least ten adult males – which is probably nearer the truth. In any case, for some time after their departure, no native encampments were to be found within the vicinity.

Father McNab's desolation and sense of futility can be imagined, for apart from finding himself completely alone in a silence broken only by the screaming of sea birds and the wash of the restless tides, he knew that no one in this godless land really wanted or understood his mission. It seemed that even his friends in the south had lost faith in his work, though for himself he still believed that, given support and some authority as a protector of Aborigines, he could do much to prevent the exploitation and eventual extinction of the peninsula tribes and might yet succeed in helping them find a place in their radically changing world. In his more sanguine moments he had visions of a fishing industry operated by the Aborigines with boats they had built themselves. He pictured native villages, farms, market gardens and a growing tradition of local handicrafts – all the dreams of all the missionaries who ever hoped to bring the stability of Christian life to this drifting soil.

Tortured by intermittent fever and infected bites of sandflies and mosquitoes, his old eye trouble returned and in his agonized loneliness he invoked the aid of St. Michael, 'one of my special protectors, I believe at any rate'.[16] Like an answer to prayer the boy called Knife, whom he had met some time before, turned up at his camp, offering to act as 'an associate and kind of interpreter'. True to his name, this youth, himself a member of the Bard tribe, proved sharp enough to explain to his people that the priest had come as their protector and friend. When told of his idea to have land reserved for them by the government 'they seemed highly pleased and expressed willingness to settle down, to catch and cure fish, to cultivate gardens and send their children to school'.[17]

For Father McNab, like Robinson Crusoe on finding his Man Friday, life was again supportable. He and his young friend after selecting a tentative mission site near Goodenough Bay, about forty miles south of Swan Point, went on horseback to Derby, hoping to meet the long-promised assistant. A letter awaited him, saying that Father Gibney's desperate efforts to find a priest had so far failed but that he had managed to send some stores, a pocket compass, an ecclesiastical directory, some sacred relics and a cheque for

£13 17s. 3d. This was apparently the net result of the Australia-wide appeal but Father McNab was assured that another drive was about to be launched. He replied with some resignation: 'I expect a pathetic appeal on behalf of the Aborigines but little more. I speak from past experience.'[18]

It was noted in *The West Australian* of 3rd December 1885:

> The Rev. F. McNab has gone overland to the mission reserve on the West side of King Sound. He wants to interest the natives in gardening if possible, as well as fishing. It will be very hard work for the natives will never do anything for their living if they can rob him without much trouble, and now that the pearling boats have left he will be all alone up there.

The lugger that was to have brought the priest's wet season supplies was wrecked in a 'cockeye' that destroyed much of the pearling fleet and the overland route being blocked by flooded rivers he was left with only what food could be obtained from the pindan scrub and the sea. All the natives he had been feeding, with the exception of the faithful Knife, thereupon lost interest and went bush.

In April 1886, Father William Treacy, the long-promised helper, arrived at Goodenough Bay with a small boat, a quantity of stores, a spring cart and some building and farming equipment.[19] This young man, formerly chaplain at Fremantle jail, had been the only volunteer for the north-west mission, possibly because he was the only priest available for whom removal to this rigorous assignment had offered a brighter outlook. In any case, he and the goods that accompanied him had taken nearly three years and all Father Gibney's persuasive powers to get hold of. The Australian public was not notably ungenerous, but it would contribute to missionary causes in China, India or Africa much more readily than to any concerned with the Aborigines of its own land.

Now that rations were again available the tribespeople

returned to the vicinity and with their occasional help the two priests erected a small church and house of timber and spinifex thatch, fenced and ploughed a garden plot and sowed seed. They were under no illusion regarding the natives' renewed interest in the mission site but they were encouraged by the fact that, although quite indifferent to goings-on in the garden, the people would sometimes gather, unprompted, at the doorway of the church during Mass and Benediction.[20] This was not surprising for ritual, unlike agriculture, being an intrinsic aspect of their own culture, its manifestation in any form must have touched in them some chord of understanding.

Before long they were singing hymns with enthusiasm if not comprehension and Father McNab attempted to translate some verses into their own language. From the beginning of their association he and his boy Knife had been working together on a dictionary of the Bard tribe. The Nimanboor people of Goodenough Bay, however (as indeed each of some ten tribes of the peninsula), spoke a different tongue, which had meant starting all over again.

The priest had soon realized that Bishop Griver's plan for having the gospels translated for all the tribespeople of his diocese would require nothing short of a team of anthropological and linguistic experts. 'There are simply no terms in their language fit to express our religious ideas,'[21] he wrote, and attempted to explain that not only would the scheme require the mastery of at least one hundred major tribal tongues but that the gospels would need to be translated into meaningful idiom and to be contained within the limits of Aboriginal experience. In this Father McNab was up against the same problem that had bedevilled his work on the Queensland reserves and that was to frustrate the many missionaries to follow him. In order to interpret the Christian message it was necessary to educate the people to some extent in European ways of life and thought whereas education, unless in segregated circumstances, had been found to incline them more readily to corruption.

Still, the two priests persevered in this labyrinth of

contradictions, praying for divine direction and drawing some comfort from the parable of the fruitful earth:

> ... This is what the kingdom of God is like. A man throws seed on the land. Night and day, while he sleeps, when he is awake, the seed is sprouting and growing; how, he does not know. Of its own accord the land produces first the shoot, then the ear, then the full grain in the ear.[22]

At the end of five months together they felt that they might have sown a small seed here and there and Father McNab set off in better heart on a business trip to Derby. News awaited him there of the gold rush to Hall's Creek that had started in the middle of that year, and hearing that many prospectors were dying of fever and privation, he set out on a three hundred mile journey to render what comfort he could to members of his flock.

During his absence from the mission Father Treacy went down with malaria, was brought by lugger to Derby in a delirium, and thence shipped back to Perth. When Father McNab returned he found his mission deserted, the buildings burnt to the ground and the garden gone back to the scrub. Some said it was the result of a bushfire; others that it was the work of a hostile pearling crew. Another version had it that the mission people, finding both the priests gone, had decided to ransack the stores and burn the evidence.

Hearing that he had returned and was lying, weak and stricken, among the ruins of his mission, the people came back and made anxious efforts to comfort him, even offering to help him start again. He soon rallied sufficiently to muster his horses and ride with the devoted Knife to Derby where the doctor insisted that he was no longer fit for work and must leave the north at once. Instead he went to Darwin to 'recuperate', as he said, with a band of Jesuit missionaries and there to await instructions from the bishop. His health, however, continued to decline and at the end of 1887 he took ship for Victoria where, surprisingly enough, he lived on at Richmond, Victoria, until 1896.[23]

His uncompromising honesty had recognized no short cuts to the goal of Christian conversion. He had baptized a few natives at the point of death, but he claimed no converts in Kimberley and probably thought his work had been to no avail. This was not the case, for the sincerity of 'poor old Father Mac-a-nab' had sown a seed of trust that spread among all the tribes of the peninsula. Never again would a missionary, whatever else his trials, find himself shunned as a stranger by the native people of that strange land.

# CHAPTER FOUR

## 1886 – 1890

WHEN Pope Leo XIII, 'in intimate reunion with his hierarchy',[1] first raised the matter of a mission to the Australian Aborigines Dom Sebastian Wyart, Abbot of the French Cistercian monastery at Sept Fons, found the eyes of his fellow prelates turned speculatively upon himself.

'I hid myself straight away as best I could,' he later told his community, 'and made signs to implore them to keep quiet and that it was impossible for me to undertake this task.'[2] But two years later there was his confrère Dom Ambrose Janny, tall, ascetic and bearded, with little Father Aphonse Tachon, swarthy and volatile, bouncing at his side, their white, cowled habits drawing curious glances from the crowd on Fremantle wharf as they disembarked.

Their arrival in May 1890 was the result of long negotiations set in motion by Bishop Gibney, as he now was, and backed by Cardinal Moran of Sydney.[3] It was also the outcome of religious persecutions in France that had caused the essentially contemplative Cistercian or Trappist Order to seek ways and means of establishing itself in other lands. The Pope himself had urged them to take up missionary work and during the 1880s several monasteries had dispersed to China, North America and New Caledonia. By so doing they had hoped to attract local postulants and to raise undeveloped communities to a point where the monks could once more withdraw from the world into their quiet monastic life.

Their ancient agricultural tradition and many other skills seemed a sound basis for the practical training of backward peoples but the experience of centuries had left them with no illusions about the effect on their rule of too much pre-occupation with wordly affairs. It was not forgotten how, in medieval times, the vitality generated by St. Benedict's simple precept of work and prayer had led to such material prosperity that the abbots became more respected for their worldly influence than their spiritual fervour. But the flame of original inspiration, never entirely extinguished, had been fanned into new life during the Reformation.

The Reformed Cistercians, although divided into two congregations practising slightly different rules, had long since returned to the essential spirit and zeal of their 'Golden Age' and, fortified with the warnings of history, had embarked on this new phase of active missionary work resolved to maintain it.

Little wonder that Dom Sebastian had hidden himself from the pontifical eye when the subject of an Australian foundation was raised, for, with a struggling establishment in French New Caledonia and another shortly to be launched in Palestine, his resources were then strained to the limit.[4] Other European Orders were evidently similarly placed, for two years later none had come forward in answer to Bishop Gibney's appeal.

In 1889 Dom Ambrose Janny, Abbot of the Trappist mission in New Caledonia, had returned to Sept Fons to report that, after ten frustrating years, his small community felt their efforts to have fallen on barren soil. It was decided therefore to suppress this foundation and to investigate the situation in Australia where Church authorities, seeking missionary helpers, had reported the natives to be 'numerous, intelligent and tractable', lacking only Christian teaching and instruction in simple farming principles.

Bishop Gibney, overjoyed at their coming, had arranged to accompany them by ship to Derby without delay. At his consecration, after the death of Bishop Griver in 1886, he had pledged himself to 'promote every possible mission of mercy for the sick, the poor, the natives, the outcast and the sinner' and he had since become more than ever a dynamic force in the community. While exhorting his flock to greater interest and participation in public life he vigorously defended their rights and expounded the views of his Church on all major issues of the day. Travelling on horseback, by buggy and coastal steamer, he kept in touch with his enormous diocese, selecting meanwhile the best sites throughout the growing colony for Catholic churches, schools and orphanages and pressing the cause of the Aborigines at every opportunity.

Dom Ambrose and his companion had only a few words of English between them and Bishop Gibney rather less of French. They were able, however, to the astonishment and edification of their listeners and their own amusement, to communicate to some extent in Latin. In this tongue, aided by an eloquence of mime and gesture that surprised himself, Bishop Gibney managed to convey something of the vast empty land for which they were bound and of the million-square-mile colony of only 50,000 people of which it was a part.

The sight of Derby, principal outlet for West Kimberley's total white population of 100 men and fourteen women, must have proved shattering to the French monks. Father Alphonse went down immediately with an attack of malaria, to which – a legacy from their East Indian mission – both were subject, and Dom Ambrose became faint from the effects of the heat. Residents, no doubt a little in awe of their unusual visitors, were sympathetic and helpful, the inspector of police giving positive encouragement by assuring the bishop that Father McNab's influence had made the task of his force considerably easier on the peninsula.[5]

George Rose, manager of a nearby station, lent the party a wagon and told them of an area of good natural springs on the western side of Dampierland that he had seen when droving sheep from Beagle Bay to the Fitzroy River. Beagle Bay was a popular lay-up base for the pearling luggers, but the inspector was optimistic of the government's declaring the area a mission reserve, in which case he considered – though by what means he did not say – that the crews could be controlled.

The greatest help of all came from one John Cornelius Daly, a thirty-year-old police trooper and shareholder in a struggling family property on the Fitzroy. An impressionable young man, strong in the faith of his Irish forbears, he could hardly have been in his element among the tough men of the Kimberley force. Some of these were reasonably humane and conscientious but others had become hardened to the extent that the natives were of little more concern to them than kangaroos. The bonus given for every suspect native murderer, stock spearer or 'witness' brought in to trial had, moreover, encouraged the rounding up and bringing in of as many natives as could be trapped or tricked into custody. Daly, as an Australian of his time, does not appear from his subsequent correspondence to have had much faith in the Aborigines' potential as citizens but he was probably unable, in conscience, to remain a party to injustice and cruelty. He may even have been suffering some remorse on this score since he at once offered his services to the abbot, not as a mere helper, but as a postulant.

This seemingly hurried decision, which, as it happened, he was never to recant, was a great encouragement to the monks, for that a vocation should have come so readily seemed a promising omen for a foundation in Australia. Daly was strong and practical, experienced in bushcraft and with stock. He could handle a team or a boat, had a good knowledge of the tidal and climatic hazards of the coast and enough education to act as secretary and executive for the monks in their local negotiations.

He quickly procured horses and a native guide, and the party, consisting of Bishop Gibney, Dom Ambrose and John Daly (Father Alphonse being too weak to travel), set out to explore the wilds of Dampierland. They rode south over the broad speargrass plains of the million-acre Yeeda run, stopping to rest in the broad shade of grotesquely shaped boab trees, weaving their way through termite castles that studded the grey flats. The abbot, in the brown working habit of his Order, its pointed cowl protecting his tonsured head, rode in quiet contemplation of the outlandish scene, bearing patiently with the heat and the

57

tormenting insects until he too succumbed to an attack of malaria. The party had then reached the Fitzroy River which, owing to unusual mid-year rain, was impassable for three or four days, by which time the monk was able to continue.

Their route then lay to the north, along the east coast of the peninsula, through a tangled pindan wilderness of pandanus palms, wattle, eucalypt and tea-tree scrub. Near Goodenough Bay, some fifty miles north of the Fitzroy, they surprised a small group of natives who fled into hiding at sight of them but who, on being followed and informed by the guide that these men were 'brothers belong Father Maca-nab', emerged with beaming smiles and friendly gestures. Signing for the white men to wait, they went off, to return soon afterwards with gifts of fish and large mangrove crabs.

> In turn [the bishop wrote] we gave them bread, tea and some tobacco of which they are passionately fond. They showed us where the priests' log house had been. . . . There lay, scattered about, the remains of a cart, buggy, ploughs, harness, and a great variety of utensils all devoured by the flames. . . .[6]

These relics of failure did not unduly depress the bishop for he saw in the welcome of the natives the brightest prospects for a new mission.

William Dampier who, two centuries before, had put in for water thereabouts had reported of the same race that:

> . . . setting aside their human shape they differ little from apes. Their eyelids are always half closed to keep the flies out of their eyes. . . . From infancy being thus annoyed by these insects they do never open their eyes as other people and therefore they cannot see far. . . . They all of them were of the most unpleasant look and the worst features of any people that I ever saw and I have seen a great variety of savages . . .[7]

58

But Bishop Gibney saw them as 'a splendid race of men'.

> Certainly [he wrote] some of the young men were perfect pictures, of an average height, well-shaped limbs, good, round heads, high foreheads and large, dazzling eyes. They knock out the two front teeth and wear a bone in the nose. . . .[8]

However they might appear to others, the Aborigines, in the eyes of this loyal and consistent friend, were comely, warm-hearted and by nature of high moral principles. Cynics declared that he would change his tune in the light of further experience, but twenty years later, reporting to his friend Daisy Bates on the mission she had helped him save, he could still write: 'The history of European civilization does not afford an instance of any such lovable and docile race.'[9]

The news of these 'brothers' of the good men who had once lived among them went before the travellers from tribe to tribe and they were everywhere received with the same gestures of goodwill. The Njul Njul people near Beagle Bay led them through the pindan to a park-like area of spreading white-gums and paperbarks where spring-fed pools, lily-covered and set about with palms and ferns, attracted flocks of wild duck, parrots and cockatoos, ibis, brolgas, cranes and twittering flocks of jewel-bright finches. Wreathed in early morning mist and touched with the glow of sunrise it was a place of such wild beauty that the abbot, like the prophet Moses beholding the Promised Land, fell on his knees and gave thanks to God. Here, in the desolate wilderness, was at last a place of fertility, a site where they might one day build an abbey to 'swim upon fountains' like the ancient monastery of Fontenay in the distant woods of France.

Satisfied with this promising discovery, the party returned to Derby and obtained the use of a police boat. In this the bishop and Father Alphonse brought on supplies to Goodenough Bay and there awaited the arrival of the abbot and

59

John Daly with the bullock team. This gave the bishop a chance to become better acquainted with the tribespeople of the peninsula whose numbers he had estimated, somewhat recklessly, at from five to six hundred. He found them cheerful and willing helpers in clearing a track for the team and opening up wells for the animals. 'A hundred times these men could have killed us if they had a mind,' he wrote in answer to those who accused the natives of inherent treachery. 'I was practically alone with them when out, and the priest whom I left behind was alone, and neither could say we ever saw a frown from any one of them.'[10]

When the team arrived part of the load was taken across country to Beagle Bay and the rest left in charge of an Aboriginal. 'And although he ran short of provisions – the team not returning as soon as expected – the poor fellow never forsook his post, nor did he touch a thing in the tent.'[11]

Then began the task of hewing out a foothold in the virgin scrub. Tree felling, fencing, hoeing and digging, with the help of the curious Njul Njul people, soon produced a 'goodly sized garden plot' in which to plant the seeds and tropical plants sent from the famous botanical gardens in Darwin.

The bishop, having been granted the privilege of grubbing out the first tree, hacked away with a will, pleased to demonstrate to the French monks that an Irish priest could also employ his hands to good effect. Used enough to the bush, he took the heat and the rough life in his stride but there was one hardship to which he did not submit so stoically. John Daly, in his eagerness to embrace the Trappist life in all its austerity, had overlooked the fact that his lordship had taken no vow of abstinence from meat, salt or condiments and he had not included them in the supplies!

When the time came for him to leave for Perth the bishop invited all the local families to a 'feast' improvised from their stocks of flour, rice, sugar and tea. The guests, seventy in all, straggled shyly in, the men dressed for the occasion, with carved pearl shells dangling from hair belts, the women naked, but coyly peeping from behind bunches of leaves or pieces of bark which they carried in their hands. This the bishop accepted as a sign of innate modesty and the fact that they had with them only full-blood children, as an indication that this tribe had so far escaped corruption. He left with a happy sense of achievement, confident that before long the *spiritus lenitatis* of the white monks would spread its influence through the crude and cruel land.

# CHAPTER FIVE

## 1890 – 1891

ABBOT AMBROSE lost no time in establishing a Trappist routine of work and prayer in the wilderness. Although strict monastic silence was necessarily relaxed for missionary purposes, he and his prior, Father Alphonse, with the novice, John Daly, now Brother Xavier, faithfully abstained from meat and kept as closely as possible to their austere rule. They rose at two in the morning for matins, lauds, and meditation and at daybreak Father Alphonse blew several blasts on a conch shell to make known, for those who would hear, that Mass was about to begin.

While the abbot and Brother Xavier Daly went off to work in the gardens or to cut timber in the bush, Father Alphonse cooked porridge for the people. Later, for the midday meal, he made wheaten bread, a stew of emu or kangaroo meat for the natives and a vegetable hash of sorts for the religious. The monks broke their fast at noon for the first and only time of the day, then took a short siesta and prayed for half an hour before resuming work.

At sunset the conch shell sounded out again and the people gathered for hymns and rosary, returning to their camps at night with their evening meal of bread and meat and on Sundays with a ration of tobacco. Their acceptance of this prayerful regime was not, as sceptics maintained, solely on account of the accompanying benefits, for as Father McNab had observed, they undoubtedly enjoyed singing hymns and listening, with or without understanding, to doctrinal instruction. The monks, hoping in the tradition of the Church, to graft a vigorous Christian growth on to a judiciously pruned tree of native culture, began studying tribal customs and beliefs and Father Alphonse, undeterred by the fact that the six other main tribes on the peninsula, averaging only about 150 members to each, spoke different tongues, soon claimed to have translated into Njul Njul the *Pater*, *Ave Maria*, *Gloria*, *Credo*, and one of the gospels.[1]

Within six months several boys, versed in the Latin responses, and clad in red soutanes and white surplices, were already serving Mass. Their teachers judged them quite as receptive to learning as European children of the same age and thought their elders far more amenable to reason than the New Caledonians.[2] From the beginning they had been courteous and welcoming, often bringing gifts of food and, though admittedly not to be depended on, helping to cut and carry timber, open wells and cart water. They would take themselves off without notice into the bush and were easily enough enticed away by intruding pearlers but the monks had little doubt that when they gained confidence in the missionaries as their guide to salvation they would settle down to a satisfactory Christian pattern of life. The monks, as French nationals, could not be given official jurisdiction over the Aboriginal reserve, but Bishop Gibney assured them that a protectorship, soon to be granted to Brother Xavier Daly, would enable them to act against intruders and to recover any natives taken or enticed away.

Abbot-General Sebastian wrote from France of his satisfaction at progress reports and at the 'vivid interest' of the West Australian government in their new foundation. He also stressed to the bishop his confidence in Dom Ambrose as a 'courageous and enterprising man, well able to contend with the obstructions put up by the evil one always ready to thwart pious enterprises'.[3]

As the months went by, however, the missionaries themselves saw little evidence of local enthusiasm for their undertaking. The Aborigines Protection Board[4] had approved the grant of a 100,000 acre mission reserve, rent free, but the subsidy of a mere £350 for the current year, on the guarantee of a community numbering no less than ten

63

members within twelve months, was a shock to them. The abbot estimated the cost of supporting ten religious and an unspecified number of Aborigines at some £2,000 a year, with another £1,000 for equipment, freight, passages and the purchase of some cattle and sheep. Cardinal Moran in Sydney had promised £500 a year for some time to come and Bishop Gibney what other support he could raise, but this would by no means meet the bill. Failing support from societies in France and Rome, 'Shall it be necessary,' the abbot asked, 'to commit myself entirely to Divine Providence?'[5]

Evidently the bishop, for all his own simple faith, thought not. He redoubled his fund-raising efforts and promised that he would never permit the mission to want for the necessities of life, but with typical optimism, he anticipated that 'the land being rich and its extent so great ... by cattle rearing alone a large income may soon be counted upon with reasonable certainty'.[6]

For himself Abbot Ambrose had already grown wary of counting on anything with 'reasonable certainty' in this unpredictable land. Dr. Maurice Holtz had sent, from his renowned botanical gardens in Darwin, a quantity of young plants, cuttings and seeds, many of which, especially the tobacco, grain crops, melons, snake beans and radishes, promised well but they were destroyed by night-raiding kangaroos that defied ordinary fences. By the time a high brushwood enclosure was completed it was getting late in the year and the newly established garden shrivelled in the first blast of summer heat. The monks, reduced to a diet of rice and porridge, soon became afflicted with scurvy and recurrent fever.

For the abbot, however, the greatest disappointment of all was the lack of response to his Australia-wide appeal for Trappist novices, since, after all, the desire of his Order to establish a mission for the Aborigines had been secondary to that of implanting its tradition on Australian soil and of attracting local religious. This aim had been encouraged by reports of the devotion to their faith of the many Australians of Irish origin but it was not foreseen that these, being mainly working people of a practical pioneering outlook, were unlikely to be drawn to the intellectual and mystical aspects of the Trappist life. Their first drive had netted only one novice, Brother Stephen Montague.

In February 1891, just under a year after his arrival in Australia, Abbot Ambrose went to France to report that the mission needed further recruits and funds from home if it was to carry on. Father Alphonse, left in charge in his absence, threw into his task all the love and enthusiasm of his volatile nature but lived in constant dread of a decision from France that the mission should be abandoned.

He reported regularly and at length to the bishop, pouring out, in confused and tumbling sentences, his hopes and fears. Mid-year he wrote that he had heard nothing from Abbot Ambrose since his return to France and was 'very astonished and somewhat afraid with his silence'.[7] Brother Xavier had been suffering from fever for some weeks but had not spared himself on that account. A small church and monastery were already completed. They now had cells and beds but sleep was often difficult as 'during some weeks the mosquitoes hurt even truly dreadful and we have been obliged to make fires with cow dung close [to] the altar for celebrating Mass'.[8]

He himself, except for sore eyes, had recently been blessed with exceptional good health and was able to work long hours at building, gardening, learning the native language, sewing clothes for the people and cooking for the community.

Although for every sign of success there was a score of failures and frustrations Father Alphonse saw them all as obstructions raised against his work by the powers of darkness. The evil one had sent a mid-year frost to destroy the garden just as it had again promised well and had also brought into the mission a number of outside tribespeople who, while taking all the rations they could get, talked against the missionaries (generally referred to by the natives as 'the Hail Marys') and the doctrines they preached to those already inclined to favour them. Father Alphonse dared not send the trouble-makers away for fear they would kill the stock.

Brother Xavier had been granted a protectorship but this entitled him to do no more than report on specific instances of exploitation and abuse. His reports were presented to the Aborigines Protection Board which, in due course, submitted them to the police, who eventually carried out an investigation and reported back to the board that owing to the lapse of time and lack of evidence nothing further could be done.

Now in some doubt of converting the tribal elders, the priest concentrated his efforts on the younger generation which, together with a young man named Norengbor, whom they called Felix, he was confident would soon accept the faith. Felix and his old father Cormar, otherwise William, who as a head man or elder of the tribe regarded himself as their chief friend and protector, worked 'very constant'[9] for the missionaries.

There is no knowing the truth of the story that Felix had not long before sanctioned the killing and eating of one of his own children as a gesture of hospitality to visiting tribespeople.[10] He had, however, so taken to heart Father Alphonse's teaching on the sacredness of human life that he had presented the priest with an ailing child who would ordinarily have been considered better dead. The monk had devoted himself to her care in vain but her baptism at the point of death had made her the first Christian of her tribe. She had been buried with all the ritual of the Church, the natives being issued for the occasion with the clothes – 'trousers for the men, petticoat or camisole for the women'[11] – on which Father Alphonse had spent long and devoted labour. The people had been greatly impressed with the ceremony and the clothing had delighted them but the men were soon afterwards seen wearing the 'camisoles' rolled up under their armpits, the women trailing trousers

from their heads. Within a week all the garments had vanished – given away to outside relatives or 'burned in the
night fires.'[12] None the less, the influence of 'the little soul
in heaven' had seemed at once apparent in the sudden
success and abundance of the garden, in the increased diligence of Felix in working for the mission and in the devotion of the younger band of catechists.

It was at this promising stage that an Irish priest named
Father James Duff, while touring the Kimberleys, spent a
few weeks at Beagle Bay where he assisted the solitary
priest, prepared a progress report for the Catholic *Record*,
and incidentally provided some lively comments on the contemporary pearling scene. He had travelled from Broome to
Beagle Bay in the schooner *Ethel*, whose skipper he found
as 'kind as he was enterprising'.[13] This was the same Captain Ridell who, with his eighteen-year-old son and first
mate was murdered on his schooner by his Filipino crew in
1901. At the time of Father Duff's visit Ridell employed
about sixty men, Japanese, Malay, Filipino, Chilian and
South Sea Islanders, mostly engaged from Singapore at
wages ranging from £1 10s. for crew members to £5 a
month for divers, with a bonus of £20 per ton of shell
brought up. The priest discussed with him and his mate
Barnes the idea of the mission later entering the pearling
industry, which both thought worth trying.

Father Duff left Beagle Bay full of enthusiasm for the
mission and its people and the remarkable progress of the
children, especially in religious knowledge.

But alas, the crop of Christians Father Alphonse had
hoped to harvest was soon nipped in the bud, enticed away
by an artful pearler who, being 'very good in words', had
come to the mission ostensibly to attend Mass, actually to
make contact with the natives:

> After the matins he tells them that if they come to us I
> shall kill them at some time, that I am not a whiteman but
> a blackfellow and consequently cannot be their master,
> but he only . . .[14]

67

This reference to Father Aphonse's swarthy complexion, that was no doubt accentuated by long exposure to the tropical sun, also alludes to the natives' refusal to accept authority, other than in matters of tribal law, from one of their own race. Father Alphonse, however, was not then concerned by the problems this might augur for the future education of native leaders. He saw only the immediate alienation of his hard-won flock:

> The diving pearler strives to get all of them from the mission. And he succeeds. He gives them plenty. He got last year £1,100 of shells. . . .[15]
>
> If these pearlers have extra good at least for the material of the coloured man he will be a great drawback to the mission. Their immorality is great. . . . He employs the natives for diving . . . and he does give them tobacco and drink. . . .[16]

Some of the master pearlers, to be sure, had been of service in delivering mail and cargo to the mission free of charge, but even the best disposed could not control their crews. To these the women and girls were a constant prey, some going willingly and with the connivance of their men, others chased and intimidated.

Father Alphonse wrote of one child who had been chastised by her tribal husband after refusing to share the money she had been given by a Malay. Of this ill-treatment, interpreted by Father Alphonse as a protest against the girl's loyalty to the mission, the husband evidently repented soon afterwards:

> Some little girls having climbed a tree to escape them they [some Malay divers] followed them there and took down one to satisfy their passions. Among them was the little one so ill-treated by her husband lately. He was with his tomahawk on the spot. The Malay asked [for] his wife. No, no, he replied. She belong to Hail Mary and they fled away frightened.[17]

Bishop Gibney replied always with warm reassurance: 'Rome was not built in a day. . . .'[18] The prior rallied each time to his encouragement, only to be cast down by further setbacks and cruel contradictions. What of the trouble-makers among the natives themselves who came in and talked against the mission? Could they be forbidden to enter the mission area which was after all part of the reserve set aside by the government for all Aborigines? If be-friended and encouraged they would seduce those inclined to Christianity, if rebuffed they would go off and kill the mission stock.

. . . Would it be possible to get Government guarantee we will not be molested in our work? . . . Some law to keep out the trouble makers, to hinder the black women from going on the boats and to punish the seducers?

If the natives are taught in English they will be always more inclined to get to the boats and the white men. Would it be good to teach only to read and write in their own language as the Jesuits did in Paraguay? . . . The mission is about impossible if they come in contact with these outside. . . . If they remain at the mission even some time and afterwards work for the white man, all the work and hardship of having them in religion will be almost totally lost. The black fellow is too weak to struggle against the corrupted white civilization. Only if the mission should be segregated would we have more success. . . .

I hope dear Father, you will remember my poor soul at the sacred altar. Sometimes I get a little bit dark . . .[19]

# CHAPTER SIX

## 1891 – 1892

BACK in the ordered silence of Sept Fons, Dom Ambrose, while seeking avenues which might lead to support for his mission, had become enmeshed in a serious dilemma. Since his departure for Australia the pending reunion of the two main Trappist, or Cistercian, branches had re-focused the interest of his Order in Europe on the simple definition of monasticism. The abbot, who in his younger days had taken the Holy Father's direction into the missionary field as a means to an end for his Order, now found himself torn between his attraction to the purely contemplative life and his commitment to the benighted Aborigines.

One suspects that the Australian mission had already become a cross he would prefer might be lifted from his shoulders, for not only was he in poor health but he was aware of many facets of the situation that did not obtrude themselves on Father Alphonse's simpler and more extrovert definition of their task. As a disciple of holy poverty the abbot was clearly pained by his enforced pre-occupation with raising money, to which, since he had begun to doubt the mission's ever being able to pay for itself, he could see no end.

What required careful explanation at Sept Fons was that although the Australian bishop had not actually misrepresented the situation, he had certainly emphasized only its more hopeful and positive aspects. The extent of the mission area was indeed enormous by European standards but in north Australia where pastoral properties were reckoned in millions of acres, it was a mere pocket handkerchief. Australians had too little regard for their Aborigines to grant them land that was good for much else. Indeed were it not for the fact that the natural pasture of the area was too poor to fatten stock and contained a weed that was poisonous to horses it would have been taken up long before by big company interests such as occupied all the accessible good land in the north-west and Kimberley districts. A limited area around the natural springs seemed suitable for growing fruit and vegetables but even so much had yet to be learned about the soil, the seasons, and the control of innumerable pests.

The Aborigines too presented difficulties that had not been anticipated, for they were in many respects more puzzling in their disarming friendliness than the truculent head-hunters with whom the same missionaries had failed in the East Indies. It would have been wishful thinking to liken the Australian natives to the Africans of Natal, among whom the Cistercians were meeting with such success, for there were significant differences between the two racial cultures. The Order had found in Natal a native tradition of land husbandry that had been firm soil on which to build, and progress was already leading towards an adaptation of the Trappist rule in that area to a far from contemplative situation.[1] The Australian environment, on the other hand, had produced a nomad, food-gathering people for whom a change to land and animal husbandry was no simple matter of application. It required in fact a complete reversal of an attitude to life, a denial of the law that had sustained them from time beyond memory.

Though not taciturn or wanting in merriment and human sympathy they were quiet and restrained in comparison with the ebullient and emotionally responsive Africans. Only at night in a wild chanting and stamping that disturbed the monks' few precious hours of sleep did these strange people show evidence of a passionate energy that was, in the case of the Africans, being directed into Christian activity. The latter had at once welcomed Christianity as a new and wonderful message of hope and love, but so far even the most amenable of the Aborigines regarded it not as a substitute for but as an addition, and with reservations at that, to their tribal beliefs. The Abbot-General, however, was assured that confidence in Divine Providence, backed by adequate funds and a good working force of monks and brothers, could overcome such initial difficulties. He instructed Dom Ambrose to write to Bishop Gibney that his Order was most interested in the Australian mission but that their carrying on was largely dependent on finance from the West Australian government of which they had so far heard nothing promising.[2]

Bishop Gibney, while continuing his campaign for an increased subsidy, sought to make the mission self-supporting by obtaining licences for pearling and for working the rich guano deposits on the Lacepede Islands[3] and he also urged the monks to consider the experimental processing of turtle meat and emu skins. These suggestions were received without enthusiasm at Sept Fons, for mining was contrary to the Trappist tradition and it required some sophistry to define the gathering and marketing of shell and the excrement of sea birds in any other way.

More to their liking was the news, received early in 1892, that the bishop had purchased, for the sum of £500, a 100,000 acre property named Lombadina,[4] about fifty miles north of Beagle Bay and which the original owners, Harry Hunter and Sidney Hadley, had sold not long before for £150. He had at the same time managed to secure for the mission a grant of reserve land containing 2,002 acres of freehold in the vicinity of Disaster Bay on the eastern side of the peninsula. These acquisitions had trebled both the mission area and its native population, while stock listed as 332 sheep, fifty head of cattle, a few horses, a number of pigs and some poultry, together with a pearling plant of two luggers and equipment, had been part of the bargain.

This and the promise of a grant from the Society for the Propagation of the Faith in France turned the scales in favour of the continuation of the mission with an increased community. After eight months' absence the possibilities for the foundation in Australia seemed considerably brighter to

Abbot Ambrose who, now content to return, resolved to launch a more resolute drive for Australian candidates and to embark more forthrightly on educating the natives to conduct their own affairs.

The seven religious chosen to make up the stipulated 'minimum community' of ten members were Dom Ambrose's younger brother, Father Jean Marie Janny who had been with him in New Caledonia, Father Anselm Lenegre, a gentle scholar who had had no previous missionary experience, three middle-aged French brothers, Etienne Pidat, François d'Assise Jorcin, Felicien Chuzeville and a young Hollander named Brother Bonaventure Holthurin. The party also included the sixteen-year-old boy John Berchmans, who had been dedicated to the Order as a child and was soon to take the habit. They left France early in March 1892, trans-shipped at Singapore to a steamer bound for Broome and there boarded the mission lugger *Jessie*[5] for Beagle Bay.[6]

Their arrival was a quiet one, for provisions had run short at the mission and Father Aphonse had been forced to send the people off to live on bush food until further stores arrived. He had hoped they would return for Mass on Sundays but they had not done so. As one old man had bluntly explained, it was a case of 'no more tobacco, no more h'Allelulia!'[7]

Recharged with optimism by the return of the abbot with fresh recruits, Father Alphonse assured the new arrivals that this need not depress them, for despite the many counter-influences to which they were subjected a number of natives now showed a sincere inclination to accept the Christian outlook. He, for his part, after some study of their customs, kinship divisions and tribal taboos, had been careful to respect their beliefs except when he considered them contrary to God's law. Having learned that men and women within certain degrees of tribal relationship were forbidden to look at each other he had put up a curtain in the church to divide the sexes so they could make no excuse of having to break their law by entering the house of God. This he regarded as a tactful and harmless concession, but such practices as infanticide, polygamy and the ritual initiation of the boys he lumped together as 'the futile works of darkness' with which St. Paul had warned his people to have nothing to do.[8] So far the elders had refused to listen to the suggestion that they should abandon all but one of their several wives. The monk believed, however, that he had convinced them that Christian baptism should henceforth take the place of tribal initiation and he planned, when the people returned, to proceed with the instruction of a number of boys whom he thought almost ready to be received as children of the Church.[9]

His optimism on this score was soon again to be belied, for when he and Father Jean Marie went to inform the people in their camp at Bungadok that the mission stores were now replenished, they stumbled upon the full-dress man-making ceremony of their cherished catechists. Hidden in the scrub, a wild chanting and thunder of sacred bull-roarers throbbing in their ears, they watched the boys, their faces and bodies drenched with blood, drinking from the pierced arm veins of the elders.

They returned thoughtfully to the mission, but the news of fresh supplies did not take long to spread. Soon the people came trailing back, laughing and calling joyful greetings to the abbot and his new helpers. Not all the women who had given birth during their absence had babies in their coolimons and when questioned they shrugged and said the little ones were 'finished' or had been 'rubbish ones' – half-caste Malay or Chinese.

The young initiates, washed clean of all signs of recent rites, put on their red soutanes and white surplices and greatly astonished the newcomers by their seeming piety and the fluency of their Latin responses.

The abbot's determined drive for postulants took him, soon after his return, to most of the Australian capitals where, an impressive figure in his monastic habit, he had been received with respect and not a little awe. His English,

74

however, was too limited for easy conversation or public speaking and even the most devout Catholics were at a loss to understand what he thought he could do for the Aborigines. Any inclined to enter religion recoiled from the austerity and 'foreignness' of the Order he represented and decided they could do more good elsewhere. Only one young man, of little education and no special ability, who had dramatically prostrated himself at the abbot's feet, offered himself as a recruit and came to Beagle Bay where he took the name of Brother Bernard.

By the time Dom Ambrose returned to the mission the last of the horses had died and stock work was impossible. The cattle ran wild in the scrub, and the sheep, though carefully shepherded, showed little sign of increase. The Lombadina property of which the bishop had been so optimistic had also proved disappointing. The land itself comprised an almost useless expanse of tangled pindan scrub, paperbark swamp and tidal marsh. The homestead and outbuildings were completely derelict and there was little or no stock to be found. According to the former owners, Hunter and Hadley, most of the sheep and all the horses had died in the drought since the sale, the cattle and pigs had strayed and were too wild to muster and there was no sign whatever of the 'poultry'. Worst of all, the natives one and all had departed with their former employers to a new base on Pender Bay.[10]

The only real asset from the transaction had been the lugger *Jessie* that, repaired at considerable expense, had been the one part of the 'pearling plant' worth salvaging.

The natives, except for three or four who remained faithful, continued to drift in and out as the whim seized them and it was obvious that only by greater material inducements could they be won from the pearling camps and encouraged to settle at the mission. The abbot was therefore forced to sink his Trappist scruples and to sanction the mission's embarking on the sale of pearl shell, guano and emu skins. He also inquired into the possibility of processing turtle meat but discarded the idea on learning of the dismal failure of a French company that had previously set up a factory for this purpose on the Lacepedes.

Responsibility for the new enterprises was relegated to Brother Xavier Daly, on whose uncomplaining shoulders fell an ever-increasing burden of work, negotiation and correspondence. The bishop must have gained great consolation from his letters as he alone of all the missionaries wrote with real optimism. He never neglected to thank his Lordship for having encouraged him to enter the Order and praised the mercy of God in having permitted him to continue 'even so far'.[11] He also considered himself privileged to have been able to contribute to the misssion some sixty-eight head of cattle, his share of the stock on his family's Fitzroy property. He reported briefly and in typical Australian style on the natives. There were as yet no conversions amongst them and they continued to be 'very inconsistent'.[12] For the success of the local foundation, however, he seems to have entertained no doubts and wrote in detail of the regular Trappist life that had begun in earnest soon after the arrival of the new recruits. News from Sept Fons of the longed-for reunion of the three separated Cistercian communities had seemed a good omen to the missionaries who hoped that the Order, in its renewed strength, would be able to help them to a firmer footing in Australia.

But, for all his absorption with the Trappist way of life, Brother Xavier appears to have thrown himself dutifully into the mission's 'temporal enterprises'. To skipper the pearling lugger *Jessie* and organize the Aboriginal crew he secured the services of one Harry O'Grady, an experienced seaman who had a pearling base of his own at Cygnet Bay. He also did his best to explain to the natives that the missionaries intended this pearling project specifically for their own benefit and hoped that it could soon be given entirely into their control. Many of them had already some experience of diving, shell-opening and packing. Harry O'Grady was to instruct them in seamanship and navigation, Brother Xavier to explain to them the financial aspect and to train them in the handling of money. Shell

76

being then plentiful and bringing a fair price, and with the added prospect of finding valuable pearls, the venture seemed fairly foolproof. The catch was that owing to the poverty of the mission the quantity and quality of rations provided did not come up to those offered by private pearling concerns. A long range economic plan was quite meaningless to the natives and they decided that if they must dive for pearl shell they might as well do so for those who offered the richer immediate reward.

Bishop Gibney, staunchly upholding his protégé, interpreted the failure of his cherished scheme as further proof of the iniquity of the pearlers:

> ... I was of the opinion that when gently used by the missioners, and well fed and clothed, they would get to understand that they were working for their own benefit, which, on land, they did not object to. But the idea had to be abandoned, as ... the natives refused to go on board, and thus the industry which would have helped the mission had to be relinquished. The former contact of the aborigines with pearlers had evidently struck terror into their minds, and so militated against those whose kindness they acknowledged on shore. ...[13]

None the less the natives were by no means reluctant to board the mission lugger to collect guano on the Lacepede Islands, which, since turtles and eggs were plentiful there, had always been a favourite haunt of the local tribes. Negotiating their crude mangrove rafts had, however, been difficult and dangerous and the chance of going by lugger, even with the obligation of doing a certain amount of work, delighted them. They cooked all they could eat while there and returned with a feast for their people who gathered on the beach to welcome them.

One after another of the bishop's bright schemes to make the mission self-supporting failed. During 1892 eight tons of guano and a large bundle of cured emu skins were brought to an agent in Broome but neither commodity was found salable. In the same year a few bales of mission wool were shipped to England but scarcely paid the cost of transport.

No further effort was made to market guano but the abbot's brother, father Jean Marie Janny, quickly put it to use in the mission garden with splendid results. Before long the community was enjoying fine paw paws, bananas and a great variety of vegetables as well as plentiful honey from a hive of imported bees.

Brother Xavier reported this with his usual enthusiasm and it might have been assumed from his letters that living conditions at the mission left little to be desired. To one used to bush life and to sleeping in a swag on the hard ground, no doubt any sort of bed and shelter seemed comparative luxury, while a diet of fresh vegetables and wholemeal bread stood in good stead of the salt beef and damper that had been his former staple fare. To the French monks, however, for all the austere standards of their normal monastic routine, life at Beagle Bay must have been almost insupportable. As the season gathered its forces for the breaking of the monsoon the garden withered and insects descended in their countless myriads. Infected bites brought complications to add to the miseries of dysentery, conjunctivitis, and fever (kept in constant circulation by the busy anopheles), that made the normal procedure of clearing and ploughing, fencing and building, an agonizing test of endurance.

How much hotter could it get? At what temperature and at what state of weakness and fatigue did human will-power reach breaking point? How, in this upside-down world, where the trees showed neither fall nor spring, were they to match the rhythm of the seasons to the liturgy of the Christian year as monks in the old world had done throughout the centuries? Sometimes during the long hours of prayer in the stifling little church one of the community would slump in a faint and as December drew on and the dry bush panted in the cruel heat the familiar words of Isaiah, proper to the season of Advent in a winter landscape, took on a newly literal sense: 'Send victory like a dew, you heavens, and let the clouds rain it down. Let the earth open for salvation to spring up.' (*Isaiah* 45, 8)

As the storms gathered the skies proclaimed God's glory in billowing mountains of cloud that flashed with unearthly light and crashed with portentous thunder. The monsoon broke with awesome majesty and fierce gusts of wind-driven rain turned the parched earth to quagmire, set running a network of shallow creeks and brought on a quick growth of high, rank grass.

> Let the wilderness and the dry-lands exult, let the wasteland rejoice and bloom, let it bring forth flowers like the jonquil, let it rejoice and sing for joy. . . .
>
> Strengthen all weary hands, steady all trembling knees and say to all faint hearts, 'Courage! Do not be afraid'. . . .
>
> For water gushes in the desert, streams in the waste-land, the scorched earth becomes a lake, the parched land springs of water. . . .

When the fury of the first cyclone had spent itself Brother François d'Assise went out to find some sheep that had strayed away. By nightfall he had not returned to the mission and searchers next day found his body trapped in the debris of a running creek, a drowned lamb in his arms. It was remembered that he had taken the habit at the little abbey of Tamié, in the high Alps of Savoy, and had been one of the small band that set out from that monastery for north China in 1883. There he had tended the sheep and survived the perils of towering mountain ravines and rushing torrents to come to his death in a shallow creek on the scrubby flats of Dampierland. Only the old natives who were children then remember the circumstances of his death and recall the place of his burial.[14]

In the motherhouse at Sept Fons the trials and frustrations of the Australian community were paraphrased to snippets of careful understatement for the newly established journal *L'Union Cistercienne*.

*August 1892*. We have heard news of our monastery in Australia. Our fathers (some eight men) were somewhat frightened by pains in their eyes and limbs, but otherwise things seem to be going well for them. A curious feature of these parts is that around the Lacepede Islands tortoises of more than twenty lbs have been seen dying on the shores. May we add that in this new foundation where everything has to be started right from scratch, each day brings ample opportunities for really heroic sacrifices.

*November 1892*. We have received a very long letter from Dom Ambrose the Abbot in the Australian House. He emphasized especially the difficulty of civilizing, much less Christianizing the natives whose custom he finds very distressful. For example, the mothers sometimes kill and eat their own children. Yet he hopes that prayer ... will enable himself and his confrères to do some good in these parts. His little community is a source of consolation to him. ... They are praying that God will send them good vocations. ...[15]

# CHAPTER SEVEN

## 1892 – 1894

IN 1892 criticism of the treatment of Aborigines on station properties had roused north-west pastoralists to defend their attitude and to demand more authority in dealing with native offenders. At a meeting called for this purpose one speaker was reported as saying that the question 'was a difficult one to handle, owing to the sentiment of a large portion of the English-speaking race, who were bereft of their reasoning powers. ... Having suffered so heavily himself he knew only too well what was necessary. ... If the lash had not been used they would all have been murdered years ago. ... The natives only study destruction of life and property. ... He likened [them] to dingoes because they had always destroyed the herds, and always would do.'[1]

Some advocated longer and more severe prison sentences for stock-spearing or absconding from station employment, others the removal of all Aborigines to outlying islands. Another suggested shorter prison sentences and more severe floggings 'at the beginning and end of term', remarking that 'the official "cat" used on a native simply wiped the dust off him'. 'It should be remembered,' he said, 'that a native had a hide, and not an ordinary skin like ordinary human beings.'

Forthright criticism was voiced against the government for being so 'frightened by the clamour that was being made in the colonial and English papers' that 'already the flogging of natives was becoming the merest farce'.

As might be expected these sentiments drew Bishop

Gibney into the arena with all his gladiatorial zeal, his diatribes against the northern settlers and pearlers triggering off a spate of correspondence probably unparalleled in heat and verbosity in the local press. Letters to the editor, published in full from introductory preambles to final declarations of humble and obedient servitude, ran column after column for months on end, some of the bishop's statements, made in the heat of controversy and the indignation of his soul, having drawn the red herrings of theological interpretation and the ubiquitous Irish question across the clear trail of justice for a neglected people.[2]

North-westers in general proclaimed the blessings of civilization they had brought to the unenlightened savage, though settlers were prepared to admit that 'certain atrocities' had been committed by the pearlers, and the pearlers that ill-treatment of the natives often occurred on pastoral properties. 'Eye-witness' accounts were denied or justified on all sides, one pastoralist writing in spirited defence of a punitive expedition for which a number of special constables had been sworn in to help the police:

> The settlers that were in that party were as justified in obeying orders as British soldiers when they shot at either Kaffirs, Zulus, Abyssinians, or any other inferior race, and for which they are frequently decorated with medals, iron crosses, etc., and their names sounded forth as heroes and brave soldiers, the pride of the nation. . . . Now what was the result? Never afterwards in that particular part of the district for miles around, was there any further trouble with natives. They became henceforth good servants, on the most friendly terms with the settlers, and soon gave up bush life and poverty to enjoy plenty of good food and other luxuries.[3]

Premier John Forrest, anxious to reconcile the ideals of British justice and his esteem for the Catholic bishop with the settlers' demands for increased protection against wholesale sabotage, observed that there seemed to be 'a screw loose somewhere'.

The bishop's forthright attitude, while standing to his credit in history, had set against him a powerful section of contemporary society and the fact that some members of the Aborigines Protection Board had pastoral interests in the north did not help him in the conflict he continued to wage on behalf of the Beagle Bay Mission.

In 1893, having failed to get any satisfaction from the board, he wrote to Governor Robinson, giving him a full account of all missionary efforts in the north up to that time.

> Sir, [he wrote] with grief I admit the native race is dis-
> appearing ... but so far from recognizing under all cir-
> cumstances the correctness of the doctrine of the
> Aborigines Board that the European must efface the
> black race, I am bound to declare, after thirty years of
> missionary labours in this colony, that ... if more pains
> were taken to introduce [the natives] to not alone the
> curses but also the blessings of civilization, and if the
> funds at the disposal of the board were properly utilized
> ... this effacement would be largely checked. ...[4]

His case for a subsidy at least equal to that granted to Protestant missions in the south was clearly justified and the governor handed on his letter to the board with a friendly recommendation.

In January 1894, still no further forward, the bishop decided to go over the heads of local authorities. He sent a well documented memorial[5] through the governor to the Secretary of State for the Colonies in London pointing out that whereas members of the Board considered a paltry sum adequate for an establishment to assist the natives, they had recently granted themselves £155 8s. each for annual attendance fees!

Bishop Gibney had no doubt hoped that the Secretary of State, the Marquis of Ripon, being a Catholic, would give his cause favourable consideration. In a despatch[6] to Governor Robinson the marquis requested him to inform the bishop that while sympathetic to his cause he could not interfere since a clause of the Western Australian Constitution Act provided 'that the Board may spend their money at their discretion under the sole control of the governor of the colony'. At the same time Cardinal Vaughan, to whom Bishop Gibney had also appealed to plead his cause, replied from London that he had seen Lord Ripon who explained that he could use his influence in the matter only, in a private capacity.

A press statement at this stage accusing the missionaries of condoning the wanton and cruel destruction of turtles on the outlying islands could hardly have been more unfortunately timed. In this the Commissioner of Fisheries declared himself to have been 'a practical witness'[7] to the fact that hundreds of animals had been turned on their backs and left to die by the Beagle Bay natives.

A spokesman for the mission replied that the islands were much frequented by pearling crews that often remained for three weeks, that Captain O'Grady and Brother Xavier always accompanied their natives and were careful that no turtles were left to perish. The report was ascribed to those who, having once held undisputed sway over the Aborigines, resented the mission and took every opportunity of maligning it.

Bishop Gibney appealed to John Forrest to carry out an investigation and was later assured that the reports were found to have been based on hearsay. The Commissioner of Fisheries wrote that he regretted having been misled and published an apology, but his irresponsible assertion, tossed off in an unguarded moment, had already helped to turn the scales between public sympathy and disregard for the mission and probably served to strengthen the case of the board for refusing an increase of subsidy.

In the middle of 1893 Abbot Ambrose, summoned to attend a General Chapter at Sept Fons, had sailed again for France, leaving in charge Father Anselm Lenegre, who had been prior from the time of his arrival a year before. Sadly disappointed by his failure to attract Australian postulants and in worse health than before, the abbot could hardly have been expected to present an encouraging picture of the mission's prospects to his superiors, but it appears that he had found 'les black-fellers', at first so strange to him as to seem almost, as their detractors maintained, of another species, increasingly human and likeable.[8] The tears they had shed at his leave-taking had touched him deeply, as had their habit, when he or members of his community lay ill, of passing their windows with murmured words· of encouragement and sympathy and the assurance of their prayers. He had even begun to find, in their naked struggle for existence, a curious dignity and to perceive in the pagan jumble of practices from which he had shrunk a sort of elemental common sense.

It could not, of course, be claimed that these poor people were free from iniquity – far from it – and yet none of the seven deadly sins could be very convincingly applied to their simple, law-fearing, savagely communal lives. What chance had covetousness and envy with a people not only lacking in but totally indifferent to worldly goods? The sin of sloth, to which many considered them prone, must remain meaningless to them until they had accepted the virtue of industry in a civilized sense.

The monks had, of course, condemned polygamy but further study of tribal customs indicated that this was not necessarily dictated by lust, in which respect the Aboriginal was no worse than the average European and a good deal better than many. As their means of communication had improved, so had the native tendency – in a quaint mixture of English, French and their own tongue – to argue the virtues of their own beliefs and practices. The elders were quite unmoved by the monks' condemnation of polygamy with what they saw as the attendant evils of child marriage and the subjection of women, for did this law not, the natives argued, assure protection and a place for all in the pattern of tribal life? Nor did it always break the male's way, for, as in a levirate marriage of the Old Testament, a man was obliged in certain circumstances to take over his deceased brother's wife or wives, even though they might prove a burden to him. No woman, however ill-favoured or infirm, was rejected in tribal society, while the older women, when questioned, implied that it suited them to have younger bodies to bear their burdens and to fetch and carry for them in their declining years.

It had been found so far quite useless to hold up to them the ideal of the Virgin Mother of God. They themselves claimed some spirit hero[9] who had arisen, fully mature, from the sea, without any parents at all. They agreed, therefore, that this sort of thing could happen but they saw no reason why a woman who had never known a man (a concept quite impossible in tribal life) should be held in high regard on that account. None of the older people, though some bowed in veneration before the Blessed Sacrament, and might even recite the rosary with seeming devotion, showed any regard for the statue of Our Lady in the mission church.

The people fought among themselves from time to time but their anger was controlled and quickly cooled by the practice of striking blow for blow or throwing spear for spear in accordance with tribal protocol.

They might be held guilty of the sin of gluttony on such rare occasions as there was more than enough food for all, but the greedy man, who exceeded his lawful portion, was ridiculed out of countenance.

This left only the sin of pride of which, apart from a certain essential pride of tribal tradition and status, the Aboriginal was singularly innocent.

Father Alphonse, with much painstaking search for meaningful local idiom, had translated the Sermon on the Mount which they claimed they understood very well and found completely in accordance with their own law. Had they not always taken example from the plants of the pindan and placed the fullest confidence in all their needs being provided by supernatural means? Did they not believe only too firmly that tomorrow would look after itself and that clothing, except as a protection from the cold, was of no account? Was sharing not so strong a precept in their law

86

that they were obliged, even against implicit instructions, to give their mission issues of clothes and blankets to outsiders who had none? These people had, in fact, so little inclination to store up treasure upon earth, a prey to rust and a temptation to thieves, that the monks feared they needed rather a precept to explain the new practical necessity to plan and to save, to aspire to the ownership of plots of land, stable homes and the basic worldly goods that went with them.

Nothing of this, however, actually convinced the abbot that the mission should be continued nor did it help to inspire the confidence of his superiors, for in August 1893 Bishop Gibney received the following letter, written in Latin, from the Abbot-General, Father Sebastian Wyart:

Most Reverend and Illustrious Lord Bishop:

The Reverend Father Dom Ambrose, Abbot of the Trappists in Kimberley, has told me of the difficulties of maintaining his monastery and states that it is impossible to stay in Australia any longer for the following reasons:

(1) The Aborigines are a race of people such as it seems impossible to convert to the true faith.

(2) Vocations of novices are non-existent and there is no hope of there being any in the future in these remote, pagan and abandoned regions.

(3) It is doubtful whether we will ever get the financial support promised by the Australian Government. Obviously it is not possible for the most Eminent Cardinal in Sydney to obtain the money previously bespoken by the government for the monastery.

(4) Experiments have proved that the soil of those regions is infertile and barren. Under such conditions therefore, with no hope of converting souls, without financial support and on account of the barrenness of the land and the poorness of the crops, life is impossible even for the frugal Trappist.

Such is the opinion of the Reverend Father Dom Ambrose, Abbot.

What do you feel about this? How do you respond to the points raised and the difficulties to be faced in continuing?

I humbly beseech you, frankly and unhesitatingly to tell me as soon as possible what you think of his opinion of this recent establishment in Kimberley so that our General Chapter can judiciously deal with the present condition of the monastery and make plans for its future. . . .

Father Maria Sebastianus, Abbot. O.C.R.[10]

The bishop, shocked and hurt that the monks he revered should have adopted an attitude as defeatist as that of the Aborigines Protection Board that he despised, prevailed upon Cardinal Moran to join him in urging the Trappists on. The cardinal wrote[11] stressing that missionary work among primitive people must always be difficult at first and cited the success of the Spanish Benedictines at New Norcia with the same race of which the French monks despaired. They also pointed out that similar trials were being bravely met by the Jesuits at Daly River in the Northern Territory[12] and by other missionaries in New Guinea. To have obtained three candidates for the brotherhood was, they thought, an encouraging response from a pioneer colony still lacking in tradition. Vocations were not yet to be expected here as in Europe and, in any case, surely the aim of the foundation had been to help the Aborigines rather than to build up a strong centre of cloistered monks?

Australian soil, even in the now prosperously settled areas, always appeared sterile until its special requirements and the local seasons were understood. Had the garden at Beagle Bay not already produced splendid fruit and vegetables? As far as finance was concerned there were avenues within the Church itself, such as the Society for the Propagation of the Faith, that might be called upon for further monetary assistance, while the colonial government would no doubt be more generous once the mission had proved its worth. The case ended with a heartfelt plea that the Trappists might show to the community as a whole an example of perseverance and trust in the goodness of God.

This impassioned appeal moved the Abbot-General to reconsider his decision and he wrote to the three monks at Beagle Bay asking them to nominate a successor to Abbot Ambrose. It had by this time been mooted that the Kimberley mission field should be declared a vicariate apostolic with its superior as bishop, a role that none of the three in question was inclined to accept. When they replied that they could arrive at no decision, Dom Sebastian, completely at a loss, called on the Cardinal Prefect of Propaganda, offering the mission, without indemnity, to any congregation that would take it over.[13] According to his own account his eminence refused to listen to this suggestion.

'It is the Trappists who are there,' he insisted, 'and that by the will of the Holy Father. They must keep at it and you must do all that depends on you to develop the mission.'[14]

The Cardinal Prefect further encouraged Dom Sebastian by the promise of financial help from his society and the use of his influence in getting five or six English-speaking German sisters then attached as tertiaries to the Trappist mission of Marrianhill in Natal.

Smaller donations from other sources quickly followed. A Spanish secular priest[15] and three postulants to the brotherhood entered Sept Fons in the expressed hope of joining the Australian project and a number of professed Trappists earnestly volunteered for the task. These turns of event were accepted as a sign of the Divine Will being in favour of the mission and Dom Ambrose, greatly heartened, agreed to return as abbot until another of the community was elected in his place.

At Beagle Bay meanwhile the priests had tried to keep the unsettled state of affairs from the working brothers but in so small and enclosed a community it was impossible to conceal their disturbed state of mind. The new recruit, Brother Bernard, who, after the death of Brother François, had been put in charge of the sheep, began asking awkward questions about the return of his beloved abbot and when reminded that a good Trappist spoke only when granted permission, fell into a brooding silence that he stubbornly refused to break. It was then recalled that he had shown symptoms of instability when, not long after his arrival, he had suspected that a mischievous native boy who kept peeking at him from behind trees had been set to spy on him. This matter had been cleared up but as the wet season of 1893 dragged on it became obvious that he was no longer in his right mind. At last he wandered off into the bush where he was found by the natives in a state of exhaustion and carried back to the mission.

'What to do?' Father Alphonse wrote to the bishop. 'We cannot now admit him to Profession. . . . He already scandalizes the natives by not attending Mass.'[16]

The bishop solved the problem by arranging for the unfortunate man's return to his family. Father Alphonse, deeply grateful, tried to write cheerfully to his good friend, making no mention of the fear in his heart of the missions being abandoned: 'If trials and crosses are a good sign for a new foundation, then we have, thanks be to God, a good prospect.'[17]

# CHAPTER EIGHT

## 1895 – 1896

FATHER JEAN MARIE JOSEPH, one of the ten new recruits chosen for the Australian mission, wrote for the Cistercian journal a detailed account of their departure from France and the events that followed:

> Our fathers and brothers [he began] have seen for themselves how many trials God wanted to put Dom Ambrose through before granting him the reinforcements of personnel and funds he had come back to Europe to seek. He has had no lack of suffering, both physical and moral, but they turned out to be the seed-bed of blessings. Though there had been a year and a half of inactive waiting for men and means, when they did come they came both speedily and in unexpected ways that bore the stamp of a God planning mercy for the unfortunate Aborigines ...
>
> Our brothers witnessed too the final preparations and the generosity with which the missionaries threw themselves into the great sacrifice. Dom Ambrose had taken care to dissipate any likely illusions, repeating over and over that there were no consolations to look forward to, only hardships, trials and crosses of every sort. But far from discouraging us, their warnings only inflamed our will for the path of sacrifice ... and no one has quit it, because it is for all the path of obedience and love. ...

The writer told how on 2nd March, 1895, in accordance with Trappist tradition, the travellers united themselves with their community before the Blessed Sacrament at

Sept Fons. They then set out by carriage for the convent of the Trappestine Sisters at Macon where Dom Sebastian Wyart was to bestow on them a final blessing. He stood awaiting them with outstretched arms while the nuns, from behind their convent grille, raised their voices in a song composed for the occasion. The verses, in translation and the light of after knowledge, seem somewhat extravagant but Australia was indeed the wildest of antipodes to these French religious and the days of martyrdom for Christian missionaries were not after all at an end.

### Chant de Depart

*Partez, héraults de la bonne neuvelle,*
*Voici le jour appelé par vos voeux . . .*
*Frères, volez sur les ailes des vents;*
*Ne craignez pas, Marie est votre étoile,*
*Elle saura veiller sur ses enfants.*
*Respecte, ô mer, leur mission sublime,*
*Garde-les bien, sois pour eux sans écueil,*
*Et sous ces pieds qu'un si beau zèle anime*
  *De tes flots abaisse l'orgueil!*

### Choeur

*Partez, partez, Frères, pour l'Australie!*
*Portez là-bas le Nome de notre Dieu!*
*Nous nous retrouverons un jour dans la patrie,*
  *Adieu, Frères, adieu!*


Go forth, heralds of good tidings,
Here is the day ordained by your vows . . .
Brothers, fly on the wings of the wind.
Fear not! Mary is your star,
She will watch over her children.
Respect, o sea, their sublime mission;
Guard them well; be for them without foam,
Under these feet animated by such fine zeal
  Abase the pride of your waves!

Set forth, set forth, brothers, for Australia!
Carry down there the Name of our God!
We will meet again one day in heaven,
    Farewell, brothers, farewell.

Hasten your steps towards those teeming races
Without truth, without God, without hope . . .
Hasten to this holy mission.
Give to God your suffering and your toil,
For suffer you will and your lives
Will be expended in rough work.
Perhaps too the blood will be spilled from your veins.
These feet of such beauty[2] perhaps will wear their chains
    And your bodies be given up to the executioner.

Set forth, set forth, for your brothers are failing.
Time and death will soon diminish their ranks.
Must not one replace those who fall,
Cut down by the heat of summer and by the years?
If you would share their victory
Follow always the imprint of their feet.
God calls you and from the heart of glory
    All the saints hold out their arms to you!

We your sisters shall hasten in your steps,
Seeking to share with you the saving of souls,
And to this end, across the space that divides us,
We will know how to suffer and pray.
O missionaries, in holy transport
    We kiss your feet so fair. . . .[3]

The Abbot-General's address was more down to earth.
He told the travellers that there was little chance of the sort
of martyrdom referred to in the nuns' *envoie* but that they
would not lack daily crosses to test their fortitude.

'You will be carrying on the glorious tradition of the Cistercian Order,' he told them, 'for our Fathers, since the time of St. Bernard, have worked among people as uncultured as those to which you are bound. . . . Love God, love one another, support one another in great charity and humility. . . . Oh, if we could but practise this charity – what marvels! what paradise! . . .'[4]

At this point, we are told, the Abbot-General could no longer restrain his emotion and with tears streaming down his cheeks he turned towards the sisters in their enclosure.

'My dear daughters,' he said, 'in your farewell song you told us of a great desire to kiss these "feet so fair" of the missionaries, who are off to proclaim God's peace and gospel to an infidel population. Well, the grille keeps you from fulfilling your wish, but ourselves out here can do and will do it both for ourselves and for you.'[5]

Whereupon, amid the tears of all present, the Most Reverend Father prostrated himself and kissed the feet of the departing missionaries. Other priests and brothers present followed his example, 'while we', the missionary-scribe continues, 'were obliged to undergo this humiliation, but with the thought that it was not to us, but to Our Lord and his Apostles that the honour was being paid'.[6]

They were then invited to bless their sisters whose sobs were audible from behind their enclosure, whereupon the Reverend Mother bade them good-bye on behalf of her community and the Abbot-General presented them with souvenir medals especially blessed for them by the Holy Father.

The steamship *Salazie* took the party from Marseilles to Singapore where, before trans-shipping to the *Australind*, the abbot cabled the Broome telegraph office to send a courier to the mission asking for a lugger to intercept them offshore. As there was no entrance for larger vessels into Beagle Bay and no way of knowing whether their message had been received they were 'half-way between hope and dread' when a sail was sighted in the expected area. This proved to be the provision boat for a pearling fleet that gathered to meet it, thirty luggers strong, sails billowing in a stiff breeze, coloured crews like pirate bands scrambling in the rigging to wave and shout to the *Australind* as they skimmed past.

Soon, however, the lugger *Jessie* was sighted struggling out towards them, Father Alphonse's white robes and black scapular flapping at the prow.

Transferred with their belongings on to the lugger the new arrivals had their first experience of the tides to which the people of the peninsula learned to adjust their activities:

> It was 2 p.m. when we left the *Australind* and set our prow straight for Beagle Bay. Having the wind and tide with us we managed to get within a mile of the shore by 5 p.m. when we had to drop anchor and wait for the 11 p.m. high tide. ... We then drifted slowly shorewards with the rising tide and a gentle breeze. At 11.30 Dom Ambrose and a party of newcomers got into the *Jessie*'s dinghy and set foot on shore where they immediately intoned the 'Ave Maris Stella' and sang it through, alternating with us who were still on the schooner. Then the dinghy came back for the rest of us and brought the whole group together to recite a number of prayers and invocations before setting off for the mission site. Dom Ambrose led us off on the nine-mile walk into the midnight. ... That was how God led us on, right to our beloved mission. The valiant founders had been far from expecting such re-inforcements. They saw in our arrival an evident proof of God's will and blessing that put to flight the doubts that had sometimes arisen about the future of the mission and they responded straightaway with a great peal of bells. ...[7]

The mission more than satisfied the newcomers' expectations of hardship. The buildings, all of bush timber, bamboos and paperbark were 'so scorched by the tropical sun that they could take fire in an instant'. The beds, strips of canvas nailed to wooden frames, were without mattresses and the pillows were sacks filled with straw. Each man was provided with a cheese-cloth net – 'no luxury but a downright necessity' since mosquitoes haunted the mission like the special legions of Lucifer, 'the Holy Place, where we can least defend ourselves, being their stronghold'.[8]

Horizontal poles across the dormitories served as clothes hangers and the door was made from pieces of old sail:

> Don't look for anything else, because there isn't anything, not a vessel, not a piece of furniture, no carpet but just the plain old floor of sand the way God made it, dark grey and very fine ... Back in France I had always believed that it was all right to be poor but never dirty, though here it is impossible not to be dirty even though one washes several times a day.
>
> The poverty of the house is so extreme that for the twenty persons we have only thirty towels which can only be washed fortnightly, and at table one would have a hard job to find the shadow of a table napkin under our beards. What a lovely thought it would be of some kind person to send us this indispensable linen. . . .
>
> The dormitory serves also as an infirmary, and is shared by the sick with the roosters and hens that make themselves at home there and with the pigs that have their permanent domicile on the verandah and there they entertain us with their scarcely soothing snorts. The mosquitoes give no sick leave from their bothersome operations and the good Blackfellows throw them in a helping hand. . . . Then there are the bells at the entrance of the dormitory that are big enough to upset the sick as each new exercise is announced upon them. . . . Then try to imagine what the Lord inflicts on those He visits with fever or similar diseases. I am speaking from experience and all the new arrivals have shared my fate. . . . However, none of this keeps us from gaiety in the service of God ... and Dom Ambrose, good father and religious that he is, has already taken in hand the construction of a new dormitory and church more spacious and suitable than the present ones.[9]

Singularly enough, in this long and detailed account, ending with assurances of the unflagging routine of their prayerful lives, the only mention of the people who were the reason for their being there at all is the passing reference to the disturbance they contributed to the snorting of the pigs and molestations of the mosquitoes!

Bishop Gibney, seeing in the strengthened mission community a chance of relegating part of his enormous responsibility, wrote the abbot with 'fervent and fraternal greeting' that:

> You have now priests enough to send out to the various places where people reside . . . I claim nothing but to have the work done as well as you can.
>
> You may soon expect advice from Rome giving the jurisdiction of the Kimberley district to your Holy House

This letter revealed a basic misunderstanding between the points of view of the secular and monastic religious and the bishop was shocked and surprised when the abbot, without reference to the matter of leading priests for outside work, replied that he had 'now neither the strength nor the zeal' to undertake the administration of a vicariate.[11] Where the bishop saw the monastery as a supply centre to meet the needs of the area, to the abbot it was a stronghold besieged by enemies – the pearlers and their lustful crews, the worldly pastoralists, the indifferent government, the obdurate tribal elders and now the bishop himself. What chance had a Trappist establishment in a land where even Catholic churchmen could suggest dispersing members from their powerhouse of prayer?

One by one all the doubts that the abbot had been so determined to cast aside returned to torment him How could the monastic regime, ordinarily lived in healthy harmony with nature, be supported in a land where sickness thrived on a Trappist diet and the seasons made a mockery of their rule? How was even a temporary compromise possible between the roles of missionary and contemplative?

97

The maintenance of the mission, far from becoming simpler, required an ever-increasing weight of working priests and brothers and as their strength failed it became necessary to relax traditional austerities until too little of their rule remained.

Racked with fever and troubled with a heart complaint, Dom Ambrose wrote to France asking that the Abbot-General, if in favour of their accepting the Kimberley vicariate, should himself name a successor to administer it. None of the Trappists then in Australia seemed able to fill the role. Prior Anselm was neither forceful nor enterprising enough to administer a vicariate. Father Alphonse lacked the physical strength and his English was too poor for such a public task. Father Jean Marie's great agricultural skill and increasing influence with the natives were too valuable to be spared from missionary work and he would never willingly have accepted the position. The two ex-secular priests, Father Ermenfroy Nachin and Bernard Le Louarn, were both strongly opposed to the Trappists having any part in outside administration, while the Spanish Father Nicholas Emo, then acting as parish priest of Broome, could hardly be spared from that post. Father Marie Joseph, the mission chronicler, who had come out strongly in favour of continuing as a separate missionary foundation, had declared himself willing to undertake this responsibility but the abbot did not, for some reason, consider him suitable.[12]

Dom Ambrose was much relieved to hear at last that the Abbot-General was not, on further consideration, in favour of their taking over the vicariate. For Father Marie Joseph, however, this news was the breaking point. He claimed to have received private advice that the Abbot-General's opinion was quite the reverse and early in 1896 he took himself back to Europe to protest, presumably against what he considered the duplicity of Abbot Ambrose.[13] There is no available evidence to indicate whether he was an emotionally unstable character or an able zealot disillusioned by the vacillation of his superiors. At all events, he thereafter left the Order and his name does not appear again in Trappist records.

This disturbing influence removed, the abbot again resigned himself to continue in office until a successor was found. None the less his community had been badly shaken by the issue of the vicariate and he was aware of a widening rift between those in favour of concentrating their forces on missionary work and others who believed this policy a betrayal of their contemplative vocation.

# CHAPTER NINE

## 1895 – 1899

THE abbot's brother, Father Jean Marie, although truly a Trappist at heart, believed that his order's first responsibility in Australia was to the Aborigines who, from the time of his arrival, had singled him out for their special reverence and confidence. Those who remembered him from their childhood days described him as tall and broad, his beard golden in the sun, his hands strong on the axe as he hewed at the pindan scrub. They told how his spade and plough worked miracles with the reluctant soil and how he coaxed more honey from his cultivated bees than was to be found in all the wild hives on the peninsula.[1] The natives may well have formed an exaggerated impression of his outstanding physique in a community of otherwise fairly small men but they still speak of him as wistfully as of a great dream-time teacher whose law they also failed to keep.

Galalang lived a long time ago. He came from far away to the country of the Nimanboor on Disaster Bay. He sat down beside a big freshwater lake called Londyemargan, which means 'the place of the paperbarks', and he allowed only good people with him in this place. In that lake were many fish, turtles and lily roots. Flying foxes and birds also came there. Wild turkeys, cranes, ibis, brolgas, cockatoos, pigeons, finches and ducks all came to this place. Kangaroos and lizards came here. Oh it was a good place this one in that time.

Galalang was before Minau who brought the ceremonies of circumcision and subincision to the Njul Njul.

100

He was before Djamar and his three sons who brought the first *galangarau* (*tjuringa*) and the first blood drinking ceremony to Dampierland. Galalang gave his people songs, dances and good laws but no magic. This is how he spoke to the Nimanboor: 'Now, you are all good, strong people here. You do not lie. You are not cannibals as others. You men have one wife only and you do not exchange this wife for others. When you want a wife you see she is the right woman. You know that to kill another is bad. You help others half by half and not by selling. When you kill a kangaroo you give half of it away, but you do not take payment. You young people must eat the smallest fish. No one should be greedy or keep the best food for himself.'

The law of Galalang was simple and straight. He gave the people two classes only, *djando* and *yenar*, not four as they now have. When they did wrong he punished them by sending lightning and hurricanes. Minau brought the Njul Njul the new man-making laws and gave them magic and secret songs and the Nimanboor heard of these things. Some did not like them. They said, 'No good,' and turned away but others took to them straight away. They said: 'This is a good way. We want this one.' Then Galalang made that channel. He pulled a log from the lake to the sea and drained off the fresh water, taking away also the turtles and fish. The people were afraid to see him so angry and they said: 'We must keep his law. He is strong this one.' Then by and by they went over to that other way. 'We have to get rid of that old man,' they said. So they sneaked up at night and speared him at the place called Gurmiri and threw him in the sea. They heard him call out, dying: 'You keep away from the shore now, all you turtles and dugongs, except in the breeding time.' Then the sharks tore his body to pieces and his blood stained the sea.

Galalang is now at Bangaranjara, the place of the dead. He is those shadows in the Milky Way. . . . He does not return to the people. They belong now to those others but

101

they are heart-crying for that good teacher and they remember him in this song:

> At Gurmiri you have been killed,
> You are resting stretched out on the sea.
> At Gurmiri you have fallen.
> Stretched out on your back
> On waves you can rest now.
> The fighter is dead.
> At Gurmiri you have fallen. . . .[2]

As the mission people were constantly going off to an
inter-tribal meeting place about five miles away, Father Jean
Marie thought it a good idea to form thereabouts an experimental branch mission or 'grange' which signified, in Trappist terms, a small dependency with neither abbot nor prior.
Having gained permission for this move, he took with him a
young professed cleric who, to distinguish him from probationer brothers, was already known as 'Father' Narcisse
Janne, and together they set up a small church and hermitage near the tribal camp at Bungadok. That the natives
showed no resentment towards this intrusion on their sacred
intertribal meeting ground was cited as proof of the regard
in which the missionaries were now held. This was no doubt
so, but in any case the natives had by this time accepted the
futility of physical resistance to any move the white man
might choose to make. It was obviously better to acquiesce
and accept such benefits as might accrue, in this instance not
only food but the protection of the sanctuary lamp to which
they attributed the power of warding off evil spirits in the
dark night scrub.

No demands were made on the people but they helped
spasmodically to cart timber, case a well, put up troughs for
a few head of sheep, cattle and goats, fence off a poultry run
and a garden plot. Some came to Mass and Benediction of
their own accord and often after evening prayers the monks
would sit by their camp fires, learning the languages, songs
and legends of the Njul Njul, Nimanboor and Bard.

Preferring this voluntary exile to the growing atmosphere

of disharmony at Beagle Bay, Father Jean Marie and his companion made such a success of their branch mission that the area adaptable for cultivation at Bungadok soon became too limited to support the growing community. A new site was selected around the spring country of the Nimanboor on Disaster Bay, a few miles south of Father McNab's mission that had been abandoned some ten years before and in which place long ago the great Galalang had gathered his people. Bishop Gibney with typical foresight had already secured a grant of reserve land with 2,002 acres of freehold embracing this area and before long, with the help of various tribal groups, a path had been cleared for the wagon, the stock and equipment moved, and work on the new branch began.

In this enterprise the monks had a staunch friend and helper in Thomas Puertoallano, a young Manilaman who had come to Broome as a diver. He had recently married a half-caste girl named Agnes Bryan whose Irish father had placed her with the missionaries at Beagle Bay, and the couple now wished to settle down on the land and raise a family. Although small in stature Thomas brought to the task all the enthusiastic faith of his Filipino heritage and worked with tremendous energy under Trappist direction. A garden quickly sprang to life around the natural springs of Disaster Bay and the graceful tops of bananas, paw paws, coconuts and Indian bamboos waved above a tangle of coastal vegetation.

The little mission of the Assumption of Our Lady, named for the day's Feast, set among scrubby dunes within sound of the sea, was opened on 15th August, 1896. The garden at Bungadok, particularly the flourishing melon and pumpkin patches, was also kept up for some time and the church and hermitage were occasionally used until demolished by fire many years later.

It suited the nomadic habits of the tribespeople to wander from one to another of these three mission establishments and gave the missionaries a better chance of keeping in touch with them. The Njul Njul, however, tended to remain longer at Beagle Bay, the Nimanboor and some of the Bard to gather at Disaster Bay, while all three groups continued to meet together at Bungadok. Things appeared to have taken a hopeful turn at last. The garden at Beagle Bay, responding to the increased number of skilled workers as well as to the use of guano and a greater understanding of climate and soil, was becoming talked about as second only to Maurice Holtz's botanical wonderland at Darwin, and the natives showed signs of settling down.

Up to August 1896 the only name in the baptismal register was that of Felix's baby, Maria Norengbor, but from this time on baptisms and marriages were recorded regularly at both Beagle Bay and Disaster Bay missions. In October, Brother Xavier wrote to Bishop Gibney of the happy occasion on which the first twelve members of Njul Njul, instructed in their own language by Father Alphonse, were received into the Church by Abbot Ambrose and of the deep impression this had made on all who witnessed it.[3]

Brother Xavier forbore to mention less edifying aspects mentioned in Father Alphonse's jumbled reports from which it emerged that the 'conversions' were causing trouble between the youths and the tribal elders. The concern of the old people can be appreciated for, although anxious to come to terms with the missionaries, to have abandoned their initiation rites would have amounted to no less an apostasy than had the monks themselves renounced their holy vows. The many stages of initiation, beginning when a boy was eleven or twelve, continued until he was a man of mature years, by which time, although no novice in sexual experience, he was entitled to claim his rightful wife or wives. The first and most important stage, known in the Dampierland area as the *Balleli*, extended, under ordinary conditions, over an impressive period of weeks or months. This began with the piercing of a boy's septum with the sharpened bone of a kangaroo and the removal of his two front teeth. Then followed a period of separation from normal tribal life, during which the youth was anointed, adorned, sung over and finally circumcised. The deeply symbolic significance of these ceremonies, in the course of which the boy passed through ritual death to be reborn to adult status in the life of his tribe, impressed at once the importance of the individual and his oneness with all creation. Through physical endurance and the gradual unfolding of secret and sacred traditions a man became indeed a warrior, proud in his own self-mastery, humble in his relationship to his country, his fellow men and their creator spirits. A terrible responsibility therefore weighed upon the elders to prepare the young to become trustworthy custodians of the law, properly versed in the rites that in tribal concept assured the increase of species and the survival of their people. Previously, although a boy had looked forward, with mingled fear and awe, to the mysterious ordeals that awaited him, he had accepted them as inevitable and necessary and endured them, for the most part, with fortitude. The missionaries, however, had shown the boys that there was an alternative to this age-old procedure and one moreover that could be justified on the grounds that the trials awaiting them were the work of Satan and hence displeasing to God. Little wonder that this had become the basis of endless arguments between the young people and their elders though few if any of the boys had so far managed to elude the *Balleli*. Sometimes a youth, by remaining close to the mission and thereby foregoing all the interest and excitement of tribal activities and 'walkabouts', contrived to avoid it for some time, but he was bound, sooner or later, to be caught off guard, and if still inclined to resist, to be unceremoniously circumcised on the spot rather than allowed to suffer a lifetime of manifest unworthiness.

Father Alphonse by no means underestimated the powerfully formative effect of the initiation rites. He understood that once a boy had become *Ballil* by undergoing the first man-making ceremonies he would remain for the rest of his life basically subject to the authority of his tribal law and thereby, according to orthodox Catholic reasoning, cut off forever from the source of divine grace and the hope of salvation. The monk wrote Bishop Gibney of his efforts to substitute the authority of the Church for that of the tribal devils:

> These young fellows now show a little zeal for religion and there is sometimes fighting. . . . One night all the camp became on fire, women and married men were jumping, vociferating like furies while all the young fellows were joining together. One old man was then running with a bundle of weapons . . . I struck him with the hand on the face and put an end to the combat. . . .[4]

The incident, for all its disturbing aspects, spoke something for the priest's influence, for the anger of the elders, once aroused, was not always as easily controlled. Station employers of native labour considered that any interference with camp quarrels or native law was not only unwarranted but dangerous to their own safety. Father Alphonse, however, denying the former premise and scorning the latter, reported soon afterwards that his firm stand was showing promising results. Some of the mission women had since actually approached him begging for protection from the attentions of the lugger crews during the coming lay-up. He had accordingly organized the building of a dormitory in which the more responsible women had asked him to lock them up at night to keep the flighty from temptation.

Abbot Ambrose, despite the continued difference of opinion in his community, still had sufficient faith in the continuation of the mission to decide to map its territory and to complete a wagon track between Beagle Bay and the port of Broome. He embarked on this task, with the help of six brothers and eight natives, in the middle of the wet season, when the pindan was a steady quagmire and the heat almost insufferable. They managed somehow to explore and map the country and to cut through some fifty miles of scrub between the mission and a neighbouring station from which a track had already been made into the port. The abbot several times collapsed from exhaustion but always rallied to say Mass and insisted on remaining with the party until the job was completed.[5]

Tales of woe awaited him on his return to the mission. Some of his newly baptized Christians had after all been won over by the elders to undergo a further stage of initiation. The women, including those who had asked protection from the lugger crews, had one night escaped like mice through the high narrow windows of the dormitory and had not been seen since. An Australian diocesan priest and a promising young teacher, who had come with the idea of joining the community, had left after only a few weeks and one novice had scandalized the community by confessing himself the father of a half-caste child.

The abbot did not, however, now despair of the mission itself so much as of the possibility of implanting the Trappist tradition in that environment. He had warmed more and more to 'les blackfellers', many of whom had shown him such true affection and compassion in his sufferings, but when he learned that the Kimberley district had at last been declared a vicariate apostolic he realized that he could no longer carry on as superior. He left for the last time in June 1897, believing that he did not have long to live,[6] and on his return to France discussed with his superiors the establishment of a rule more suited to the missionary field, the sort of 'Order within an Order' that was then evolving in Africa. He now saw no reason why they should not in Australia proceed as in that other outpost to develop their Benedictine apostolate of 'prayer and labour, of liturgy and the plough' but no longer under the strict rules of silence and fasting that governed the pure contemplatives.[7]

The Abbots Sebastian Wyart and Baptise Chautard, again faced with the bitter choice between betrayal of the monastic ideal and the betrayal of a defenceless race, at this stage requested every member of the Australian community to write confidentially what he thought of the prospects for their foundation. Fathers Alphonse, Anselm, Jean Marie and Nicholas were in favour of persevering. The majority,

107

however, believed that the compromise between the contemplative and active life had failed, that outside missionaries and enclosed religious could not exist without disturbing each other and that to place increasing emphasis on the practical side was to lose sight of the ideal for which the Order had spent a century in fighting to regain.[8]

The Abbot-General, on the point of making a final decision to relinquish the mission, was once more confronted by the persuasive and sanguine Australian bishop, this time in person. Bishop Gibney may already have acted unsuccessfully on Cardinal Moran's suggestion that they have done with these vacillating people and offer the Kimberley vicariate, through the Irish college in Rome, to Don Bosco's Salesian missionary society. His interview with Dom Sebastian, however, in which he insisted that the mission's pioneering stage was already giving place to an era of definite progress and prosperity, appeared to have gone well and he returned to Australia assured of having definitely settled the mission's precarious future.

The sudden increase of population after the discovery of gold at Coolgardie in 1892 had greatly increased the bishop's responsibilities and he was much relieved when, in 1898, Father William Bernard Kelly was consecrated bishop of a second diocese extending from the port of Geraldton into the Northern Territory. This put the Beagle Bay mission out of Bishop Gibney's official control though he continued his work for his cherished project as forthrightly as before.

When the Aborigines Protection Board with which he had done battle for so long was abolished in 1897 the bishop was not the only one who failed to mourn its loss. Even the conservative *West Australian* newspaper had described it as 'an irresponsible body whose proceedings are enshrouded in mystery and which, if it so pleases, can fritter away £5,000 a year without anyone to say it nay'.[9] The British Government, however, even after granting the colony responsible government in 1890, had been reluctant to entrust it with the full responsibility of its native people and had maintained nominal control of this board for a further seven years. This had caused considerable resentment, especially as it had originally been stipulated that the board's annual expenditure on native welfare was to be 1 per cent of the colonial revenue, or the sum of £5,000 if the latter was the greater amount. At that time it was, but after the discovery of gold 1 per cent of the revenue amounted to nearer £30,000 a year, a sum considered out of all reason for such a hopeless and unpopular cause. Even had Britain insisted as the price of responsible government that this amount be devoted to native welfare it is doubtful whether any great benefit would have then accrued. Since there is nothing so inviting to private exploitation as the distribution of ration grants and there was no general policy or belief in the efficacy of native education, ways would no doubt soon have been devised for diverting the money into more profitable channels.

Paul Hasluck, at the conclusion of his history of Aboriginal administration to this time, sums up the situation in these terms:

> With nearly seventy years of practical experience to give them the advantage of information and the disadvantage of preconceived opinions, with the settled idea that the natives were dying out and were of inferior class, and without a single shred of idealism, the people of Western Australia received into their care the sacred charge of several thousands of human beings. The Imperial Government ended its rule of uncertainty, inconsistency and neglect and handed on a charge that was ill-kept, contaminated, hopeless and despised.[10]

Harsh though this judgment might appear it was more than justified by subsequent events. Bishop Gibney, long frustrated by the board's discrimination in favour of Protestant missions, officially on the grounds that the Catholic institutions derived considerable income from their vast, rent-free holding, now hoped for fairer treatment for Beagle Bay. Instead, following a report that the Trappists were so preoccupied with their spiritual affairs that their gardens were deteriorating and the cattle running wild, the subsidy for the following year was cancelled altogether. To what extent this report was true one can only judge from the evidence.

Poor little Prior Anselm, under the impression that the bishop while in Rome had 'definitely settled the future of the monastery and the mission',[11] wrote with unshakable faith in his influence:

> A kind friend you have been in the beginning, a kind friend you have proved yourself in the recent arrangements and now we humbly request your Lordship not to give us up. Our funds are not in a very prosperous condition, principally because the government did not this year give its usual subsidy. But a kind word from your Lordship will work wonders and this is our humble request, that you speak in our favour to your great friend Sir John Forrest. ... Humbly asking your blessing for myself, the community and the Catholic natives of whom there are now 150 and who look to you as their best friend and benefactor ... I etc.[12]

The bishop, evidently hoping to shame the government by showing the mission to have been almost totally subsidized from charitable sources, largely from outside Australia at that, asked the prior to send him a financial statement. This showed that in their nine years at Beagle Bay the Trappists had received the sum of £9,066, only £2,270 of which was supplied by the government, and a further £13,437 from the Order itself, which had gone into 'permanent improvements'. Besides this, evidence was produced of an 'adequate and stable' community and promising agricultural development.[13]

That this failed to convince the government of its further responsibility to Beagle Bay probably helped to persuade the Abbot-General that the Trappists' duty in this regard had also come to an end.

# CHAPTER TEN

## 1895 – 1899

In their final decision the Trappist superiors were no doubt swayed by the impetuous return to France, in September 1899, of Fathers Bernard Le Louarn and Ermenfroy Nachin, both ex-secular priests who had come to Australia for the prime purpose of implanting there the seed of contemplative life. The picture of distintegration they painted must have been grim indeed, for their testimony struck at the vulnerable point of responsibility for the spiritual welfare of the exiled religious. The Abbot-General later stated his conviction that he had withdrawn the community just in time. 'All indicates that the Australian climate has profoundly affected most of our religious' he wrote. 'In general fathers and brothers were not able to render any long service. Intellectual and physical unbalance were accentuated. . . .'[1]

This judgment may have been somewhat extreme but there can be little doubt that the community was suffering sadly for want of a strong superior and that ill-health had magnified their differences and undermined their mutual forbearance.

Abbot Sebastian, pressed with the problems and financial needs of a growing number of outside communities, was now anxious to suppress the Australian foundation as quickly and quietly as possible. He had still, however, to choose an executive capable of determined and incisive action and this was difficult. It did not seem that Fathers Anselm, Alphonse or Jean Marie, although all in favour of continuing the mission, would prove forthright enough to withstand the protests of the local prelates who had defeated previous efforts to withdraw. This left only Father Nicholas Emo who had carried out his solitary role as parish priest in Broome with uncomplaining fortitude, and who, having had little to do with the mission itself, seemed less likely to be emotionally involved.

Father Nicholas came of an influential Spanish family of the province of Castellon and had studied medicine for some time in Paris before his ordination to the priesthood. At the age of forty-five, after twelve years as a missionary in Patagonia, he had returned to France, eager, because of what he wrote of as 'the secret attraction I felt for this unfortunate race,'[3] to devote the remainder of his life to the cause of the Australian Aborigines. It was with this intention that he had entered Sept Fons as a novice in 1894, though the Trappists seem rather to have considered him an answer to Bishop Gibney's request for a Spanish-speaking monk to minister to the many Filipinos who had flocked to the pearling fields.

Soon after his arrival at the mission he was asked to take charge of the parish in Broome, then a lugger journey of about a hundred miles from Beagle Bay and from two to seven days' travelling, according to wind and weather. This port had been proclaimed in 1883 but its site had been used as a lugger base for at least ten years before. It had by this time taken over from Cossack as the principal supply centre for the 150 vessels and 1,500 men then employed in the pearling industry and was also the main port of contact for shipping between Australia and Singapore.

The town at the time of Father Nicholas's arrival was lively and cosmopolitan, but not yet the flourishing, white-painted trading centre of its hey-day. Of its fifty permanent white residents, only six were women, though the wives of a few master pearlers, living with their husbands on 'mother' schooners, came into the port from time to time. Most of the population, then reckoned at 500, was Japanese, Chinese and Filipino but representatives of most countries in the world visited on one pretext or another. Pearl buyers of various nationalities came to purchase gems for big businesses or for the private collections of crowned heads and other wealthy patrons, while traders from Singapore used the port as a stepping-stone to the Australian market.

The more rigid immigration laws were not then in force and many Japanese who had come in originally as divers had remained to form co-operative pearling groups. These, behind an official front of eating houses, stores and laundries, and with the help of renegade whites paid to act as 'dummies', were contriving to gain a firm hold on the industry and had staked their residential claim on a sandhill that sloped up from the business centre of the town. A track known as 'Sheba Lane', that ran between their flimsy establishments, was already redolent of Oriental mystery and intrigue. Some of the Japanese women who had come on the pretext of working in the various little businesses actually did so, but most remained hidden from the public gaze behind tinkling bead curtains, their thin, high-pitched singing and the soft plucking of their geisha lutes sometimes faintly heard against the harsher noises of the port.

Below the Japanese quarter spread the Chinese shops and gambling houses raised on concrete stumps. There were also two shanty hotels and a general store. Straggling along the sandy mangrove beach and the muddy banks of Dampier Creek were the iron shacks of the lugger crews, the shell-packing sheds and the lean-to workshops of Japanese shipbuilders, while the homes of the few resident master pearlers and the substantial headquarters of the Eastern Extension Cable Station were set apart from the Asiatic *hoi polloi* above the curving beach of the bay.

There were everywhere signs of the port being expected to develop along the lines of a neat town plan. Chain gangs of Aboriginal prisoners were busy clearing the smoky coastal scrub, covering the carefully parallel thoroughfares with white shellgrit that dazzled in the sun and glowed like phosphorus under the moon. Pearlers returning with indentured crews from the Far East, the Celebes, the Indies or the

Philippines, had brought blossoming shrubs and trees to give shade and colour to the gardens and road verges. Already the scent of oleanders floated on the warm air, and poincianas glowed like fire against a background of turquoise sea and emerald mangrove scrub.

Father Nicholas, a short, thick-set, black-bearded little man, devout, emotional and at some pains to keep his naturally extrovert nature within the bounds of Trappist convention, hid his disappointment at being thrust into much the sort of mixed community that he had left behind in Patagonia. The savages to whom he had yearned were not the poor bedraggled natives camped on the outskirts of the port in humpies thrown together of brushwood and slabs of rusty iron from the rubbish dumps, living mainly by prostitution and cadging from the pearling crews. Sometimes he caught a glimpse of the type of tribesmen he had visualized – and who by a stretch of the imagination might be considered Aboriginal counterparts of the Californian Red Indians converted by Spanish Franciscans in the eighteenth century. These were among the native prisoners brought in, on sheep and cattle spearing charges, from the remoter Kimberleys – tall, erect and proud, their torsos slashed with raised parallel cicatures, walking with an air of aristocratic disdain between their red-faced warders. Father Nicholas was by no means the first to believe that if Christianity could only be brought to such as these, within their own environment, they would come to reject the darkness of their savage ways and be fortified against the evils of civilization. In an initial approach to win their confidence he visited them at the prison, bringing tobacco, sweets and some New Testament illustrations through which he hoped, in his simplicity, to introduce them to the basic ideals of Christianity. A few forthrightly rejected his gifts. Others took them with polite detachment but communication was impossible as their English was more limited than his own, and the local tongues, spoken through an interpreter, were equally unintelligible to them.

The white and coloured people of the town at least paid

him the compliment of their curiosity, but it was clear that most of them found something out of place, faintly suspicious, about the appearance of a solitary monk – a Trappist above all – complete with habit, cowl and cross, in the rowdy, go-getting little port. His elaborate Spanish courtesy and curious English soon became a byword, to be imitated with varying success by the town wags.

Only the Filipinos accepted him without question and welcomed him as their Father Confessor and friend. These were a people apart in the polyglot community. Culturally neither Asiatic nor European, they were reputed by the pearlers to be less industrious than the Chinese and Japanese but more so than the Malays and Islanders. They made warm friends and bitter foes, played sweet music and fought with knives. Rodriguez, Corpus, de la Cruz, Puertollano, Santimera, Musoleon, Raymundo – their names and their features were to be perpetuated in generations of part-Aboriginal people along the pearling coast.

Too hot-blooded for the celibacy kept by many of the exiled Chinese and Japanese but staunch in their Spanish-type Catholicism and by tradition good family men, they were ill at ease in the passing relationships and casual begetting of children by native women. They had, therefore, inclined to establish themselves in little family groups in and around Broome and close to the scattered lay-up bases of the pearling fleets. Most of the men worked on the luggers during the shelling season, leaving their women and children to tend their little plots and herds and to sell goat's meat, milk, poultry, eggs and vegetables to the pearling crews. The arrival of a Spanish-speaking priest was a profound relief to them, for although few of them really knew his language they were able, with the assistance of two or three of their better-educated countrymen, who were actually of some Spanish blood, to confess their difficulties and set about getting their irregular relationships straightened out.

They helped the priest put up a little timber church on the beach behind Streeter's general store and to build a shack for himself on the sandhill above the town. This was at least some place of refuge for the solitary monk who by rising at two in the morning could abstract himself, sometimes finding consolation in the ebb and flow of the restless tide and the symbols it suggested to his devout imagination. At neaps the sea lay far out in a silver band and the rippled mud of the bay shone under the moon like a staircase to heaven while big king tides came flowing into the town like a cleansing grace, spilling out around the little shacks and shops, covering the scattered Binghi camps and lapping about the Mohammedan mosque on the edge of the marsh. What matter if they also brought with them an infestation of sandflies and mosquitoes and an army of scavaging hermit crabs to nibble at the monk's sandalled feet and raid his meagre stores?

Before long Father Nicholas had established a small school for the native children and a hostel for half-caste girls and had enlisted the help of the pious Filipino, Caprio Anabia and his remarkable wife. A half-caste Aboriginal, this young woman had escaped the usual fate of her kind by being taken to Perth as a child and brought up in a good family. Her marriage to Caprio had been arranged by her guardians before she returned to Broome, where she had shown an unusually strong sense of responsibility for her mother's people. She had gone into the native camps ministering to the sick and trying, in their own language, to teach them Christian principles and the basic rules of hygiene.

Now, in her many-sided role of hostel matron, nurse and schoolteacher, she did her best for the little waifs brought in by Father Nicholas from the outlying camps. The priest spent much of his time bargaining with the native mothers for the part-Aboriginal babies that they frequently killed and according to his and the other missionaries' testimony, often ate as well. Some he succeeded in placing with the respectable families in the town. Others were cared for at a hostel with older half-caste girls who attended the little school for both full-blood and part Aboriginal children and where the girls were taught to read and write, trained to look

116

after a house and to take some pride in their appearance.

The spruce little group that was every Sunday shepherded through the town to the church soon became the talk and envy of the pearling crews. The girls themselves, born in the corrupt outskirt camps, were often enough an easy prey and proved extremely ingenious in outwitting their devoted guardians.

Even some of the Europeans of the town enjoyed the joke of the service rendered the community by 'Madam' Anabia and her priestly protector. The story grew; the money made from their enterprise and the relationship between them was 'established' beyond a shadow of doubt, and practical jokers recommended newcomers to the hostel where they were assured of being able to hire girls for a small fee. One South Sea Islander, having been sent about his business, took umbrage, set alight to the mission school and hostel and burned them to the ground. The culprit stood his trial and was deported and sympathetic people helped the mission to a new start, but not long afterwards, a group of coloured boys, incited by tales of the priest's claiming all the local girls for himself, burned down his church.

Father Nicholas struck a carved stone cross in the sandhill near his new school and, with the support of loyal Filipinos, put up beside it a second and considerably larger church and a small presbytery. Despite setbacks, the sincerity of his work had by this time made an impression on the majority of Broome residents and when a government official named Marsden reported unfavourably on the mission to the Aborigines Protection Board, mainly because of gossip concerning its half-caste matron, they rose staunchly to his defence. Twenty-seven prominent residents (few of them Catholic) added their signatures to that of H. W. Brownrigg, J.P., in a letter testifying that the priest's establishment had 'greatly improved the condition of the natives, morally and intellectually'.[3]

Corporal Thomas of Broome added to this that he had 'always found the mission scrupulously clean' although 'the house is not a mansion and would no doubt be better if larger'. Of the matron he reported in glowing terms as 'a good housekeeper, cook, laundress etc.,' who had looked after his own home when his wife was ill. 'Mr. Marsden,' he concluded, 'never reported the matter to me. ... He had ample time and opportunity while here to have ascertained the falseness of the rumours which he scarcely himself believe.'[4]

Father Nicholas, in answer to a heartbroken letter to Bishop Gibney, received a comforting reply from his lordship's vicar-general: 'Do not, on any account let it worry or annoy you. It is no wonder that things are said. Are there not some who would like to see the school put an end to altogether? ...'[5]

Marsden's report, however, had blighted the priest's hopes of financial help from the board for the erection of better premises. Some years later, asked by Commissioner Dr. Roth why he had abandoned his school and hostel, he replied that 'the very fact of his [Marsden] having made such a slanderous statement did a great deal of harm, with the final result that, disgusted and disheartened, I gave up this particular school and distributed the elder girls into service amongst the European ladies in Broome'.[6]

He continued to teach and support the boys and younger children and forged ahead with a plan to house married native couples on allotments made over in their own names. These blocks he had purchased for £20 each from public subscriptions and what he referred to as 'a private source'[7], possibly the sale of native artifacts and geological specimens to Australian museums.

Besides this he had secured, for a rental of £3 a year, some ten acres on a headland within the town boundary which served as a clean, quiet camp for sick and aged natives whom he visited each day, bringing rations and medicines. He kept a record of sorts of the people who were blind and 'deff', the prostitutes and the 'coquettes'[8] (he apparently made some distinction between the two) whom he was treating for syphilis and other diseases. As early as 1897 he wrote of a 'man and woman with the leprosy' and of

118

another old woman 'her left arm being with the leprosy'.[9] It is now thought likely that he misread the symptoms and that these natives were suffering from yaws, for by all known rules had leprosy been spreading unchecked from this time it would have become alarmingly obvious long before the thirties. In any case, as no one wanted to believe him, he isolated his 'lepers' as well as he could and when they died buried them himself in an isolated spot and set fire to their camps.

But his greatest hope during this time remained the establishment of a mission among natives not yet contaminated by the diseases and vices of civilization. He knew that Abbot Ambrose had considered the possibility of moving the Trappist mission to somewhere near the Prince Regent River, but for himself Father Nicholas was in favour of maintaining Beagle Bay as well as opening a more remote establishment. That he should at some time be allowed to undertake pioneering mission work was his dearest wish and one in which he had been encouraged by Father (soon to become Bishop) Kelly when the latter was on a visit to the north. Of this Father Kelly had written to Bishop Gibney:

> . . . I look upon Kimberley as the pick of Western Australia and this part between King Sound and Cambridge Gulf as the pick of Kimberley. Already several speak of expeditions to explore it. They may not do this for some time as they fear the natives, but in the meantime it would be well for the Trappists to seize the opportunity which may never offer again.[10]

Bishop Gibney was at that time finding Beagle Bay difficult enough to keep afloat without considering a second or alternative proposition but Father Nicholas suspected nothing of the Trappists' inclination to close the Australian foundation. He took a trip up the coast with his friend Filomeno (Pat) Rodriguez, a Spanish pearler from Manila, and found what he considered a good site for a mission near the mouth of the Drysdale River. Full of enthusiasm for the proposition, he was planning a letter to the motherhouse when he received a communication from the Abbot-General informing him that he had been put in full charge of the Australian mission – for the purpose of terminating it! Father Alphonse, then acting superior, had been advised that he must return to France with all but two or three lay brothers but, as opposition was expected if the local prelates came to hear of the decision, he was given no reason for the order. Father Nicholas was instructed to say nothing, until after the main body of religious had left, except that the mission would be held as a 'grange' until things improved.[11]

# CHAPTER ELEVEN

## 1899 – 1900

FATHER NICHOLAS carried out the wishes of his superiors with a heavy heart. Nothing had confused his own objective in joining the Australian mission and he could not appreciate the ideological difficulties of his fellow Trappists as much as the distress their departure would cause their loyal supporters. To make matters worse he had been asked, in effect, to pull the wool over the eyes of these faithful friends until it was too late for them to intervene.

It was while taking a holiday with Bishop Kelly in Geraldton that Father Alphonse received notification from Sept Fons of his 'release' from the office of superior and his recall to France. Having worn the Trappist habit for twenty-seven years, done service in New Caledonia and, alone of the religious sent out, given ten years' unbroken service to the Australian mission, the only reason he could think of for being displaced by a mere novice was that Father Nicholas had reported against him to his superiors.

He returned to Beagle Bay to find the Spanish priest carrying out his charge in grim silence and all the religious, except Brothers Xavier and John Berchmans, preparing to take their departure. Father Jean Marie and young 'Father' Narcisse had been summoned from Disaster Bay and informed that they must return to France with the others. Father Jean Marie probably realized the truth of the situation but anticipated obtaining permission from his superiors to return and carry on at Disaster Bay for a time at least. Before leaving his mission he had assured his people that he would soon be back, and charged them, under the leadership of

Thomas Puertollano, to look after everything until his return.

Some of the religious no doubt hoped, for reasons they had already expressed to their superiors, that their sudden recall meant an end to their long and irksome compromise. Others were deeply troubled in conscience for the future of the natives. An Irish-Australian priest who had joined as a novice not long before had, on receiving the order to depart, applied to Bishop Gibney to be allowed to remain in Australia as a secular. His request was apparently taken as a weakening of his missionary resolution and he received a terse reply. He then wrote again, implying that he had no desire to leave his Order if they were to remain in Australia and asking whether there was any prospect for the foundation of a new Trappist house in the southern diocese. He received, for his pains, an even more testy letter from the Vicar-General informing him that there was no question of such a thing. The letter continued:

> You were, likely, most well aware of the fact. . . .
>
> You ask, 'What will become of the new Christians? There are close on 300.' If they are abandoned, you with your Order will answer for it . . . God will know where to sheet home the blame.
>
> 'Nine of us,' you say, 'are ordered to Elathroun, – half-way between Jaffa and Jerusalem.' If this be so, pray go there without delay. The Bishop gave you clearly, by telegram, to understand that there is no place in this diocese for runaway missionaries. . . .[1]

Since the name of the inquiring priest does not appear among those who sailed for France, it can only be assumed that he shared the Vicar-General's opinion of the move and left the Order.

But most bewildered and heartbroken of all was no doubt Father Alphonse Tachon whose early efforts at Beagle Bay had characterized him as not only zealous and hard working but normally realistic and not lacking in humour. As time went on, however, the devout little man had developed the inordinate but unconscious possessiveness towards the Aborigines that they so often evoke in their white associations. It seems that he had come to regard himself as the divinely appointed custodian of the Australian mission and, not without justification, as its real founder. The fanatical diligence with which he strove to hold his divided community to the strict observance of their ancient tradition and to wean the Aborigines from theirs had been noted by the more down-to-earth Australian clerics and was more than hinted at by the Vicar-General in a letter imploring the Benedictine Bishop Salvado, then in Rome, to try to prevent the Trappists abandoning Beagle Bay. In this he states:

> ... All the trouble, as far as we know, is with the superior. Father Alphonse Tachon is most unfit to rule as he is half crazy with scruples, but troubles of this kind should not be dealt with by running away. ...[3]

Father Alphonse now saw in the tormented Spaniard the personification of the powers of darkness that had for so long contrived to destroy his mission and the souls of 'les pauvres sauvages' whose feet he was guiding along the path to salvation. There can be little doubt that he was driven, through the bitterness of his personal hurt and disappointment and fear for his native flock, to a state of mental breakdown. Bishop Gibney, reporting privately, later in the year, on the state of the mission wrote:

> At the commencement of the present year half of the buildings was blown down or pulled down and the College destroyed by fire. A considerable part of the Church was pulled down by one of the Fathers, without authorization.[3]

It would be unfair to assume from this that the priest in question was Father Alphonse, but the suspicion is strengthened by the accounts of the older mission natives, and an ambiguous telegram sent to Perth by Father Nicholas shortly after the departure of most of the religious. This read:

January two large buildings Beagle Bay refectory of Chapter destroyed by storm. Large building Father Alphonse destroyed by fire. . . .[4]

Whatever the true story it is clear that the departure of the pioneer Trappists from Beagle Bay was both dramatic and emotional, and that such buildings as were not destroyed by fire, accidentally lit or otherwise, were demolished or damaged in a hurricane that pounced like the wrath of the Lord – or of Galalang – as the monks and brothers were about to leave.

Father Nicholas, sorrowfully surveying the scene of ruin and desolation over which he was now superior, must have decided that, for the sake of all concerned, he should now break his silence. His letter to the Vicar-General sent shortly after the departure of the religious and quoted anon suggests that, in a last minute effort to make his peace with Father Alphonse, he disclosed the secret reason for his sudden rise to authority. In the same letter he mentions entrusting this monk with a petition to his superiors and asking him to further defend the cause of the mission in his name.

The natives recall how Father Alphonse, wasted with fever and fasting and bent with toil, collapsed near the end of the eight-mile walk to the coast and how, weeping for his and their own grief, they had carried him for the rest of the way. Whatever arguments they had had with him or however eccentric he may have become they knew that he had acted always from motives of true goodness and for this they honoured him. In a mixture of French, English and their own tongue, then the *lingua franca* of the mission, they had murmured assurances that he would soon grow strong and come back to them. He had nodded mutely under his cowl, knowing as well as the natives themselves that this was the last he was to look on the tangled Dampierland scrub and the strange wild people he had come to save and grown to cherish.[5]

Very different the desolate little band that boarded the lugger at Beagle Bay from the eager recruits who had been welcomed to the mission with a peal of bells a few years before. Prepared to face suffering, even martyrdom, with the strength of glorious certainty, their worst agony had been, after all, the result of doubt and indecision. The environment had rejected their rule and the savages to whom they had offered the enlightenment of a doctrine of love had humbled them by their own understanding and charity. The native people, in all their simplicity, had baffled their would-be teachers and caused them to reflect on aspects of the human heart never revealed to them before. Had they come indeed for love of their primitive fellow men, or for devotion to a highly evolved ideal of spiritual detachment?

But even those who had been most dubious of their missionary role looked back in desolate regret as the wind caught the lugger sails and the dark people, waving from the beach, struck up the song that had been composed for the Trappists' departure from France by their sisters at Macon:

> *Partez, partez, Frères, pour l' Australie!*
> *Portez là-bas le Nom de notre Dieu!*
> *Nouse nous retrouverons un jour dans la patrie,*
> *Adieu, Frères, adieu!*

Only when he had seen them on their way was Father Nicholas free to reply to the urgent inquiries of the two bishops. He wrote in Spanish to the Vicar-General:

> ... After all that has happened with Father Alphonse in relation to Beagle Bay mission whose direction has been entrusted to me despite my reluctance, now at last I can write to give satisfaction to His Lordship and to your Reverence. Please tell the Lord Bishop on my behalf that I have felt the incident deeply in my soul ... I will say nothing to excuse myself but I should let you know, in the cause of truth, that never did I aspire to the charge of superior, nor have I taken the very least step towards acquiring it. On the contrary, I remain very antagonistic to my appointment, but in accepting it I have

125

not done more than to obey the final and unconditional orders before which a religious is able only to incline his head.

Father Alphonse believed he found in my telegrams *contradictions* that existed only in his imagination and on reading them again in my presence they gave him cause to repent ... the poor Father tortured himself and was the victim of his imagination. ...

It is certainly not for me to assume to judge the actions of the superiors nor to enter into discussion of the motives that prompted such a strange and unexpected resolution. ...

It is only an unfortunate combination of circumstances that has given this bad appearance to the proceedings taken and that obliges me to explain and justify them. ...

Well, dear Father, although ignorant of the cause of this order, I confess that it has grieved me profoundly, especially because of the love I profess for the blacks for whom I have always sacrificed myself. I came to Australia for the secret attraction that I felt for this unfortunate race and for whose benefit I made the sacrifice of my life to God. Our Superior-General allowed me to entertain the hope that I might live and die in this country and therefore I blessed God with all my heart when I became aware of his Lordship's visit to our Father-General in Rome and of the salutary effects that followed. To receive the present order that put me at the head of all, not to build and consolidate, only to destroy, that is to say, to disband the community, has been a hard blow to me and one I will not easily forget. And who would believe that the charge of Superior in such circumstances could be in any way enviable?

I suspect that that the information presented to the Superiors by two of our sick and discontented religious who returned to Europe declaring that the mission was not able to support itself in the least and that our efforts on behalf of the blackfellows [sic] would have remained

126

sterile has been the cause of this contretemps. I believed it my duty to send Father Alphonse to Europe in my name and with my letter, to defend the cause of the poor black-fellows and to explain *verbally* to the Superiors the true state of the mission. . . .

The only thing I fear is to receive a new order to proceed immediately with the liquidation. In such a case would it not be better for his Lordship to come to an understanding with me to buy for himself, from the government, the mission territory with its springs and gardens and existing stock to save our natives from falling into the hands of Jews and Protestants? His Lordship, with Monsignor Kelly might place here some zealous priest like Father Martelli to minister to Broome and Beagle Bay, or some faithful Catholic who would take care of these places until the arrival of another religious community.

I myself would willingly remain if it were God's will and my Superiors consented, at least until another community replaced us.

. . . Immediately after the departure of our religious a Protestant pastor established himself at the entrance of King Sound.[6] I fear he is working with the government to claim our mission property. Jews and Protestants wish to buy the breeding cattle on our pastures but I tell everyone that I have no intention of selling. . . .

I wish now more than ever that they [Bishops Gibney and Kelly] would come immediately to Beagle Bay and put me *unconditionally* under their orders. . . .[7]


Bishop Gibney readily exonerated Father Nicholas from all responsibility for the sad affair but news of the Trappist decision could scarcely have reached him at a worse time. The Kimberley mission, though so close to his heart, was after all only one of his many concerns. Community activities occupied him in every direction, for not only the population increased following the gold strike but the end of government aid for denominational schools by an 1895 Act

127

of Parliament[8] had added tremendously to the financial and administrative strain of his office. His reputation as a just and wise man also meant that his advice was called upon in political problems such as the serious labour dispute of the previous year in the settlement of which he had played a leading part. To hear, shortly after learning of the near destruction of the mission by fire and hurricane, that all but three of the Trappist religious had been withdrawn was a severe shock to him. Having publicly refuted rumours that the Trappists planned to abandon their mission the news surprised, angered and embarrassed him. He managed, none the less, to turn a confident front on the doubting world and insisted that the monks were faithfully holding the fort until the arrival of another missionary band. He realized, however, that it would be difficult either to persuade the Trappists to return or another community to replace them without the guarantee of a government subsidy and the long promised, but still unsettled, freehold tenure of the 10,000 acre mission. In reply to renewed representations he was informed that neither would be considered until the stipulated £5,000 fixed improvements had been proven, in which seemingly impossible stipulation the authorities no doubt saw an end of the whole affair. In this they had not reckoned on the bishop's determination and unconquerable optimism for he decided in this case to go himself to the mission and put things in order before the arrival of the official valuer.

The Vicar-General was left to explain to Cardinal Moran his Lordship's absence from an important Catholic meeting in Sydney at that time.

Your Eminence should know [he wrote] that there has been a great upset at the Trappist mission. It was most unexpected as everything seemed to be progressing peacefully and favourably. The bishop was nothing short of indignant when it came to be whispered about that several of the fathers and brothers had left and when finally it came to be known that the rest of the community were preparing for flight by selling off all the stock and other

128

belongings of the place. Not all that had been promised the missionaries had been done for them. The government especially were in default; yet it seemed to the bishop a shame that the Trappists should as lightly abandon their great enterprise. How different their French levity from the Spanish constancy of Bishop Salvado and his Benedictines through years and years of discouragement and trial of every sort. . . .

Dr. Gibney is now away in the wilds and perhaps Propaganda may not hear of what is going on. Would it not be well for Your Eminence to let them know at Rome of the impending danger. . . .

It is clear that the missioners at Beagle Bay have been eminently successful both from the financial point of view and – which is of more consequence – from the consideration of the great good, well done, for many poor neglected souls. For them to fly now and abandon the natives would be a disgrace and a calamity affecting the Catholic Church throughout the Colony.[9]

Early in August, when almost ready for departure with the Italian priest, Dean Martelli, the bishop had been approached by Mrs. Daisy Bates, an Irish journalist, who had come out for *The Times* some two years before to report on the condition of the Aborigines. Although herself an Anglican, this enthusiastic young woman impressed the bishop as a sincere and eloquent ally of the native people and he agreed that she should accompany his party to Beagle Bay.

Detailed accounts of their experiences, first as articles and later in her book, *The Passing of the Aborigines*, have been written by Daisy Bates herself, her style striking an oddly lighthearted and feminine note in a story of so much zealous masculine endeavour, earnest soul-searching and bewildered study of native customs and psychology. Aboriginal behaviour never greatly puzzled or surprised this extraordinary woman who was to become their beloved Kabbarli, grandmother and counsellor of the desert tribes.

It is not hard to picture her as she was at this time, for in fact she changed little in her long and active life. Always small, slim and quick-moving, she clung to the fashions of her youth, dressing even in her bush camps in long, tight-waisted frocks, dust coat and buttoned boots, Queen Alexandra toque, gossamer veil, and neat white gloves.

The bishop's party was met in Broome by Father Nicholas and his friend Filomeno Rodriguez who put himself and a lugger at their disposal. Rodriguez was one of the most colourful personalities in an area already renowned for its 'characters'. He had come from Manila as a humble diver but he had claimed the hand of his employer's daughter, Maud Miller, when she was only fourteen years old and his fortunes had grown with his family. His eldest son, Giovano, born, like the rest of his ten children, on his mother schooner *Pearl*, was the first name in the Broome baptismal register. Rodriguez, now a big man in the pearling game, was a good friend to his Church and his less fortunate countrymen and generous to the cause of the Aborigines.

His schooner *Scree Pas Sair* that was to take the party to Beagle Bay was a lugger with a history. Originally the floating palace of Rajah Brooke, it had been bought from him by Lord Delaware for a cruise to the South Seas and there sold to Edward Cockayne Chippendall, ex-naval officer and adventurer son of an English clergyman. Chippendall manned it with a crew from the Solu Archipelago north of Borneo with whom he introduced 'dress diving' to the Australian pearling grounds. His experiments paved the way for more modern and efficient methods of procuring shell but most of his crew perished and he himself died, presumably as a result of foul play, in 1886[10]. His partner eventually sold the lugger to Rodriguez but the bishop's party soon discovered that fifteen years in the pearling trade had stripped her of all pretensions to luxury.

Father Nicholas, obviously somewhat nonplussed, had explained that there was no accommodation whatever for a woman at the Beagle Bay monastery and that according to Church law, no woman except a queen or the wife of a Head of State could be allowed within its walls.

130

However [Daisy Bates wrote] there I was, and the dear little acting abbot [Father Nicholas] took it upon himself to grant a dispensation, and went out to see what furniture he could buy for me, making wild guesses at what a female might need. His bewildered and exaggerated idea of hospitality filled me with astonishment. . . .[11]

At the end of three days' voyage they found horses and a bullock wagon awaiting them on the beach at Beagle Bay. The horses, we are told, were 'Trappists, too, skin and bone in their poverty, and stopped so often for their meditations and devotions that the bullock-team arrived before us.'[12]

The mission Daisy Bates described as 'a collection of tumble-down paperbark monastery cells, a little bark chapel and a community room of corrugated iron, which had been repeatedly destroyed in bush fires and hurricanes'.[13] She met there Brother Xavier, Sebastian Alkaleno, a Filipino who had become a Trappist novice to help Father Nicholas, and little Brother John Berchmans who, having been with the monks since childhood, fled at sight of her 'as from the world, the flesh and the devil which I represented'.[14] Before she left, however, this boy had overcome his distrust to the extent of making her a pair of kangaroo skin shoes and sleeping trustfully in her company when camped in the bush.

Small and disorganized though the Trappist community then was, they maintained their long night vigils, their meals of pumpkin and rice, with sometimes a little beer brewed from sorghum, and slept on the same comfortless beds. Their fluctuating native congregation, reckoned all told at about 150, still struck the visitor as being half wild – their front teeth knocked out, bodies slashed with ritual scars and wearing bones through their noses – but the conch shell reveille brought most of them straggling up at dawn to sing hymns and prayers. Only a few young people now used the dormitory that Father Alphonse had put up for the protection of the women. All the others slept on the ground in hollows scooped out and warmed with hot stones on wintry nights.

Since the recent exodus of religious the reduced staff had been able to cope with no more than the basic needs of the people, so not only were most of the huts and buildings in ruins but the wells had fallen in and the gardens had sadly deteriorated. The bishop, however, outwardly undaunted by the task of presenting £5,000 worth of improvements to the government within three months' time, set everyone to work. From morning to night, their hands blistered by rough gardening implements, the community toiled in the blazing sun. Father Martelli, who was in delicate health, sometimes fainted with heat exhaustion, but the bishop, with Father Nicholas, the brothers and a few native men, and Daisy Bates with her band of women never flagged.

When the valuer arrived the last corner had been cleared, the wells cleaned, fences and buildings straightened up. The sheer courage and enthusiasm of the bishop and his helpers must have won the support of this official who embarked on his task in a spirit of warm-hearted co-operation.

He was surprised [Daisy Bates records] to see a thriving property where he had expected ruin and decay. Every screw and post, every fruit and vegetable, buildings, wells, trenches and implements were meticulously valued, and with the livestock on the run, the supplies in the store, the sorghum and sugar-cane fields, the tomato and cucumber patches, and the orange, banana, coconut and pomegranate groves, the sum reached over £6,000. Even one Cape gooseberry bush and one grape-vine had to be valued. The Mission was saved for the natives!

All together and in much jubilation we made the first bricks of sand and loam and a clay for the new convent and monastery, of which I laid the foundation brick . . .[15]

The 'fixed improvement' issue settled at last, the mission could now officially claim the promised 10,000 acre freehold, which, in the absence of a government surveyor, the bishop and his helpers set out to measure with an old lugger compass and a chain. Daisy Bates' account continues:

The bishop and I were the chainmen and we walked in a steamy heat, of 106 degrees at times, sometimes twelve miles in the day. Over marsh and through the pindan, now lame from the stones and prickles, now up to our thighs in bog, we plodded on. . . . We were always hungry. Brother Xavier, in charge of the commissariat . . . would forget the salt or the bread or the meat, or the place where he had arranged to meet us, or that we existed at all; but in hunger and hardship we managed to keep our good humour throughout our whole long stay, strange companions in the solitude of the bush.

On the night walkings, rosaries were chanted all the way home, the natives and brothers responding. I often stumbled and fell in the dark but that rosary never stopped. . . .

I compiled all the survey notes at night. Those notes were later a source of great amusement to the bishop and his staff, but the bishop received the title-deeds of his 10,000 acres, so the mud-stains and blots scarcely mattered. Later, in Perth, he presented me with an inscribed gold watch, in memory of our survey work and the saving of the mission for the natives. . . .[16]

Their last task was to visit the little mission at Disaster Bay that Father Jean Marie and young 'Father' Narcisse had left some six months before. It was a gruelling two days' journey, walking beside the bullock wagon, through heavy sand and scrub, but they were rewarded on arrival by a touching welcome. Thomas Puertollano had taken a temporary job with a pearling fleet to help maintain the mission, but the natives had meanwhile kept open the wells, watered the gardens and guarded the supplies of rice, tea, flour, sugar and sugar-cane that had been left in the unlocked store.

I should scarcely have credited [Daisy Bates remarks] that the natives could know there was food within reach and yet refrain from touching it out of regard for, not fear of, the missionaries.[17]

When the people asked how soon their beloved fathers would return to them, the bishop, not wishing to deceive them, said that the Trappists might not be able to come back but that other good priests and brothers would take their place. This the natives were not prepared to believe, for Father Jean Marie had himself told them he would return. They had worked hard not to disappoint him and were confident he would not disappoint *them*.

Here, as at Beagle Bay, the tribes people had not seen a white woman before and Daisy Bates was a source of wonder and delight to them. The women and children crowded around the doorway of her open hut to watch her dress:

> I have always [she tells us] preserved a scrupulous neat-
> ness and all the little trappings and accoutrements of my
> own very particular mode of dress, sometimes under
> difficulties, but I think I never made a more laughable
> toilet than that one. Every motion of mine, as I laced my
> corset and eased my shoes on with a horn, brushed my
> hair and adjusted my high collar and waist-belt, was
> greeted with long-drawn squeals of laughter and mirrored
> in action, though the slim black daughters of Eve about
> me had not even a strand of hair string between the whole
> thirty.[18]

On the last stage of their journey, when walking from the mission to meet the *Scree Pas Sair* at Beagle Bay, the bishop's strength at last gave out. He was carried aboard the lugger almost delirious, but managed to rally briefly to admonish a naked Malay to put his clothes on!

Daisy Bates, loyal to the bishop's cause, later wrote an optimistic report of the mission. She described the garden, after their three months' work, as again 'a Chinaman's para-dise',[19] with eight thousand heavily bearing banana trees, fifty-two coconut and sixty date palms, plantations of sugar-cane and rice for local needs, flourishing citrus fruit and every known variety of vegetable. She claimed that much of the stock 'would have carried off prizes at a show' and said that the difficulty of keeping horses, owing to the prevalent poison weed, had been overcome by introducing couch grass and hardy Timor ponies. She confessed herself wrong in expecting to find the mission native 'a sneak and a sycophant – a sort of flour and rice Christian', and described the faces of the people as expressive of the change that had come into their lives and the sincerity of their religious devotion.[20]

From the book, written in her later years, it is clear that she was truly touched and impressed by the mission and its people, but even more so by the great-hearted man who had fought so hard for them and closed his eyes to their weaknesses. In loyalty to him, and to help his cherished mission to its feet again, it would seem that she had even been prepared to wear rose-tinted glasses in writing her contemporary report. When it could no longer harm his cause, and perhaps in the light of her own later experience, she revealed that she had few illusions about the wild people's devotion to work, the wholeheartedness of their conversion or the reality of their Christian 'marriages'. Close contact with the women at Beagle Bay had convinced her that most of those whose marriages to Manilamen had been blessed in all good faith by Father Nicholas regarded themselves as being merely 'on hire' from their rightful tribal husbands. She did not make this public at the time but she claims that her evidence to the bishop and Father Nicholas decided them to inquire more closely in future before consenting to such mixed unions.

Her summing up of the Trappists' contribution, though warmly appreciative, was somewhat ironical, in view of their high spiritual aspirations:

[They] did the greatest service in the State of Western Australia, for they demonstrated in the most practical manner the suitability of the Kimberley area for any kind of produce. These little Trappists may be justly ranked among Australia's finest pioneers.[21]

# CHAPTER TWELVE

## 1901

MEANWHILE Bishop Kelly on a visit to Europe had managed to interest Father William Whitmee, Vicar-General of the Pallottine Pious Society of Missions in Rome, in the idea of taking over an established mission in Australia.

The Pallottines were founded in 1835 by the Italian priest Vincent Pallotti who had recruited a number of missionary priests and lay people with the avowed intention to 'revive faith and enkindle charity so that Christ may be known throughout the world'. Since that time the Society had spread from Italy to other parts of Europe and also to England and Ireland and in 1890 a house, committed to establish a mission in the Cameroons, was opened at Limburg in Germany. There seemed no reason, however, why they should not also branch out into the Australian field. When the matter was broached to the Superior-General he had thought at once of Father George Walter, a German Pallottine who had recently returned to Limburg from seven years on the African missionary front. Energetic, a good organizer and speaking excellent English, he seemed just the man for the job and Father Whitmee wrote to him about it at once in the brisk, matter-of-fact terms of the practical secular administrator:

Dear Father George:
... We have been offered an important mission in Australia in the Diocese of Geraldton, Western Australia. Geraldton comprises about one-third of Australia and

hence is a diocese that must be divided into several others in the near future.

The mission is near the coast and a German line of steamers touches weekly.

The Australian Government has reserved 600,000 acres of land to the mission . . . which was given in charge to the Trappists. They stayed about nine years and have just left because they say they cannot observe their rules there. The bishop is now in Rome and I am trying to arrange things with him . . . I think you would be the person capable of taking charge. . . .

The work would be just the same as in the Cameroons, caring for the natives and trying to civilize them. There was a little steam boat belonging to the mission and a means of support would be the raising of cattle, pearl fishing and supplying perishables to the different steamers which call.

We could begin in a small way and the mission would grow fast provided it has a capable man at the head. Australia, as you know, is a very growing country. There is much commerce.

The mission is 1,200 miles from the bishop and would be quite a diocese in itself.

I hope F. Kugelmann will have nothing against your leaving because he can do a great deal in helping afterwards with some lay brothers who will be wanted or at least would be very useful. Also Sisters later on will be required. I have received a nice letter from the Sisters of the House of Providence. They are willing to come. . . .

Since writing the above it has been decided that if you take the mission two fathers and two lay brothers should go out. . . .

P.S. The climate is perfectly healthy. Anyone can live there.[1]

Father Walter was pleased with this proposition and Father Kugelmann, superior of the Limburg province,

137

agreed to release him. It was made clear that the Society was not in a position to subsidize the venture but it seemed reasonable to suppose that a property of such size and potential, in a growing country, could quickly be made self-supporting.

Father Walter, with three other members of his Society, left Europe with Bishop Kelly on the *Friedrich der Grosse* in March 1901. Welcomed in Fremantle by Bishop Gibney and Daisy Bates, they embarked on the *Australind* for Broome where they made a good impression by calling to introduce themselves to townspeople of all denominations. In Father Walter, tall and strong, his lean face still brown and tough from the African sun, they saw a man of confidence and culture, while Father White, an Englishman, an athlete and well up in all the sporting news of the day, dispelled the idea of the Pallottines being an exclusively German society. The brothers, although they spoke no English, were clearly strong capable workers – Kasparek, then a stocky, smooth-faced young Rhinelander; Augstine Sixt, a typical Bavarian peasant, massive, bearded, and with a great and simple faith. The newcomers themselves were no doubt relieved to find that the master pearlers seemed for the most part kindly and respectable, living conventional family lives in comfortable homes or on well-equipped schooners.

Everything pointed to a bright, new era for the Australian mission but the take-over of the Pallottines from the Trappists began with the sort of misunderstanding that was to dog all their negotiations. Father Jean Marie, who had persuaded his superiors that he should return at least until the new community was settled and their business with the Trappists finished, returned from France to Broome just as the Pallottines arrived. As senior to Father Nicholas he had been instructed to relieve the latter of his temporary authority and to draw up a contract of sale on behalf of his Order. Through one of the extraordinary breakdowns of communication so typical of these early missionary transactions, Father Jean Marie, in ignorance of a former contract drawn up between Bishop Gibney, acting on behalf of the incoming Pallottines, and Father Nicholas for his own Order, promptly drew up another one with Father Walter. Both agreements stipulated that a payment of £2,640 be made for an estimated 800 head of cattle and a few sheep, but the latter also charged for the town lots purchased by Father Nicholas and 'material of the monastery', excluded from the other agreement as 'being held in trust for the natives'.

On learning of the former contract, Father Jean Marie advised his superiors who wrote rather crossly that Father Nicholas had now no authority to act on their behalf and that his contract (less favourable to them than the other) should be disregarded. Bishops Gibney and Kelly, anxious to give the Pallottines as good a start as possible, stood out for the original agreement and finally won their point. This was one up for the Pallottines, but a mark against Father Nicholas with his superiors for having failed to act in the best interests of his Order.

The mission, despite the bishop's efforts to put things to rights, made what Father Walter described as 'a miserable impression'.[2] Father Walter conceded that the Trappists had shown what could be achieved with zeal and hard work, but reported that their gardens had, like the natives, more or less returned to the scrub. Owing to lack of resources Father Nicholas had been forced to persuade the people to fend for themselves until the new missionaries arrived, so that of the 150 or more expected to have been at Beagle Bay and 70 at Disaster Bay only a few old people were in evidence.

Unused to the contemporary standards of the Australian bush, the newcomers were shocked to find that the so-called 'monastery buildings' were no more than rough timber and paperbark huts with earthen floors and that the corrugated iron roofs of two other constructions 'had the same effect as the lead roofs of Venice in which they kept political prisoners'.[3]

Bishop Kelly wrote bracingly from Geraldton that they would quickly become accustomed to the 'novel appearance and conditions of the country'. He assured them that 'the more one knows it the better one likes it' and that they would soon come to lose their 'dread of it'.[4]

Whether or not they believed this possible, the Pallottines set practically about assessing the situation and planning to get the mission on to a self-supporting basis. Their finances were precarious but they felt assured that substantial government and private support would soon be forthcoming. In the meantime, on the grounds that this money had been intended for the mission, they had no scruples about taking over 3,000 francs that had been allocated by the Society for the Propagation of the Faith to the Trappists, but that had not become negotiable until after their departure.[5]

They did not know of the behind-scenes battle Bishop Gibney was waging to establish the right of the mission even to the small subsidy that had been denied Beagle Bay since 1899. Not long before he had written the Chief Protector of Aborigines:

> It was bad under the Aborigines Board, very bad, but under you it is worse. . . . There is nothing so invidious as to slight one institution and liberally help another where both work for the same object and bear in mind my institutions are far out in the wilds and yours at home.[6]

In order to concentrate the activities of their own religious, the Pallottines had obtained permission from Sept Fons for Fathers Jean Marie and Nicholas to stay on as 'auxiliaries', the former at Disaster Bay and the latter at Broome, for an indefinite period; and for Brothers Xavier and John to remain in charge of the stock for a few months.

They had little difficulty in persuading the natives to return, the elders to work on the gardens and buildings, the young people to resume their lessons under Father White. It seemed to Father Walter that they would be the least of his problems and he reported on them in optimistic vein:

The Christians hereabouts are much more unassuming and submissive than those of the Cameroons. Compared with the African negro the Australian Aboriginal is industrious, and by no means talkative, often speaking scarcely a word for days. The children laugh and jest freely, their elders now and then joining in with a hearty laugh. They work gladly for the mission without remuneration (except their food and a little tobacco) and their disposition towards us is friendly. . . . So all things considered the prospect of existence is not too bad, although money, devotion and perseverance will be needed as everything must be started afresh. . . .[7]

It was not long, however, before Father Walter realized that the natives, though seemingly so amenable, were lacking in a serious application to work or a proper understanding of its importance in the accomplishment of God's will for man.

He decided that the former missionaries had lacked discipline. They had professed a policy of 'no work no tucker' but had evidently not stuck to it and had imposed no penalties on the shirker or the wanderer. The routine he established was not very different from the former – a time for prayer, a time for work and a time for play – but a firmer hand had taken the helm. There was more insistence on time-tables and tidiness and before long not only the school children but their elders were in uniform – the women all in blue gingham, the men in khaki trousers and shirts.

Some of the natives disliked the new state of affairs and took themselves and their children off to the pearling camps or found jobs on the adjacent sheep or cattle stations. Others found no more against the new Order than the old. They had loved the gentle Trappists and would remember them with tears as long as they lived, but there was much to be said for this quick-moving man who left them in no doubt whatever of where they stood, what was expected of them and what would happen if they did not come up to scratch. His punishments were swift and just – a few strokes of the rod, so many hours solitary confinement on reduced rations. (If the pastoralists held their people by these methods in the name of commerce, why not the missionaries in the name of God?) The worst punishment of all – complete banishment from the mission, which was also their tribal ground – he never inflicted and for this the natives praised him, not realizing the importance of numbers to a mission's prestige and its claims for financial aid.

Extensions to the garden, for the sowing of grain crops, and the erection of new buildings were organized with military efficiency and soon Father Walter was able to report to Bishop Gibney:

> ... At first the work was slow and hard and more than once the natives wavered under the continual strain. But by dint of persuasion and example we kept them together and have succeeded in making more than 20,000 bricks. We shall want at least 50,000. ... I have collected about eight tons of shells to be made into lime and have ordered three tons of sheet iron from Singapore. ...[8]

The bishop's hopes that the new turn of affairs would strengthen the mission's case for government support were dampened when a medical practitioner from Brisbane, named Dr. Joseph Lauterer, then Chairman of the Royal Society in Queensland and a prominent member of ANZUS,[9] was quoted as having said, after a visit to Kimberley, that mission natives in that area were being taught in French, German and their own tongue. His observations, probably made from hearsay and not intended as derogatory, caused such a spate of public comment on the ineffectiveness of this type of education that Mr. G. S. Olivey, Inspector of Native Reserves, was sent to report on all missions in the northwest.

He left Beagle Bay after two weeks' sojourn, admitting that it had completely altered his conception of missionary education and of the mental capacity of the Aborigines. He had found Father White teaching a school of thirty cleanly-dressed, happy-looking children and, seemingly under the impression that their education had started only two months before, he was naturally astonished to find them already able to read from elementary books, to write neatly, and to count up to a hundred. They showed remarkable talent for singing and sport. Some of the boys had the Latin responses of the Mass by heart, the seventy adults attending church sang hymns translated into their own language by the Trappists, while Father White's sermons were interpreted to the people by one of the older boys. The inspector thought the standard of food and medical care very good and found the people all well-mannered and industrious.[10]

Father Walter had been much encouraged by the inspector's praise of his mission and his estimation of its value as 'very much over £5,000'. He expected this report to result in a healthy government grant but received no more than a niggardly hand-out of £250, and this only through the strenuous representation of Bishop Gibney. Having anticipated keen public interest and solid government support for his venture this was sadly disappointing but Father Walter still saw great possibilities of the mission's soon developing its own source of income. That the other-worldly Trappists had failed in this direction seemed no reason whatever why the practical Pallottines should not succeed.

# CHAPTER THIRTEEN

## 1901 – 1902

DIFFICULTIES increased as the months went by. The Pallottines found, as the Trappists before them, that grain crops could thrive only by an extensive system of rotational sowing and the use of expensive fertilizing agents. No further guano could be obtained from the islands until money had been found for the repair of the mission lugger but even had all the necessary finance, equipment and labour been available, the land capable of cultivation was limited to the areas of natural springs.

The shortage of missionaries was also a tremendous handicap for although a number of mission Aborigines were now reasonably good gardeners, stockmen and handymen it had soon been found that work in any department came to a standstill without white supervision.

When Father Walter first made known his plan to develop leaders by putting the more dependable natives in positions of authority, Father Nicholas told him that this would not work. He explained that the Aborigines, though in many ways so biddable, had a hard core of resistance to anything contrary to their idea of correct social behaviour. In this respect, the priest warned, he had found from experience that they would stand firm against any form of persuasion whatever and it was therefore better for one's own prestige to give in quickly than to be forced to do so after a long and abortive struggle. 'To think you will win,' he said in the advice he was to repeat to the missionary nuns on their arrival some years later, 'is to make one great mistake.'[1]

The problem had its roots deep in tribal life wherein the

status of leadership was achieved only through stages of initiation that eventually won a man the right to interpret and administer the law. Even this, however, did not mean that he could issue orders on matters of everyday life, for ordinary tribal tasks were matters of tradition and protocol of which few needed reminding.

The natives voiced no objection when Father Walter put one man in charge of the garden, one of the stock camp and another of the workshop, but before a week was out only the selected leaders remained at their posts. The explanation was much the same in each case: 'I can't tell them what to do; that's not my business.' Insistence that they should make it their business was of no avail and Father Walter was forced to accept the fact that team work was possible only as long as a white man remained in charge.

It was a great loss to the Pallottines when, six months after their arrival, Brothers Xavier Daly and John Berchmans were recalled to join their own Order. It had been hoped that they would apply for release from their Trappist vows and join the missionary society, but neither had shown any inclination to do so. Little Brother John had been reared in the Trappist tradition and missed the monastic life, while Brother Xavier had grown increasingly eager to embrace it and to remove himself from all worldly concerns. Before leaving Australia he wrote Bishop Gibney that he was soon to join a branch of his Order in the Holy Land:

God's mercy has now sent a more suitable body of men to continue this your dear work. They are devoted, efficient and heartily willing. The very Rev. Father Walter appears to me a very pushing, practical man and Rev. Father White most spiritual and the two brothers are not afraid of work.

I hear Father Walter finds great difficulty to get money assistance from Europe, however I hope and pray that God's great mercy and the strong faith of the Beagle Bay missionaries will make those mountains of difficulties disappear.

At the eve of my departure I could but view with edification the good work of Father Nicholas at Broome surrounded as he was and yet is by difficulties of infidelity. Now one sees nice families of those we have seen living in forgetfulness of God's Holy Law. ...

Rev. Father Jean Marie is trying to carry on at Disaster Bay mission which is a difficult matter. I hope and pray this good little mission will not have to be abandoned. ...[2]

The young ex-police trooper, the only local candidate to have persevered in the Order, possibly the only Australian Trappist of his time, then set sail for France and was later sent to the foundation in Palestine. He died at Sept Fons in 1934.

Father Walter was now forced to hire outside stockmen who demanded proper equipment. They refused to ride donkeys or Timor ponies, though, since poison weed still flourished despite the introduction of couch grass, good horses had constantly to be replaced.

Efforts to establish an independent footing included the hire of two carpenters to repair the lugger *Jessie*, to bring guano for the gardens and to build two new luggers, to be named *Leo* and *Pio*, for a pearling project. Bishop Gibney also made, on behalf of the mission, a successful bid for an old pearling schooner named the *Diamant* to be bartered for stores in Broome. This was some help but with so much money still going out on buildings, repairs and hired labour the first instalment of the debt to the Trappists, that was supposed to have been paid to Father Jean Marie on arrival, had perforce been deferred. Letters of increasing acrimony had since passed between Sept Fons and Beagle Bay, for, devout though they were, the Trappists saw this as a purely business matter and regarded their claim as extremely modest for their ten years' pioneering work. They protested strongly against the annexation of the 3,000 francs, granted by the Society for the Propagation of the Faith, on the grounds that this money had been declared to them before the arrival of the Pallottines who had claimed it before even

establishing their proprietorship to the mission by payment
of the first instalment on the stock.[3] The Trappists claimed
that the loss of this money was especially important to them
since religious persecution had flared up again in France.
Did it mean nothing to the Pallottines that the Carthusians
had already been banished and that the Cistercians, their
fate in the balance, were desperately trying to consolidate
their footing in other countries?

Dom Sebastian Wyart, elected head of his Order after the
reunion, had taken over the ancient Abbey of Citeaux and
was removed from the dispute concerning the Australian
mission he had launched. His successor at Sept Fons was the
dynamic Jean Baptiste Chautard who, at the time of writing
to Australia that he was 'stupefied'[4] at the non-payment of
the debt, was also engaged in pleading the case for his Order
with Clemenceau. His eloquence was such that 'the Tiger'
was moved to shake his hand and declare himself his friend,
but it remained a perilous time for the Church of France and
their efforts were being redoubled to secure foundations in
other countries.[5]

The Australian bishops, already disillusioned by the
Trappist withdrawal from the mission, were quite out of
sympathy with their impatience to be paid, or even with
their having demanded payment at all. Bishop Kelly wrote
indignantly of their attitude to Father Walter:

> ... The state gave land and money to Beagle Bay
> mission. Why? The people of Europe and Australia sub-
> scribed money for the mission. Again why? Was it to
> enrich the Trappists? Clearly it was not. ...[6]

Early in 1902 Father Walter wrote Bishop Gibney to say
that the unbearable situation with the Trappists had been
relieved by meeting the first instalment and that his first
Christmas in Australia had passed pleasantly enough with
the killing of a bullock, sports, and the distribution of
prizes. He also described having been initiated into the
terrors of that cyclonic coast when returning from a
business trip to the port.

> ... I had a terrible time of it coming back from

Broome. It took more than six days to reach Buleman Creek, with 'cock-eye-bobs' and head winds all the way. . . . A few Manilamen and myself tried to get ashore with the whale boat at Buleman Creek but capsized about a mile out and had to battle with the breakers for two hours. I felt sure it was all up with me. I lost everything – clothes, boots and a part of the mail. When we reached land I yelled and dropped. It was an awful experience. Some of the pearlers soon came on the scene and with their kind help I began to feel I was still living. I received some nasty cuts and bruises but am otherwise all right. . . .[7]

The respite afforded by part payment of the debt lasted no longer than it took another letter to come from France, this informing Father Walter that the second instalment was already overdue and that the abbot had ordered the mission stock to be held in security until it was paid. On this Bishop Kelly commented even more strongly than before:

The Abbot of Sept Fons . . . seems to forget we are living here under Australian law and not subject to the whims either of French autocracy or French clerics who may be very pious but are woefully ignorant of business. What explanation is there for the fact that French religious who cower and cringe before a handful of Freemasons in their own country assume such a masterful tone in free Australia? The Abbot must learn that since Australia is not France his threats are idle wind. . . .[8]

The bishop's criticism of the Trappists for unbusinesslike behaviour was hardly convincing in a case where business acumen would seem to have taken precedence over piety, but the forthright tone of his letter was evidently encouraging to the Pallottines. The Superior-General and the head of the Limburg House both wrote Father Walter that they hoped soon to dispatch further recruits and finance to Australia, but in this aim they had failed to reckon on the opposition of Father Heinrich Vieter, their Prefect Apostolic in the Cameroons. Father Vieter reminded them that the Limburg house was solemnly committed to the African missions and that these establishments were already under-financed and under-staffed. He strongly criticized any draining of resources to a foundation the Society had not guaranteed and should not, in his opinion, have undertaken.[9]

These objections were not unreasonable. The sharpness of the exchanges, however, suggests that the Prefect Apostolic and Father Walter may have clashed previously in the Cameroons and the need for providing two such able but strong-willed men with separate fields of operation could have influenced the appointment of Father Walter to the Australian mission.

Father Walter, aware that from the numerical point of view the importance of the African foundation was out of all proportion to his own, did everything in his power to get more people to his mission. It was this drive that led to his first falling out with Father Nicholas whom he relied upon to influence Broome natives to come, or at least send their children, to Beagle Bay. Father Nicholas, who had long since gained the confidence and trust of the majority of Broome residents, managed to persuade a number of native parents of the value of mission education for their sons. Orphan boys he shipped off on his own authority, in some cases using all the wiles of a practised blackbirder to entice them on to a mission-bound lugger.[10] Where the girls were concerned, however, he stood firm, for he had reason to know that they were even less safe from the lugger crews at Beagle Bay than in Broome and he refused to send any away before there was a community of nuns at the mission.

From the time of his arrival in Broome he had been particularly concerned for the welfare of the half-caste girls, many of whom he had bought from their parents as unwanted infants. After the dissolution of his own hostel he had placed these in the care of responsible local families or taken them south to the nearest community of nuns in Carnarvon. Some of the Broome girls had inevitably gone astray but most had become attached to their white foster parents and were very helpful in their homes. When approached by Father Walter with the idea of sending them to the mission, the Broome residents had one and all refused.

From this Father Walter concluded that they were acting on the advice of Father Nicholas, of whom he seems to have gained a poor impression from the start. The latter's simple human approach to his missionary task was very different from that of the logical and race-conscious German who, although no doubt sincerely zealous to save Aboriginal souls, never for a moment condescended to their earthly level. The Spanish monk's practice of sitting on the ground in the midst of his aged and decrepit natives, making homely jokes as he tended their sores and administered medicines, his shabby appearance and manifest humility, was suspected by the fastidious Pallottine as being blatant exhibitionism. He could not understand the respect, not to say affection, with which Father Nicholas appeared to be regarded and which, as was later demonstrated, he did not consider genuine. He had, however, no option in the circumstances than to exploit it for what it was worth.

Certain that his humble-seeming 'auxiliary' was intent on influencing Broome residents against his Society, and suspecting – correctly in this case – that he had no intention of rejoining his Order, Father Walter wrote to Sept Fons demanding that Father Nicholas be recalled at once.

To this the abbot replied that he could not leave a solitary Trappist in Australia and that if Father Nicholas left, Father Jean Marie must go too.[11]

It was vital to the Pallottines that Father Jean Marie remained at Disaster Bay until they had a priest to replace him, for if the mission was abandoned, even temporarily, the families gathered there would drift away and the total of Pallottine dependants diminish accordingly. Father Walter pointed out to Sept Fons that the Trappists, already in disfavour for having abandoned Beagle Bay, would, by forcing the closure of Disaster Bay, be held responsible for the Christians there reverting to worse than their former sav-

150

agery. He went further this time in his condemnation of Father Nicholas, recounting as truth rumours circulated by his detractors that he was a humbug, a libertine, and a hypocrite on the make. He accused the Spanish priest not only of using his influence to prevent natives from going to the mission but of giving the impression that he was acting on behalf of his Order in raising money used for his own enrichment.

This letter must have alarmed the abbot, for he replied to Father Walter that Father Jean Marie could after all remain at Disaster Bay but that Father Nicholas was to return immediately:

> If he does not go by the first boat, *ipso facto* ... he is released from his vows and he is no longer a part of the Order.
> ... I ask you to make him understand and all those who have had dealings with him that only Father Jean Marie is my delegate since his arrival in Australia. Father Nicholas has never had power other than that which he holds from *you* as your auxiliary. ... His temporal enterprises have been without one regular mandate or one permission. Sept Fons has only just heard of them. ...[12]

Father Jean Marie, instructed to see that his fellow Trappist left immediately, seemingly assured his superiors of the true state of affairs – namely, that Father Nicholas's reputation, except among a few whose opinion was held of no account, stood extremely high with people of many denominations and races. The money-raising activities referred to were the occasional fête or raffle organized by the townspeople who held his work for the natives in high regard and were satisfied that such funds were spent exclusively in this cause. Otherwise his 'temporal activities' consisted of the sale of a few geological and anthropological specimens to the Perth museum to help support his little school, provide for the aged and sick and help establish Aboriginal and half-caste couples in little homes on town blocks made over by the priest in their own names.

Enough was told, at all events, to change the abbot's mind for Father Nicholas was neither recalled nor dismissed from his Order but the fund which the townspeople had entrusted to him for the natives was given into the control of the Pallottine superior.

This concession did little to help the situation, since Father Walter, a man of normally logical mind, having formed a single illogical premise, thenceforward twisted every reverse of fortune to comply with it. His attitude, symptomatic no doubt of the severe nervous strain under which he was labouring to maintain a footing in an unfriendly land, served only to increase his problems as the community at large, always ready enough to denigrate Aboriginal missions in general, began to criticize his establishment in particular.

Bishop Gibney, evidently weary of his carping personal complaints, wrote with some impatience:

> ... Now what your community must do is this – you must have at least twelve religious there. You must of course pay off what is due by agreement to the Trappists.
>
> I am sorry I cannot promise you any further help. Rome is calling me to account for the responsibilities I am incurring and making the diocese answerable. So no more from me.
>
> Unless you can do both these things – meet the debt and get the community, take care you do not let the mission fail.
>
> I think the Benedictines (New Norcia) could take over all. They have men and means. But I would greatly regret a failure. I have been pleased to hear from you your bad and good reports. God bless and assist you. . . .[13]

The hint that another religious body might be prepared to relieve him of his cross seems to have decided Father Walter to change the tone of his correspondence. Before leaving to attend a General Chapter of his Society in Rome, at which he hoped to win his case against that of Father Vieter, he wrote to Bishop Gibney that he hoped to return with further staff and that he had conceived a bright idea for extricating the mission from all its financial difficulties.[14]

He had gone only a few weeks when the French abbot, exasperated by the long delayed payment, ordered Father Jean Marie to raise the money from sale of the mission cattle. This drastic measure was prevented by a timely letter from Father Walter advising that his Society in Germany had agreed to meet the instalment.

Father White, left in charge of Beagle Bay with an Irish secular priest named Father Russell, gives in a letter to Father Walter a straight from the shoulder account of the current state of affairs

... Father Russell ... has just written a flattering report of the mission and forwarded it to the bishop for publication.

I don't know exactly what to say about the mission. I can't write brightly about it and yet I don't want to bother you while you are on your holiday. Mr. Dwyer [head stockman] is going to Broome tomorrow to buy some more horses. I am not exaggerating when I say that all the horses are dead – at least what could be called horses. He says it would be simply impossible to bring cattle overland without five horses more. . . . He wants a cheque for about £70.

One of the luggers had been finished about a week but the sails have not come yet and the diver is growing impatient. . . .

Father Jean Marie received that long awaited letter from the abbot of Sept Fons. It frightened the life out of him. The abbot told him that he must take action at once, seize the cattle and sell them to cover the debt. I had a cable ready to send you but your letter made it unnecessary.

I had photographs by the last mail of the new church in Broome. The tower looks remarkably well. . . .

In speaking to the stockman about the sale of cattle he

153

gave me to understand that he would not be able to muster quite fifty cows and certainly not 100 bullocks. . . .

Father Russell has a peculiar way of expressing himself at times. In speaking about the mission (and he has more than a superficial knowledge of it) he said it will break the hearts of at least three men – superiors – and then things will become easier. I agree with him.

Have you made any inquiry about Sisters? Father Russell strongly recommends the St. Joseph nuns. . . . He says they would be more useful to you than six priests. He believes you would have no difficulty in getting them.

Our [altar] wine is nearly finished – just nine more bottles. Try and bring a cask with you. I trust you will feel quite yourself again when you receive this. . . .[15]

Bishop Gibney, for all he was no longer able to help financially, never missed a chance of furthering the cause of the mission. When Sir John Forrest was about to retire from the state premiership into Commonwealth politics in 1901 he had written him a last appeal on behalf of Beagle Bay:

. . . Officially I dare say this may be my last opportunity to address you. You have been so uniformly kind to me that I could not praise nor thank you too fully. I have one last request to make and I beg it from you by the love you have for the land of your birth, and by the sympathy you have especially for its helpless ones. Therefore on behalf of the most helpless of this State the Aborigines I prefer the following requests.

Before you relinquish office fix an equal capitation grant for all the children under 14 years of age born of Aboriginal women whether black or halfcaste who are kept at any mission institution for the purpose of civilization.

Declare the whole of the territory on which the Beagle Bay Trappist Mission stands and geographically known as Dampierland a native reserve when present leases expire.

154

Lastly provide that all native offenders of the North West of this State may be transported and kept by missionaries instead of being sent to any prison Government allowing for their support. . . .[16]

These proposals, aimed both to alleviate the plight of the natives and to increase the population and hence the importance of the mission, received enough consideration from Sir John to give the bishop cause for optimism. He wrote Father Walter some months later:

In the event of this coming to pass, of which I have every hope, the Government would hand over all native prisoners to those who would be willing to take charge of them, at the same time paying for their support. Your missionaries, if sufficient force be at hand, would have the first and best opportunity.

. . . What I will require to know, should I be able, with Divine assistance to make good terms with the Government, is will your people be ready to send a strong staff, say twenty missionaries? . . . I would expect hundreds of blacks would be transported into the reserve, as the settlers would have no pretence for shooting them off their runs. I may tell you the country from King's Sound to Wyndham is being all taken up by English syndicates for pastoral purposes. . . .[17]

Impractical though this suggestion was, it may have strengthened Father Walter's case for support from his Society, for the Cardinal Prefect of Propaganda, asked to decide whether the Limburg commitment should claim their full resources, at this juncture pronounced in favour of helping the Australian foundation.

Greatly cheered, Father Walter delivered a series of lectures on his mission and displayed a collection of Aboriginal weapons and other curios that had been presented to him on departure, as a peace-making gesture, by Father Nicholas. A number of private donations resulted and with the grant of half a million francs from the Society

155

for the Propagation of the Faith, the outlook for the mission again seemed promising.

In October of the same year, Father Walter sailed from Europe with the six stalwart working brothers, Henry Krallman, John Graf, Anthony Helmprecht, Mathias Wollseifer, Franz Hanke and Stephen Contempré.

Superintendents and assistant priests would come and go, but these obscure and dedicated men, as others to follow, were to remain year in and year out, stamping the missions with the imprint of their toil, passing on to the natives all they could of their ancient crafts and their enduring faith.

# CHAPTER FOURTEEN

## 1901 – 1906

THE return of Father Jean Marie in March 1901 after nearly a year in France had been an occasion of great joy at Disaster Bay. He had implored his people not to abandon the mission during his absence and they had cared to the best of their ability for the garden and the stock. They had refrained from killing the cattle and sheep, had conscientiously eked out the stores and subsisted, for the most part, as in former times, on the wild life of the sea, the beaches and the scrub. This, moreover, they had done without the supervision of Thomas Puertollano who had taken a job with his countryman, the pearler Filomeno Rodriguez, to provide for his family and help support the mission that was then getting no government subsidy. The natives, who did not understand that the meagre supplies of flour, tea and sugar received during Father Jean Marie's absence had been mostly paid for by the Manilaman, saw no reason why the priest should so warmly have welcomed him back.

Resentment, however, was soon forgotten in joy at seeing the diminished gardens spring to abundant life again and Father Jean Marie, as though to affirm his faith in the future, working with eight bullocks to the plough on areas of extended cultivation. Soon there was a harvest of melons, paw paws, barley, rye, sugar-cane and hops. Beef was scarce, as Disaster Bay cattle belonged to the Pallottines and was badly needed as a source of revenue, but goats and sometimes sheep were killed and on feast days there was an issue of sweet, light beer made from the sugar-cane and hops.

For the people life seemed rich and secure again but their

157

priest and friend had already discerned a warning tang of bitterness in the spring waters and a chill breath of hostility to his mission from more than one direction.

Although he still maintained his Trappist rule it would seem that he had grown away from his Order and wished to remain at Disaster Bay in the capacity of missionary priest. Whether or not he could have obtained this permission from his superiors, however, he was by no means sure how he stood with the Pallottines. The monetary situation between that Society and the Trappists kept him in the invidious position of debt collector and although he had been spared the embarrassment of having to sell the Beagle Bay cattle to meet the first instalment both he and the Pallottines feared that he might be forced to do so to meet the second. Father Walter, so anxious at first to maintain his services, had treated him with increasing indifference and had at last even withheld the small stipends or 'Mass offerings' that the abbot had stipulated the monk was to keep for his personal expenses. The situation emerges fairly clearly from his letter to Father Walter written soon after the latter's return to the mission in October 1902:

> ... It seems you have recently returned with a number of personnel and your Very Rev. Father General would not like perhaps this mixture of Trappists and Pallottines. You yourself, perhaps, would not have any more need of me. It seems that this is what you wished to say when you wrote Father White not to give me my Mass offerings. If it was so you can assure your Very Rev. Father General that despite my wish to live and die among my poor Christians at Disaster Bay – my attachment to this mission is not unknown to you – none-the-less if I irritate you, when you have paid the £1,600 still owing to the Father Abbot at Sept Fons, I shall hasten to disembarrass you of my useless person.
>
> But if you have need of me and if I can be of any use to you I shall be very happy to stay here, especially if your Very Rev. Father General deigns to approve and sign our contract and you keep your promises.

Someone has written me from Sept Fons that we are in full religious persecution in France. In certain districts not only the gendarmes and police but the army itself has been called out against the monasteries. For a man as peaceable as myself all this news does not attract me back to Sept Fons. Father Alphonse and Brothers John and Xavier have written me that they are all more or less sick and this too does not encourage me to join them. . . .[1]

Disaster Bay, however, seems hardly to have afforded the solitary monk the peaceful existence he desired. Tribal authority was still strong in the land and although the French priest had the respect of the majority of natives, there were some who resented missionary interference with their private affairs.

One such was a tribal elder with seven wives who while Father Jean Marie was away in France came into the mission to claim a sixteen-year-old mission girl as his rightful bride. The girl, Marie Parambor, with the support of her Christian parents, had rejected him as she planned, on the return of the priest, to marry a mission boy. The frustrated suitor one day came upon Marie while she was collecting honey from the high branch of a tree. When she refused to come down he threw a spear at her and made off. The girl died a few hours later and was buried, amid the lamentations of her people, in the bridal dress made for her by Agnes Puertollano.[2]

A pearler, to whom the murder was reported, dispatched Marie's griefstricken father with a letter to police in Derby. This was delivered, but Johnnie Parambor refused to accompany the patrol in search of the culprit. Vengeance, he insisted, was his own private business and despite warnings that he must on no account take the law into his own hands, set about it after the fashion of his tribe. The police never got near the fugitive, but for months Johnnie dogged his trail, creeping around his night camps and leaving tracks to make his presence known. The hunted man, scarcely able to eat or daring to sleep, became wasted with fear and was almost out of his mind before his pursuer was prepared to make an end of it. He then played his victim through the pindan to the water's edge where he speared him, hacked off his head and carried it in to the police headquarters in Derby. He was arrested and tried for murder but pleaded his case well on both human and tribal grounds and was acquitted.

The inspector, knowing that the dead man's relatives would then be in honour bound to carry on the vendetta, suggested that Johnnie accompany him to Fremantle until the matter had blown over. This he did and by the time Johnnie returned to die a natural death with his tribe he had made a name for himself as a black tracker in the southern police force.

As long as the murderer had remained at large, rumours that he planned further vengeance on the mission kept the community in a constant state of tension. A letter written by Father Jean Marie to Beagle Bay soon after his return bespeaks the priest's terrible agony of mind when Thomas Puertollano failed to return from a search after straying stock:

> ... You will understand my disquietude. Poor Agnes weeps. I have persuaded her that Thomas is sure to have arrived at Beagle Bay. If you would send a brother with two or three natives ['*naturels*'] who can drive the bullock cart, I will send Agnes and her children with some baggage to Beagle Bay, for if Thomas has turned up there he will not be fit to return here for several days. Myself, I do not absolutely know what to think or do and I trust that in this perilous situation you will come to our rescue. . . .[3]

It transpired that Thomas, in following a number of winding cattle pads, had crossed the peninsula and come out, to his surprise, at Harry Hunter's base on Pender Bay. Hunter fed him and lent him a horse and Thomas, oblivious of the panic he was causing, returned at his leisure, picking up the missing stock as he went along.

But of all the forces that threatened the struggling little mission, none was as strong as the fleshpots of the pearling camps. By the turn of the century pearling was netting more than £120,000 a year for the young colony and competition for the natives increased with the numbers of men based around the peninsula. The *Liber Defunctorum* of Disaster Bay, kept in the fine French hand of its hermit priest, is evidence of the fate of many such as Juanna Maggado who died in 1902, aged twenty-four:

> Juanna, the wife of Seraphim, died in very sad circumstances. Her conduct was good and she had made her Holy Communion at Christmas time. She died at Karamal, victim of the bad conduct of a Malay who, in order to use her, employed Seraphim and encouraged Juanna to drink. I have said Mass for the repose of her soul, but she was already buried by a Christian Manila-man. Mr. de D. carried out an inquiry and declared that the Malay was most blameworthy.[4]

By 1903 Disaster Bay, previously fairly isolated from the permanent lay-up camps, was becoming closed in to the north and south. Harry Hunter of Pender Bay, with his Mauritian partner 'Frenchy' D'Antoine, had at that time formed a second base a few miles north of the mission at Bulgin Creek, which had always been a popular gathering place of the Nimanboor and Bard people.

Hunter had become a sort of uncrowned king in that part of the pearling peninsula. London born, he had been a hatter by trade and after in the north-west was said to have taught himself ship-building by cutting new timbers to the pattern of old lugger pieces drawn out in the beach sand. He had joined up in Cossack with Montague Sidney Hadley, second son of an English peer, with whom he made enough from 'dry shelling' to buy a lugger and sail north with the first wave of prospectors to the pearling beds around the Dampierland coast. They had formed a base at Lombadina, but, unable to make a living from shell alone, had run a few head of stock, collected trochus, bêche-de-mer, turtle backs and natives – the latter held in labour pools on the Lace-pedes and sold to pearlers further down the coast.

161

Hadley, according to local legend, was visited by an apparition that convinced him of the debt he owed the Aborigines for his part in their exploitation. He persuaded the Anglican Bishop Hale to found a mission among 'uncontaminated' tribespeople on Forrest River in north Kimberley and in 1897 accompanied a party to this remote area. The hostility of the natives forced them to abandon this project after the first six months, but in June 1899, Hadley with two assistants established a mission for the Bard people on Sunday Island near Cape Levêque.

In his appreciation of the religious and social significance of their initiation rites the Englishman went so far as to insist on being himself put through all the rigours of the law. The natives, at first sceptical, finally accepted him as a 'proper man' of the Bard tribe, established his relationship to each of its other members, including the women to whom he was lawfully entitled.[5] It was a sincere, stoical and pragmatic means to an end that latter-day missionaries were to achieve by the longer, less painful but more painstaking study of linguistics and anthropology. None the less both he and his mission were popular with the natives, for apart from discouraging sorcery, infanticide and the cohabitation of the women with the lugger crews, he interfered little with their former pattern of life, made few rules and encouraged, but did not insist on, the wearing of clothes. His policy was defended as being based on a better knowledge of native psychology and the pace at which the people were capable of change than that of other missions, but a higher estimate of Aboriginal capabilities was to result in a higher level of achievement elsewhere.[6]

It was no help to the other missions that customs they discouraged were condoned on this nearby island and nothing could prevent the Beagle Bay and Disaster Bay people from going there for initiation ceremonies during wet season 'walkabouts'.

The breakdown in diplomatic relations between Harry Hunter and the missionaries was another unsettling factor, for Hunter, despite his former 'black-birding' activities, had considerable influence with the natives. He was proud of his numerous part-Aboriginal progeny, taught his sons ship-building, navigation and stock work, but insisted on their becoming fully initiated members of the Bard tribe. Apart from what he spent on running expenses and grog, he seems to have put everything he had into keeping his people well fed and contented and they looked upon him as something of a patriarch.

He had kept up a guarded but neighbourly enough live-and-let-live relationship with the Trappists and when acting as bailiff during the mission's take-over of Lombadina had, according to Brother Xavier, behaved towards them 'in a very open and straightforward manner'.[7] Naturally the Lombadina natives had gone off with him to Pender Bay but he had not tried to alienate the mission people and had often carried loading for Beagle Bay.

This service had been continued, with reciprocal gifts of garden produce, until a load of chaff ordered by the mission was found dumped on the beach, ruined by sea water. Hunter wrote a reasonable letter explaining that the Beagle Bay loading had been pressed upon him by the agent in Broome. He was carrying it, as usual, free of charge when bad weather had forced him to unload in heavy surf. He concluded:

> ... I did my best to oblige but am afraid the effort will result in loss to you and am sorry as suffer a good deal myself from loss through neglect of agents. ...
>
> Trusting this Explanation will dispell any misplaced Imprecion that may have entered your mind and leave us on a Friendly footing ...[8]

Unfortunately for the mission Father Walter was not pre-pared to let the matter rest at this and threatened litigation. His lawyer replied that if in fact the loading had been put on Hunter's lugger 'against his will and without his consent',[9] Beagle Bay had no claim, and the priest had therefore to drop proceedings. There is nothing to prove that this inci-dent resulted in Hunter's being less inclined to discourage the mission natives from settling in his camps, nor is there any further sign of his goodwill.

As the financial position became increasingly stringent every possible economy was used to prevent the mission's sinking further into debt. The barest minimum of cattle was killed for home consumption. Garden produce, with the exception of fruit, melons and tomatoes, was not much relished by the natives and they quietly rebelled against an increasingly vegetarian diet that included a form of pickled cabbage known as 'sauerkraut', that was as revolting to the native palate as grubs or lizards to the European.

The situation at Disaster Bay deteriorated rapidly and the natives were drawn more and more to better conditions offering around the pearling bases. When Thomas Puertollano remonstrated with them for their lack of faithfulness they accused him of having deserted the mission when Father Jean Marie was away. Resentment, that would have remained buried in happier circumstances, flared up and when the wells gave out and their help was sorely needed to move the gardens to another site the few who remained sat sulking and unco-operative.

By October 1904, the disheartened founder was forced to report to Father Walter:

    ... At the end of June about fifty natives ... went to help at Karamel. A certain number have come back and have confessed themselves. Others have gone to the coast at Lombadina. ... Those who have come back constantly refuse to work. In August after your visit Thomas and I wanted at all costs to clear a track to work in another field about twenty minutes' walk from here. No one wanted to help. ... I went to their camp several times but was unable to persuade them to do so ... in spite of all that Thomas and I have done to encourage them. They complained about the food, saying it was neither good nor abundant, though I cook them a good portion of rice in the morning and at midday and evening Thomas had given them a big ration of potatoes and tea three times a day. They asked for uncooked potatoes, saying that they preferred to cook them on their own fires ... but we found they had been storing them in a sack and eating only the rice and some roots that the women collected in the bush. They then took the potatoes to Karamel for the Malays.

Thomas and I remained alone to clear our new camp. ... We had already done a good bit of clearing when the natives began destroying the garden. They went there during Mass and at night pulling up the potatoes, melons and sorghum. It was this which completely discouraged us – Thomas and me. We told each other that if we could not prevent them stealing close to the house how could we fare with our plantations at the new camp? Under these conditions we should never be able to do anything. We therefore abandoned this new camp and continued working the old one.

Ambrose has taken to wife the two wives of his brother who died in July. ... I have done as much as possible to persuade him to send back one of his women and to marry properly. I thought I succeeded but Ambrose has now gone back to Karamel and I have not seen him since. They tell me he does not wish to return to the mission.

For Easter there were only here Thimothe, Conselme, Antoine and his family and Malachie and his wife who arrived on Holy Thursday and who have not been here for two years.

It now seems that a mission is badly placed here. There is too little for the natives to live on so they are obliged to steal or to go off to the sea to find food. It is because of this difficulty that we have always given food to all who attend Mass on Sundays.

Father White thinks that we could suppress this mission station without much loss ... but without the mission it could be a very good cattle station. Water is short, but without a mission population you would not need a big garden and you could use water from the big spring for the cattle. Also there is fine park land where the horses could find good grass all the year round.

For myself, I am feeling old and have lost heart. This abandonment of all my Christians has made me lose my missionary vocation, but I would like to retire to a little hermitage close to the Beagle Bay where I could be a little useful to the mission. . . .[10]

The monk appears to have won his point with Ambrose, for he married him to the younger of his brother's widows shortly before leaving Disaster Bay.[11] In any case, although tribally in honour bound to take over both women, the other had been old and a burden, and giving her up had entailed a conflict of loyalties rather than a personal sacrifice.

The mission was abandoned in 1905 but was used for some time as an outcamp for the Beagle Bay stockmen. Father Jean Marie helped the Puertollano family move to a place called Lumbingun near Lombadina, which property they took over on some arrangement from the mission about this time. The priest returned to France in September 1906 and was soon afterwards sent to the Maristella monastery in Brazil where he died in 1918.[12]

This time the people did not pray, as before, that he would come back because they had grown tired of him. They did not attempt to deny that they had been unworthy of his devotion or that by destroying his will to live and work with them they had done away with their priest as surely as had their forbears with Galalang in the time long past. Both had been 'too good' and their laws too austere for them[13] and both had punished their transgressions by taking away the waters on which they had once lived so well. As after Galalang they had gone over to the ways he had condemned so they now drifted to the pearling camps where work and women could be bartered for better food and the solace of alcohol.

# CHAPTER FIFTEEN

## 1904 – 1905

By 1904 fund-raising reports presented Beagle Bay as a happy, hard-working community needing only finance to put it on a firm, self-supporting basis. The staff consisted of three priests, eleven lay brothers, once school teacher, two hired stockmen and two Filipino divers, as well as twenty-six natives employed at 10s to £1 a month as assistant gardeners, stockmen, swineherds and lugger crew, and another eighty or more rendering occasional services for their keep. Thirty-one school age children were showing keenness and promise and those who had graduated were being trained in a variety of crafts including agriculture, carpentry, stone masonry, ship-building, tailoring, boot-making, baking, blacksmithing and even plumbing. Small quantities of cattle, pearl shell, and garden produce were being marketed and tobacco growing and other agricultural experiments were being carried out.

The true picture varied less than usual from the idealized, for a great deal of genuine enterprise and considerable European finance had gone into the building of the mission during the previous two years. The first and second instalments of the Trappist debt had now been paid and through representation of the Pallottine superiors to the Society for the Propagation of the Faith at Lyons, the Trappists had been persuaded to renounce the 3,000 lire in dispute.[1] The third instalment was now well overdue but the Father-General had written asking the Trappists to defer payment for another year,[2] by which time he was confident that the mission would be firmly on its feet. Father Walter was advised, this time from Rome, that rumours of war involving Britain and Germany made it even more urgent for the new foundation to become independent as soon as possible: 'The Motherhouse (Limburg) must now help even by extraordinary efforts to consolidate and expand the mission'.[3] These extraordinary measures included the raising of 2,000 lire on loan for Beagle Bay and another 10,000 from Father Kugelmann's brother on the understanding that he would receive 50 per cent of the proceeds from the Beagle Bay pearling venture.[4]

Bishop Gibney had established the mission's right to the yearly grant of £250 with special allowances for indigents. With this encouragement and the increase of staff from Germany, further buildings had gone up, the garden area had been enlarged and the lugger *Jessie* repaired, making it possible to bring regular supplies of guano and turtle-meat from the islands.

A carpenter named Higham had spent ten months at Beagle Bay, building (when sober) the luggers *Leo* and *Pio*, that had been intended for a pearling project but as the *Diamant* had come to grief in a 'cock-eye bob' in 1902, *Pio* had to serve as a cargo boat. In 1903 *Leo*, with two Filipino divers and an Aboriginal crew, had embarked at last and with high hopes on the industry from which so many comfortable local incomes were derived. The first season's take, however, coincided with a temporary slump in the market and netted only £50. The following year they did somewhat better and also found a few pearls, including one valued at £250. The natives were by this time more cooperative than when the venture was attempted in Trappist times but they fought with the divers over the pearls. The Filipinos wanted to sell them on the snide market in Broome; the natives, to whom money was then of no importance, were divided between returning them in triumph to the mission and bartering them for tobacco and grog.

Before long it could be seen that the so-called 'verandah pearlers' had more to do than sit and wait for the product to be brought in, for no one unversed in the subtleties of bar-

168

gaining for the best divers and keeping in with the Japanese, who master-minded the local intrigues and juggled the market, had any hope of success. Two years' take barely covered the cost of operations and the project was suspended as being uneconomic until the mission could afford more luggers, a full-time executive and what was known in the industry as a 'boss's eye' to supervise the opening of the shell.

Father Walter had put great store by the production of tobacco under the supervision of one H. Schmidt who came in on a half-share basis with the mission. The first crop was planted in 1903 and experiments went on for years but there is nowhere in the records any evidence of profit.

The Beagle Bay herd was then reckoned at about 1,200 head, of which fifty marketed in 1903 brought £275 and the same number in 1904 only £200.[5]

Father Walter found to his increasing dismay that nothing, in this incredible country, seemed to progress in a logical manner. Elsewhere if one put a certain amount of forethought, work and finance into a project, one could expect a certain return, but here, instead of being so much further ahead they now owed money not only to the Trappists and various benefactors in Europe, but to the two stores in Broome, where their debt stood at over £1,000, and to the local bank where their overdraft was now £1,600.[6]

The Pallottines, in striving to become self-supporting, were in fact up against the same formidable if not always tangible array of odds that had disheartened the Trappists and but for which, despite the difficulty of maintaining their rule in the environment, the Order would probably have persevered. To have admitted, however, that the nature of both the land and its people were prohibitive to their achieving financial independence would have been tantamount to an admission of the futility of the missionary task. In the eyes of contemporary society a mission's only justification lay in its becoming self-supporting while keeping the natives usefully employed and preventing their molesting the settlers and their stock. Even the broad-minded and humanitarian Premier, Sir John Forrest, believed that a civilized native was more or less unemployable, so to have publicized Beagle Bay as a place intended primarily for the civilization, education and technical training of the Aborigines would have been to jeopardize the little local support it had. It was a great pity that this significant aspect of the mission was thus generally unappreciated, for no institution in Australia could have provided better technical training than that being given the natives by the working brothers at Beagle Bay.

In school, too, the children were being well taught, according to the standards of the day, but good teachers were hard to come by. Father White had never really settled down at Beagle Bay and in 1903, hoping later to establish a Pallottine house close to Perth, took over a southern parish. He was replaced by an energetic young German named Father Rensmann who was interested in Aboriginal culture and at once began compiling a dictionary of the Njul Njul language. He had been there little more than a year when, while bathing in a waterhole near the mission, he was drowned within sight of a number of natives who had believed until too late that he could swim. They blamed themselves bitterly and never again took for granted that all people mastered the art of swimming from infancy as they did themselves.

A young English probationer who next took over the school was found to be 'unsuitable' and stayed less than a year. After that the task fell to a series of priests who, having failed 'in the matter of temperance',[7] had presented a problem in southern parishes. Bishops Gibney and Kelly had hoped that when 'removed from temptation' they would be helped by and assist with the mission at the same time.[8] The idea was not a complete failure, for these unfortunate priests were educated men and their regimes, though in the main shortlived, left their pupils with affectionate memories and a quaint smattering of classical quotations. One who remained longer than the rest even succeeded in producing a

170

Shakespearian play – which one is unfortunately not recorded – to the astonishment and edification of a visiting prelate!

None the less, keeping strong liquor off the premises was just another of Father Walter's problems. He was not so austere as to forbid his helpers a daily ration of wine, as was customary in Europe, but his secular staff was rarely content with that. They often bought liquor from the lugger crews and put temptation in the way of those who had come there to avoid it.

It was this state of affairs that lost the mission the stalwart pioneer brother, Augustine Sixt, who, censured for striking an alcoholic priest, left for Rome to put his case before the Superior General. Strangely enough, he thereafter returned and set up a little hermitage some miles from the mission where he grew and marketed excellent vegetables. In his latter years he again undertook small tasks for the mission, was brought there to die at the age of eighty-six and is buried in the mission cemetery.

Father Walter, seeking always for reasons other than the basic ones for his frustration, attributed many of his difficulties to the fact that he had not been officially granted an Aboriginal protectorship.[9] It is doubtful, however, that this office, which carried no legal status and little authority, would have made it much easier for him to control the intrusion of Asiatic crews and stockmen from neighbouring properties. His case against them was often valid, but his neighbours argued their rights to muster their straying stock in a fenceless land and the pearlers to take shelter and obtain supplies of wood and water in Beagle Bay. They were not all after the mission women and Father Walter's wholesale accusations made unnecessary enemies. In modern idiom it would be said that his public relations were bad.

Harassed by debts on all sides, he appealed in desperation to Father Whitmee who had recently succeeded Father Kugelmann as Superior General but was informed that claims from the Cameroons made further financial help then impossible. Father Whitmee's letter, however, was full of brisk advice and sympathy:

> ... Things are always difficult in the beginning but don't be discouraged. Go slowly until we can pull ourselves round. Of course every year the cattle will increase. ... What I beg you is to be on your guard, to treat everyone kindly and not show displeasure *in your face*. ... To have crosses is a good sign. ... What is most needed is a community of nuns. ...[10]

This need had been obvious to Father Walter from the beginning and he had already approached a number of European communities as well as the Dominican, Presentation, St. Joseph and St. John of God Orders in Australia.[11] Each had become interested to the point of commitment but had withdrawn on learning that no accommodation for nuns had yet been provided.

In the circumstances, a light-hearted letter from Daisy Bates asking for some water-lily seeds and notes on local languages gathered by the Trappists struck an unconsciously ironical note:

> ... How are you all and how is the mission? and are my quarters prepared for me? The New Norcia missionaries have beaten you over the advent of the nuns they've had out recently – Spaniards – and they are going to start a school. Why not do the same in Broome and Beagle Bay?
>
> All the clergy in Perth are in retreat and the sanctity which pervades the Palace deters people like myself, who breathe other atmospheres, from approaching the hallowed precincts. I rang Bishop Gibney up to wish him many happy returns of his birthday ... and we had a nice long chat. He told me Father White was in Northam for a while. ...
>
> I am sending you a series of native p.cs. which I have published ... Lady Bedford and I sent an album of them

to the Princess of Wales and I sent some to Pope Pius X and the German Emperor, mentioning the Pallottine Order as being a German one. Shall I be convicted of *Lèse Majesté* I wonder? . . .

Have you had the Superior General out yet? I would have liked to have gone up with him and seen the mission again.

With kindest remembrances to all the dear natives . . .[12] ..

Father Whitmee had written about the same time: '. . . You will be surprised to hear that I am coming to pay you a short visit. . . . When I arrive I will be able to arrange everything. . . . Keep courage. . . .'[13]

Father Whitmee was impressed with the mission and its prospects and as a result of his report his Society agreed to clear the Trappist debt and to send out a community of German nuns. He had expected Father Walter to be delighted with this news but the worried priest had hoped for more substantial backing. He seems to have blamed Father Whitmee for having misrepresented the mission to him in the first instance and for placing him in a predicament that was both humiliating to himself and belittling to the Pallottines. He argued that it was no use sending nuns unless finance was first provided to build them a convent and he must have written advising the Mother Superior of the order concerned to cancel her decision.[14]

Up to this time both prelates and priests had talked as though nuns were purely spiritual beings. In none of their previous correspondence on the subject had the matter of their accommodation and maintenance been raised and one wonders whether Father Walter's commendable-seeming honesty at this point was inspired more by exasperation than out of real consideration for the sisters' needs. Bishop Gibney was nonplussed and embarrassed by his behaviour for in order to retain the government subsidy, he had recently guranteed, on Father Whitmee's assurance, that

German sisters were already on the way.[15] Father Whitmee, harassed by his frantic cables, wrote censuring Father Walter for betraying his trust:

> ... the only way now ... is for you to write and ask them [the nuns] to come. It is on your conscience you have brought your own private quarrel into the affair and the mission you are charged with suffers in consequence. ...[16]

Father Walter remained adamant and the Superior General's interest in the Australian mission cooled in favour of the foundation in the Cameroons, under the assured direction of Father Vieter.[17] The debt to the Trappists, previously said to have been paid,[18] was left to drag on while the Society endeavoured to find another community to take over Beagle Bay. After all that had been written about the vacillation and 'levity' of the French Trappists, the stable and business-like Pallottines, after four years in the same locality, found themselves in much the same predicament.

# CHAPTER SIXTEEN

## 1904 – 1905

BISHOP GIBNEY had for some time urged a Royal Commission into the condition of the Aborigines in Western Australia and had suggested that Dr. W. E. Roth, surgeon, anthropologist and Chief Protector of Natives in Queensland, be put in charge of the job. Reports of his activities in his own State had shown him to be a man of fearless principles, great sympathy and understanding for the Aborigines and without denominational bias. He had criticized the Queensland government for the inferior quality of land provided for native reserves and certain Protestant missions for setting up on ground where cultivation was impossible, for feeding the people inadequately and forbidding them tobacco. Therefore, when his appointment as commissioner was announced in 1904, the bishop was satisfied that the state of affairs he had long deplored would be officially confirmed. He wrote Father Walter a cheerful letter, informing him that he would no doubt be called upon to give evidence and also that the State Premier had at last agreed to making the grant of 1s a day for each child attending the mission school.[1]

Bishop Kelly, obviously disturbed at reports of natives having left the mission, wrote, with unconscious irony, advising Father Walter that before the arrival of Dr. Roth he should organize an expedition to all the outlying camps, this to be undertaken by 'someone who is known to the natives and trusted by them' – Father Nicholas, for instance – 'if he were so inclined'.[2]

When Dr. Roth arrived at Beagle Bay in September of

that year, everything possible had been done to give a good impression, and the people, dressed for the occasion in clothes specially provided by the bishop, greeted the visitor with cheers and singing. Father Walter gave evidence[3] of his missionary background in the Cameroons and the take-over of his Society from the Trappists. He stated that of his staff of eleven lay brothers and one teacher only the latter, being still a probationer, received a small salary. Numbers of dependants on the mission fluctuated considerably. When the luggers were in there were from sixty to eighty adults, never less than twenty. On Sunday about 100 natives attended the mission church and received food. A point was made, however, of not feeding any who did not work, except for the crippled and infirm who received relief rations including three sticks of tobacco a week.

The thirty-one school children had lessons for three and a half hours daily and, in order to learn 'the nobility of work', were also expected to help around the mission. Although admittedly not always as well dressed as on that day they were adequately clothed and well fed.

The mission meals consisted of rice, pumpkin, sweet potatoes, with the addition of meat generally once a day – 'meat meaning fish, turtle-meat or beef'. The hard-working boys, stockmen, gardeners, swineherds and lugger crew, received from 10s to £1 a month and their keep. They got about half a pound of meat each a day and tea and sugar with every meal. The women working in the gardens were not issued as much of these items but they got plenty of rice and garden produce. A fisherman was employed for the mission and surplus fish and turtle-meat were salted and dried.

The commissioner had heard that both children and adults frequently ran away from the mission.[4] Had the missionaries any power to stop them? Father Walter said they had none whatever. He did not call it 'running away'. Their natural inclination had always been to go 'walkabout' in the bush and he thought it reasonable to let them have as much liberty as they wanted. No native had ever complained to him about the mission.

Did Father Walter admit that the mission was in trust for the Aborigines? He did. Why then had they paid the Trappists £2,640 for the property? 'It was for private property, namely the cattle which the Trappist had not included in the trust.' Did the Pallottines now consider the mission stock to be their private property? They did. The debt incurred by the Pallottines in establishing the mission still stood at over £2,600.

Asked what matters he would like to bring to notice, Father Walter replied:

'Firstly, I should like to be appointed a local protector here for this peninsula. Perhaps I am, but I have received no official notice. . . . Secondly I should like to point out . . . that the children, both half-caste and black, should be removed from those centres of vice, such as Broome and other places, and brought to this, or any other institution which is working in the interests of the blacks. Thirdly, provision should be made so that any man who has not got the permission of the mission should not be allowed to enter the boundary . . . under any pretence whatever. Asiatics, especially should be kept away as far as possible. Fourthly, I would suggest that a policeman be stationed at Beagle Bay from the beginning of September to the end of May, instead of, as at present, from Christmas to the end of May.'[5]

He had nothing else to say except that 'under the present state of the law, it was practically impossible to carry on earnest mission work'.[6]

In contrast, the evidence of Montague Sydney Hadley,[7] superintendent of the Anglican mission on Sunday Island, showed a much more free and easy attitude to finance and his task in general. He had only two helpers, a school teacher and a cook. There were 113 permanent residents on his mission, including twenty-three school children, but they received an annual grant of only £100 as against £250 for Beagle Bay. From the sale of pearl shell, bêche de mer and what he was able to provide from his own pocket they managed, however, to keep out of debt and he did not feel justified in asking a shilling a day for school children such as had recently been granted to Beagle Bay. 'I don't think,' he admitted with refreshing frankness, 'that I could give the government a *quid pro quo*.' He said that he would like to extend his sphere of influence to the Cape Levêque area at the top of the peninsula where the people were of the Bard tribe as were the Sunday Islanders. This would make his task much easier, especially if the King Sound side of the peninsula were closed to pearlers, a stipulation which, speaking as an ex-pearler himself, he did not think would be much loss to them. Such lay-up camps as were there at present could be moved to Beagle Bay and Baldwin's Creek, where there was plenty of good water, wood and shelter for repairing the boats.

Hadley's evidence does not suggest that he had any quarrel with the Pallottine mission but this last suggestion, in view of the trouble already caused by lugger crews in Beagle Bay, is hardly indicative of goodwill!

Father Nicholas, interviewed in Broome,[8] gave evidence in French of having come to Australia as a Trappist novice but with the formal promise of his superior that he might live and die in Australia working for the Aborigines. He had begun work alone and without resources in Broome: 'a tent my church, a bough shed my room'.

Asked whether he was not at some time Superior of Beagle Bay he said that he had been nominated to that position in 1898 and remained there until 1901. There had never, in Trappist times, been less than 150 people on the mission, sometimes more than 200, with about fifty children in the school. He had been empowered to carry out negotiations of transfer from Trappists to Pallottines, the money consideration being for over 800 head of cattle. These had increased from an original 150. No, the Trappists had not yet received the whole of the money due to them.

He spoke of the establishment of his school and orphanage in Broome and explained his having had to close his hostel for the half-caste girls. He told also of his care for the aged and sick, who would otherwise have been left 'to die like dogs', of the town allotments he had purchased from public subscription for Aboriginal couples, and of his visits to the natives' camps in an effort to save the lives of half-caste children.

'... I regret to state [he added] that I know of forty-four non-Christian infants who have been killed by their mothers at birth, and one child of four years old who was killed and eaten by its mother: now the latter is a Christian. I always let the blacks know that I am fond of their children and offer them so much rice and flour for any infant they do not want.'⁹

Evidence collected from pastoralists and pearlers, police and government officials, stockmen and the natives themselves showed the north-west to be an area in which the white population was for the most part either blind or indifferent to the miserable condition of the Aborigines. The commissioner found that large areas of country were being taken up with no provision whatever for the displaced people who, when driven from their hunting grounds, were doomed either to starve or to die by corruption and disease. Along the coast from La Grange to the eastern shores of King Sound he found drunkenness and prostitution ('the former being the prelude to the latter') rife in the lugger camps and he criticized many aspects of both the pearling and pastoral industries.

Where the taking of native prisoners was concerned he found 'a most brutal and outrageous state of affairs'. Since the police received an allowance for every native brought in on sheep or cattle spearing charges it was common practice to arrest as many as possible, without warrant, and to extract confessions of guilt 'at the muzzle of a rifle if needs be'. Long chains of 'offenders' were brought in for trial, with native witnesses – never for the defence – inevitably found guilty and sentenced to flogging or terms of imprisonment with hard labour.

Half-castes, despite the prevalence of infanticide, he found to be increasing in the back country, one Fitzroy

179

station alone being 'credited with from twelve to fifteen', while only rarely did he hear of these children being acknowledged or provided for in any way by their white fathers. Half-castes he thought would be better brought within the influence of missionary establishments.

In so far the report would have met with the approval of Bishop Gibney, but the commissioner not only failed to recommend an increased subsidy for Beagle Bay but suggested that its grant for the relief of indigents should be cancelled. Dr. Roth remarked a decrease in numbers of some 50 per cent at this mission from a reputed maximum of 200 in Trappist times. He had also heard complaints from the natives about the quality and quantity of the food, and he regretted the absence of nuns. Concerning the 10,000 acres in fee simple that had been promised the Trappists subject to £5,000 worth of improvements (for which the bishop thought he had long since established the claim) the commissioner observed that the improvements had been mainly applied to one location and not to the 'total area' as stipulated. This and another three blocks that the mission was anxious to obtain in fee simple, contained the only permanent waters on the entire reserve and he recommended that the Lands Department would 'take care that the property held in trust for the natives [was] not handed over to the mission'.[10]

On the other hand, the commissioner recommended an increased subsidy for Sunday Island mission, commended Hadley as a 'fine example of man who is sacrificing self on behalf of others'[11] and – making it harder than ever to endure from Father Walter's point of view – warmly praised Father Nicholas's work in Broome. Dr. Roth drew special attention to the evidence of the Spanish priest:

A more unselfish man it would be rare to meet, and the Department would do well to afford him an opportunity of increasing his sphere of influence. He certainly should not be allowed to pay rent for a reserve out of his private purse. At present he is responsible for the distribution of indigent relief to the extent of a few shillings daily, an amount far from commensurate with what is absolutely required.[12]

Dr. Roth's recommendations made on behalf of Father Nicholas and of the Benedictine mission at New Norcia, absolved him from any just accusation of denominational prejudice but Father Walter was probably right in suspecting that he had been influenced by people prejudiced against himself and his work. The sergeant of police in Broome, for one, had done nothing to help the mission and said in evidence that he saw no reason why the government grant of £250 a year should not include the upkeep of the old and indigent.

'Nothing should be paid [he said]. The mission is more of a squatting business than a mission station. ... The natives are working for them on the station, in the gardens, looking after the herds, and on the two boats, one of which is a pearling lugger. The natives work for what they eat.'[13]

This of course was foolish talk, as the sergeant later admitted in an apologetic letter, adding that he had not expected his comments to be taken 'so literally'.[14] He was shocked, however, by Father Walter's suggestion that his evidence had been influenced by Father Nicholas 'who,' he said, 'I think is above that sort of thing.'[15]

But nothing could now alter Father Walter's convictions that Father Nicholas was at the bottom of everything, from malicious rumours to harsh facts, such as the repudiation by the Labour Government, elected in June 1904, of the newly granted child allowance, which was dismissed as an electioneering dodge on the part of their Liberal opponents.[16] Examining the Spanish priest's evidence to the commission, Father Walter claimed to find a misstatement in almost every line of it.[17] His indignant letters to Limburg and to Bishop Kelly pointed out that Father Nicholas was not superior of the mission from 1898, as he had said, but had been put in temporary charge in 1900.[18] Never, declared Father Walter, as there were letters from France to prove, had Father Nicholas been empowered to act on behalf of the Trappists.[19] Furthermore, the Pallottine insisted his estimate of the Beagle Bay population in Trappist times had been totally false. Perhaps so, but it happens to correspond with figures given by Bishop Gibney in his report of 1900.[20] In short, everything, according to Father Walter's reasoning, added up to the conclusion that Father Nicholas was an enemy of the mission and that their work was to no avail as long as he remained in the country. It was proposed therefore that he be replaced by a secular priest then at Beagle Bay.

This suggestion drew vehement protests from the residents of Broome, not only on the grounds that they wanted Father Nicholas but that the priest in question was an alcoholic. From this Father Walter could only conclude that Father Nicholas had lobbied in some underhand manner for public sympathy and he lost no time in accusing the bewildered little priest of his duplicity. To this charge Father Nicholas replied in French:

> ... Never have I understood the sympathy I have among the people here who absolutely do not wish that Father ... come to Broome.... They know that he will not long resist the temptation to drink and have demonstrated strongly in my favour. If you believe, dear Father, that I should go elsewhere for the good of the Church and the mission, I will readily do so when one more suitable is found to take my place.... It would please me well to escape and to hide in the rocks beside the sea and live in solitude with God. This is the truth....[21]

Father Walter's position was a lonely one, as no one was able to see what appeared so obvious to himself. Bishop Kelly wrote:

> ... In the first place there has been no investigation into the charge made against Father Nicholas of furnishing Dr. Roth with evidence against the mission. F. Nicholas

protests that he did no such thing and I am able to bear witness that it is quite unnecessary to suppose that he did, for statements reach me even here that the natives are not so happy at the mission as formerly and some of them have even inquired of me as to when the Trappists will return.

. . . we can understand and appreciate at their face value such complaints about the mission, the fact is that they are made . . . but not by Father Nicholas. . . . Secondly it could be almost disastrous both to the cause of the natives and the Manilamen to remove Father Nicholas. It would be impossible to find one to fill his place in their regard and in the esteem of the general public. I will not therefore, for these and other reasons . . . consent to having Father Nicholas supplanted by anyone. . . .[22]

Father Whitmee wrote from Rome in his usual down-to-earth way:

. . . If you can only *keep quiet* all will come right again. You see, with Father Nicholas, had you *used* him, things would have been very different. Now he is a hero and a martyr. Don't attempt to do anything against him, otherwise the people will turn you out of the country. Use him, make a friend of him and he will help the mission at least by sending children.[23]

Rather than take this advice Father Walter asked the bishop to arrange a secret ballot that he was sure would reveal the true sympathies of the people to be with himself. This vote, however, showed 128 out of 132 Broome Catholics to be in favour of Father Nicholas.[24] Bishop Kelly then came himself to Broome, hoping as he said 'to arrive at a *modus vivendi*', and drew up an agreement[25] by which Father Nicholas was to take charge of the native and Filipino Catholics and Father Walter to minister to the others. But there was no rational solution to this clash of personalities. Father Walter demanded that Father Nicholas vacate the presbytery and also that the subsidy recently granted him for the upkeep of his aged and indigent be

183

made payable to himself. Father Nicholas submitted but he wrote to Bishop Gibney that it was no longer humanly possible for him to remain in Broome. He had in the meantime obtained dispensation from the Trappist rule[26] and proposed to devote himself as a secular priest to the coastal tribes and the Filipino crews. For this purpose he had raised the down payment on a 14-ton schooner which he told Bishop Gibney he would now have to forfeit if he could not pay it off.

The bishop, however, was no longer able to help his clergy as it had been his joy to do, for his farsighted Church projects and land purchases had run his diocese into the state of debt that was to harass and shadow his old age.

In the meantime, however, he had been instrumental in having Roth's statements regarding Beagle Bay mission criticized in the Legislative Assembly. As a result the subsidy was not cancelled as recommended, but raised to £500 a year, retrospective to 1904, with an increased grant for invalids, which made the continuation of the mission possible. With the current price of stock and shell, however, as well as the heavy cost of freight, the poor seasons and urgent need for fencing, well sinking and bloodstock, it was still unable to keep out of debt[27], the blame for which continued, as unreasonably as ever, to fall mainly on Father Nicholas.

The latter's prayers for deliverance were answered when his friend Filomeno Rodriguez came to his assistance and paid off the schooner on which he had set his heart and his deposit. The priest, overcome with relief and gratitude, named the vessel *San Salvador* and at once transferred to it his few worldly goods. Sleeping for the first time on its ample decks he dreamed that Our Lady appeared to him, 'so shining, so beautiful', and assured him that the vessel would serve him well to the time of his death and would never be lost at sea.[28] The dream was to prove prophetic for *San Salvador*, as few others of that treacherous coast, bravely weathered the seas and cyclones of the years, to be left at last, worn out, on the beach at Beagle Bay.

# CHAPTER SEVENTEEN

## 1895 – 1907

[A valiant woman] – who can find her? She is far beyond
the price of pearls. . . . She holds out her hand to the poor,
she opens her arms to the needy. . . . Many women have
done admirable things but you surpass them all! . . . Give
her a share in what her hands have worked for, and let her
works tell her praises at the city gates. (Proverbs, 31.)

IF ever there was a valiant woman in the story of Australian pioneering, such a one was Mother Antonio O'Brien.
In the first group of St. John of God[1] nuns to come to
Australia on Bishop Gibney's invitation in 1895, she had
behind her some thirty years of nursing experience and had
been in charge of her convent in Ireland.

Less than a year after her arrival she and five other
sisters had set out from Perth by buggy to nurse the typhus-
stricken miners on the Kalgoorlie goldfields. Their convent
a canvas hut, their hospital a tent, and water so precious that
alcohol was often used to sponge the sick, these Irish nuns
and a little band of Methodist nursing sisters fought the
epidemic to an end. By this time the goldfields population
had risen to over 20,000, a railway had been brought out
from Perth and a water supply conveyed 351 miles from the
coastal streams.

Mother Antonio, no longer strong enough to nurse, then
began teaching in the school established by her Order in
Kalgoorlie, but in 1905 ill-health forced her to return to
Perth. Deeply moved by what Bishop Gibney had told her
of the plight of the Aborigines and the vicissitudes of the

Beagle Bay mission, she had for some years tried to persuade her superiors to espouse this cause. Early in 1906 the St. John's nuns in Perth had been informed by Father White that money was 'no object'[2] in getting members of their community to Beagle Bay and he had assured them that sisters would be outfitted, their fares paid and a convent provided if they would undertake this missionary task. Some of the sisters had been enthusiastic, but the Reverend Mother was sceptical and wrote to Bishop Gibney that she would like these promises 'in writing'[3] before recommending the proposition to the motherhouse.

The Mother General in Ireland, inclined to favour the idea, had made further inquiries. These brought forth the information that the mission was too impoverished to provide proper accommodation or upkeep for nuns and that even Australian-born women could not endure the climate without adequate living conditions and frequent holidays. If this had not been enough to discourage her, she was definitely put off (as were superiors of many Orders before) by information that the Trappists had abandoned the mission not only for temporal but for spiritual reasons, and that the Pallottines had since had much trouble in holding their community together. Photographic evidence was supplied to uphold statements that the natives were too primitive to be responsive to teaching of any kind but that Western Australia's rapidly growing white population, mostly of Irish origin, was in dire need of the help and influence of as many nursing and teaching nuns as could be spared.

Mother Antonio's letters refuting statements against the natives were to no avail and in order to argue her case she at last agreed to take the 'health trip' home that she had formerly refused. Not long after her return to Ireland she wrote Bishop Gibney that two novices and six postulants had volunteered for the Australian mission and added that:

I myself shall willingly go with them . . . to end my days

186

in the service of God, while working for the Aborigines. ...

Our Wexford community has placed a house of my
father's at my disposal. I have been offered £180 for it
and am happy to have that sum to help on the new foundation [at Beagle Bay] ....[4]

But apart from giving a missionary branch her formal
blessing, the Mother General had insisted that it must be
completely self-supporting and separate from the main
body of the Order.

If this had seemed small encouragement, it was generous
to that awaiting the return of Mother Antonio with her five
volunteers[5] to Australia, where few, Catholic or Protestant,
could see such a mission as anything but a shocking waste of
their valuable time and energy. The Mother Superior in
Perth, struggling to get her Order on to a financial footing in
the new land, and hard put to find enough sisters for the
nursing and educational needs of the southern community,
refused to have anything to do with it except to insist that
the recruits were told frankly what they were going to and
given complete freedom to choose an alternative.

Many took it upon themselves to supply discouraging and
frightening information that disturbed and bewildered the
young would-be evangelists. One priest went so far as to
describe the natives as a sub-human species, that, since obviously not cast in the image of the Maker, could possess no
souls to save.[6] In this he overplayed his hand and aroused
the novices' Irish fire but their agonized prayers for a clear
indication of the will of God continued. One who wrote to
Bishop Gibney must have more or less expressed the feelings of the others:

... I have been strongly inclined to the mission at
Beagle Bay and would willingly and joyfully go with dear
Mother Mary Antonio if I thought the whole thing was
God's will. But really, My Lord, I am at present groping
in the dark as regards God's will and at a loss to know

187

what the work is really like. I have heard a little of some of it which makes me shudder. . . . Still . . . I am ready and willing to sacrifice my feelings for His work. . . . I am strong and healthy, T.G., and in the best of spirits to make this further sacrifice if God wants it of me. . . .[7]

Early in 1907 Father Walter, on his way to canvass for the mission in various Australian capitals, called on Mother Antonio and her little band of aspirant missionaries, in order to dispel some of the fears about the country and the natives that others had been at such pains to implant. For most of them this was quite unnecessary, as was his confession that finance was fairly stringent – a situation on which they had been well informed. He said nothing regarding accommodation and Mother Antonio did not ask about it. Bishop Kelly, however, now refused to permit the nuns to go until he was assured that they had a convent to go to and would receive adequate support from the Pallottines.

Father Walter's letters, written from Adelaide and Sydney during his fund-raising campaign, indicated that he hoped to retire to Germany as soon as possible, leaving a young priest named Father Bischoffs, who had arrived in 1905, as acting superior. He promised first, however, to get the mission on to a better financial footing[8] and hoped to collect enough at least to pay off their debts and provide a convent for the nuns. The response to his appeal was, as usual, disappointing and as his hopes began to fade of building for the nuns at Beagle Bay he suggested that they might occupy the premises of the Pallottine community,[9] though where displaced persons were to go in that case he did not say. He was able to send the nuns only £200 to cover their basic equipment and portion of their fares to Broome. Mother Antonio's small patrimony had been swallowed up in passages to Australia, but on the strength of this contribution she made tentative bookings for the north on the *Bullara* due to sail two weeks later, packed up and prayed for a miracle.

A Perth girl who had offered herself as a postulant for the

mission had had to be refused owing to the opposition of her family, but a couple of days before the ship was due to sail her parents relented. Their donation of £100 was exactly the balance required and the little company, with Father Joseph Bischoffs, who had come from Beagle Bay to look after them, set sail for the unknown.

The fresh-faced colleens aroused curious interest among their fellow passengers and were subjected to a constant barrage of teasing and questioning. Why should such lovely girls want to bury themselves in the bush? Had anyone warned them what they were going to – the climate, the tough living, the isolation, the snakes, the wild animals, the cannibal blacks? The sisters parried with Irish wit, while Mother Antonio, her arms characteristically crossed in the loose sleeves of her habit, smiled and conversed in her gently cultured way. Her broad, serene countenance betrayed no shadow of anxiety, although, lacking the financial support or even the encouragement of her Order, she was entirely responsible for their missionary project and was without the price of a postage stamp in her purse.

Of them all, only Sister Mary Benedict Courtney, who had already some teaching experience in Kalgoorlie, and Sister Mary Bernardine Greene were as yet professed nuns. The remainder were novices, most of them under twenty and from sheltered homes. One of them, looking back in later years, said they had all been 'as silly as rabbits'[10] but Mother Antonio's letter to Bishop Gibney telling of their journey and arrival bespoke only the happiest confidence:

> ... Well, to begin with we had a splendid voyage ... got out at every port and enjoyed ourselves thoroughly. Father Bischoffs is the essence of kindness and has taken good care of us spiritually and temporally since we left.
>
> We had a strange experience on the lugger. The *Bullara* brought us to the mouth of the Beagle Bay and we should have crossed to the shore in two hours, but there was no breeze to catch our sails and so we had to anchor until daylight. We had nothing to eat but a very small piece of

damper and a few biscuits and black tea. We all got sea-sick again, then remained calm and happy in sight of 'the promised land', but unable to reach it. We knelt down – those who were able – and prayed for fair weather ... but instead of a favourable breeze the wind blew a hurricane and the lugger was hurled back repeatedly from the shore.

... Father Bischoffs said Satan must be on shore driving us back but that he would be defeated. There were two small boats tied to the lugger and into these we got and set out, three in one and six in another. We were driven in opposite directions and one boat nearly capsized. However, we were not frightened.

Finally both boats landed, one seven miles and the other four miles from the brothers' cattle station [an out-camp between the mission and coast]. We had to be carried ashore and yet ours was the better landing place of the two.

Six of the sisters refused to be carried, sent away Father Bischoffs, took off boots and stockings, jumped into the bay, waded through three feet of water to the beach then walked seven miles in their bare feet and wet clothes. We three sisters M. John, M. Joseph and myself, had only four miles to walk and I was the first to arrive at the cattle station and had the pleasure of welcoming the others and inviting them to *kettle* tea, damper and biscuits.

The bullock team is now yoked going to Broome and I may not have another chance of posting for a fortnight.

We received a truly magnificent reception and a warm Irish welcome from all, especially from Father Russell and Brother James Clarke.

We feel intensely happy and delighted with our convent and its surroundings and above all with the affectionate little children.

Pray for us, My Lord, that we may be mothers and sisters to them in every sense of the word. . . .[11]


Her sisters remember how the half-caste boys had waded

out to meet them with low bows and carefully rehearsed exclamations of welcome while the full-blood people, shy but agog with curiosity, peeped from behind the sand dunes. The Aboriginal Paddy Djiagween, then a boy of about ten, describes Mother Antonio (with no intention of disrespect) as wading ashore 'like a big, white gull',[12] then going down on her knees and kissing the hot sand. He had laughed, thinking her action expressed relief at setting foot again on dry land, but he came later to see it as an act of dedication to his country and its people.

The journey from the coast was accompanied by a good deal of comedy, the poorly broken bullocks continually breaking their harness, going bush and having to be brought back again. The sisters, weak with hunger and fatigue, sighed with relief when they reached the gates of the mission. Here, however, they were told to wait and it was quite half an hour before the community, shrilling 'Hail, Queen of Heaven' above a peal of bells, returned to lead them in orderly procession to their new home.

Work begun on the nuns' house in an attempt to comply with Bishop Kelly's conditions had been suspended for lack of funds, so the 'convent' of which Mother Antonio had written so cheerfully was in truth a bark-roofed building that had been vacated for them by the brothers. The doors were covered with flapping pieces of canvas and the windows with nothing at all. A few boxes served as furniture and there were no mattresses or pillows on the greenhide stretchers.

'Heaven be praised!' Mother Antonio had exclaimed, chasing the hens from the beds where they were accustomed to roosting. 'We'll not be tempted to be sleeping in.'

She had no complaints about the total lack of comfort and privacy, the shortage of water, the poor food, and she permitted none from her companions. Tolerant of weakness in the laity, she countenanced no frailty in a religious and gave her sisters to expect no allowances of any kind. A woman of uncompromising values, she set an example of iron self-discipline. The stiffly starched coif, deep collar, cuffs, pleated bodice and other bulky features of a habit designed for a cold climate were worn with stoical compliance with tradition in temperatures often rising to over 110 degrees.[13]

Few of the sisters had much experience of house-cleaning or cooking, but under their reverend mother's eagle eye they swept, scrubbed, washed, ironed, and produced meals for the entire community. When their culinary efforts were too disastrous to be inflicted on the priests and brothers it was insisted that they were served at the nuns' board and eaten without comment, even if they choked, for to have thrown anything away would have been contrary to their vow of poverty.

Mother Antonio, although never prepared to admit it, had been, at the time of embarking on her missionary life, already worn out from years of nursing under harsh goldfields conditions and was in extremely frail health. Sometimes she would faint while working during the intense heat and would be forced to retire until evening. She would then emerge, determined to make up for lost time, and expecting her sisters, who had worked meanwhile without a break, to keep up with her.

But Mother Antonio was no killjoy. She dearly loved a good joke, even against herself, and was delighted when the most spectacular performer at a corroboree organized in their honour turned out to be Father Bischoffs, blackened from head to foot and adorned with ochre and feathers!

An excellent mimic herself, Mother Antonio would often entertain the community with amusing stories or by reciting poetry and reading from the classics. She encouraged her sisters to see the funny side of difficult situations and to perform their tasks gaily. She liked to see them enjoying themselves, but none the less held up to them as an ideal her brother Joseph O'Brien who, of her several brothers in religious orders, had always been closest to her heart. She often told with what excitement she had planned to surprise him by arriving at his college unannounced, during her last visit to Ireland. His greeting had been somewhat restrained,

1 Bishop Matthew Gibney, Taken in 1887

2 Father Duncan McNab, pioneer missionary of Queensland

3   Aboriginal elder of Western Kimberley

4   Aboriginal dancer with paper-bark headdress

5   Group of West Kimberley coastal Aborigines as encountered by the early settlers and missionaries

6  West Kimberley coastal Aborigines with a catch of dugongs or sea-cows

7  Dampierland Aborigines on a raft of mango tree trunks

8    Broome, residential area, about 1900

9    Foreshore quarters for Broome pearling crews

10
Second church
in Broome, built
with the help of
Filipino pearl
divers

11 First church at Beagle Bay mission, built by Trappist monks in
the 1890s

12  Mrs Daisy Bates in 1901

14 Mother Antonio O'Brien, taken in Broome, about 1920

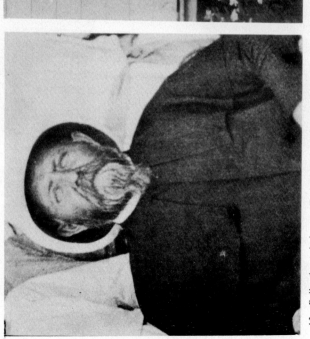

13 Pallottine missionary Father William Droste, 1923

15  Church at Beagle Bay mission, built by German Pallottines and Aborigines during World War One

16   Father Ernest A. Worms, Pallottine missionary and anthropologist

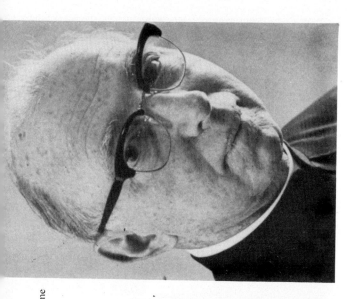

17 Father Francis Huegel, who pioneered new missions near Hall's Creek and at La Grange Bay, south of Broome

17a One of the compensations of a missionary's life is the irresistible charm of aboriginal youth

18   Pope Pius XII receiving from the Bishop Otto Raible a copy of the
anthropological works of Father Worms

19 The brothers Remigius and Gabriel Balgalai, of the Njul Njul tribe of Beagle Bay

) An old man of the Njul Njul tribe with two grandsons at Beagle Bay mission

21  Father John McGuire with an elderly couple of the Gogodja tribe a
Balgo mission

22  Old Dougal of the Bard tribe of Lombadina, with his son and two
grandchildren (Dampierland)

23 The new Church at Balgo mission—a stone fort in the desert wilderness

24 Bishop John Jobst at the controls of the aircraft he flies to keep in touch with his vast bush diocese.

but thinking him shy on account of their long separation, she had chatted brightly of her life in Australia and her hope of finding postulants for a mission to the Aborigines. He told her at last that he was sure her work would be blessed, but reminded her that they must waste no more of God's precious time in idle talk! When her novices protested at such unbrotherly indifference, the nun explained to them that his behaviour had been proof of his having learned to put first things first. She had always known, she said, that he had it in him to become a saint![14]

The natives, fascinated by the novelty of the nuns, would invent any excuse to be near them and would find jobs where they could watch their every move. Eager to please, they brought gifts of bush food and a quaint collection of birds and wild creatures which they thought they might fancy as pets. The women and girls began learning to sew and to perform household tasks with great enthusiasm while the children were frankly enchanted by these gentle white women who were prepared to laugh and play with them, bandage their cuts and sores, dose their colds and tell them stories. They followed the nuns everywhere, grasped their skirts with grimy fingers, clambering to hold their hands and sit on their laps.

Mother Antonio quickly summed up the clothing situation and decided that as far as the women and children were concerned any old thing or next to nothing must perforce do for every day, but that one good, clean dress must be kept for Mass on Sunday. Father Thomas Bachmair, acting superior in the absence of Father Walter, explained that it was one thing to make rules for these people and another to implement them and that no sooner were they given clothing than it disappeared on a long career of exchange, ending up in the camps of obscure bush relatives. This 'nonsense' Mother Antonio short-circuited by keeping the better garments under lock and key, to be doled out on Sunday mornings and returned immediately after Mass.

Before dawn on the first Sunday of this new regime she was rudely awakened to find her bed surrounded by naked

193

women, all yelling excitedly and brandishing lighted fire sticks. She shouted a warning to her sisters, closed her eyes, and prepared herself to meet her end. The screaming turned to hysterical laughter in the midst of which it was at last explained that the women had merely come to fetch their Sunday clothes.

The task of the missionary, as Mother Antonio saw it, was to civilize and to evangelize, not to be concerned over-much with the finer points of anthropology and native psychology, but as time went on she and her sisters came to learn that there were aspects in Aboriginal life and outlook that could not be ignored. On one occasion when the nuns were busy in the laundry with some of the native women a child began pulling at his mother's skirts, demanding that she come and play with him. On being told that she must first finish her work, he threw himself screaming on the ground and kicked mud over the newly washed clothes. Mother Antonio administered a reproving slap whereupon the mother picked up a heavy piece of wood and rushed at her in a towering rage. The nun coolly stood her ground: 'Go on,' she said, 'hit me if you must.' The indignant mother wavered, then dropped her weapon, gathered up her wailing child and 'went bush'. Some hours later she returned with the present of a lizard and some wild berries which she presented to Mother Antonio with tears of remorse.

The nuns learned before long that the natives considered it extremely bad form for anyone but a parent to discipline a child, and that the parents themselves were prepared to put up with almost any behaviour from their little ones. It was tacitly accepted that life would soon enough impose its own stern disciplines, for girls in the responsibilities of early marriage and boys through the ordeals of initiation.

Another aspect of Aboriginal practice that they were to learn the hard way was the extent to which restrictive taboos influenced the association of people within certain degrees of tribal relationship. When a marriage was celebrated soon after their arrival they had prepared a 'wedding breakfast' of bread and jam and strong, sweet tea and after the ceremony had carefully ushered the women to one side of a long table and invited the men to sit opposite. Suddenly the happy scene was shattered by wild shrieks of dismay, men, women and children scattering in all directions.

Father Bischoffs, having at last persuaded them to return, seated the men and women back to back. The food was then passed around and everyone was satisfied. The priest later explained that, within the complicated table of tribal relationships, men belonging to one tribal classification were forbidden to speak to or even look at the women of another. This applied most particularly to the mother-in-law son-in-law group, including boys and girls born within these classes of tribal relationship to each other. It made no sense to the nuns but they were forced to observe this taboo, even in the classroom.

Only one of the sisters found herself unable to warm to the Aborigines. She made a brave effort to overcome her repugnance but left the mission before long to join a teaching Order in the south. The rest, though they had shuddered at accounts of these primitive savages and their unholy practices, never, from the time of their first encounter with the dark people, saw them as anything else but lovable human beings with whom they shared characteristics of friendliness, compassion and a sense of fun.

Father Bischoffs, always warmly appreciative of the nuns' assistance, gave them full credit for the mission's progress from the time of their arrival[15] but it would be unfair to overlook the healthy influence of his own friendly and outgoing personality.

On being appointed acting superior early in 1907 he had established a good relationship with Mr. J. Isdell, the travelling inspector of Aboriginal reserves, and he had been appointed a Protector of Aborigines for the Dampierland area, a position for which Father Walter had long applied in vain. They corresponded at frequent intervals, discussing their mutual problems in an open and friendly way that strikes a refreshing note after so many acid exchanges between mission and government authorities. It is clear from his letters that Father Bischoffs, a staunch admirer of the Aborigines, saw their mergence into other races as something to be avoided wherever possible. Of this he writes:

> There is a great danger of a nearly white race supplanting the black fellows. The stations like to keep the boys and of course they have some reasons for it but if [they] would agree to pay about £15 a year for a child we would only be too willing to send such children back after they have been educated and found useful [occupations?] for the future.
>
> The idea of not marrying blacks with half-castes has always been our guide if we can avoid it, but sometimes the natives in the bush marry half-castes and when they come to our place we cannot well separate them....[16]

Mr. Isdell probably knew all too well how the suggestion of paying for the mission education of station Aborigines was likely to be received by those concerned. There is no record of the subject's being further considered but there is some correspondence concerning the mission's taking responsibility for Aboriginal convicts. This idea, originally mooted by Bishop Gibney to Premier John Forrest in 1901,[17] not only for the sake of the unfortunate natives who were often convicted of charges they did not understand, but as a means of strengthening the mission's claim to government support, had never been completely discarded. Father Bischoffs raised it again with Mr. Isdell in 1908 but that he was aware of the drawbacks to such a scheme is obvious from the following:

> ... Re prisoners in this place. I do agree in all you have said, because I knew it would be a great burden to the mission. I wanted to show only that if the government had no other way of escape we would open our doors. The government has helped us along and we would not want to refuse if we could help in any way.... You had raised the question in the first place ... otherwise never I would have mentioned it as prisoners would cause endless

troubles and at the same time it would be difficult for us to make it hard for real criminals. . . .

If the Lacepedes suits the government [for the purpose of a prison] it could easily become a great help to us. . . . Indeed chains are not wanted there but the deprivation of liberty will be felt there more than anywhere else. To start the turtle's business in this way would be another point worthy of consideration. . . .[18]

Father Bischoffs was the first missionary to have attempted a scholarly study of the Aborigines in Kimberley. The work done by others on the native languages and customs of that area had been solely in order to hasten the process of conversion, while this priest, though no less earnest in his vocation, approached the subject from a scientific interest in Aboriginal culture for its own sake. Basing his studies of the Njul Njul language on the dictionary left by Father Alphonse and the further work, so soon tragically interrupted, of young Father Rensmann, he made rapid progress. Two years after his arrival the scientific journal *Anthropos* published his first paper on the Beagle Bay tribe[19] and produced several more of his works[20] before the outbreak of the first world war removed him, regrettably, from the Kimberley mission field.

His report of August 1907 to the Aborigines Department was full of happy optimism. He wrote:

The great event of the year for us was the arrival of a community of nine Sisters of St. John of God. . . . Their lives are much more pleasant than even the more cheerful of their friends in the south had led them to expect, for work among so kind and affectionate a people as the blacks has many consolations.

Throughout the year we maintained about 60 children, feeding and clothing them; and of some 35 of these, who were over 7 years of age, we took full charge in place of the parents, and kept them in regular attendance at the mission school. Black people have not less natural affection than white and in the early stages of our work

197

they were most reluctant to part with their children, but as they saw the children did not suffer from the change their reluctance was overcome. I believe that at the present time we have full charge of every child over 7 years of age born on the mission country, and within a few years I hope this custom of giving us the children will have extended to all the people on Dampier Peninsula. . . .

There are now some 16 half-caste children on the mission, most of them having come from Broome. Many more of these poor children may be found, especially in the neighbourhood of bush townships and seaports. . . . I am indeed anxious to have charge of them . . . for surrounded as they are by vicious influences they cannot but grow up immoral and criminal. . . . Since the Sisters came we can afford our little charges the same education and training that is given to white children in the primary Catholic schools of Perth.

The school . . . is now in charge of two Sisters. About 35 children are in regular attendance and most made good progress in reading, writing and arithmetic. In the case of some of the bigger boys, mainly half-castes, the progress was gratifying indeed. . . .

About 300 native adults are under the influence of the mission. Of these about 200 only visit it from time to time and then go back to their camps, but the remaining 100 live with us always. . . . Over 30 women are now engaged in needlework, cooking, washing and all kinds of housework. . . . A number of able bodied men work with the Brothers. The bigger boys also spend a number of hours each day learning trades and are becoming proficient as carpenters, blacksmiths, tailors, etc.

The chief trouble during the year was contact with the Asiatics. At different times in the year about 200 pearling luggers come into Beagle Bay for water and firewood and about 100 lay up for repairs within 20 miles of it and remain there for the whole wet season. Each boat has a crew of about five Japanese, Malays and Manilamen. . . .

The financial position at the beginning of the year was gloomy indeed, with a Government grant of only £500. ... However Father Walter began a tour of the Eastern States to make an appeal ... and so far he has met with so generous a response that he is almost sure of paying off the more pressing debts within two or three months. ... The position at the end of the year is therefore much more satisfactory and we look towards the future with a great deal of hope.

Father Walter's private account of his money-raising campaign was far less cheerful. In fact he wrote to Bishop Gibney at its conclusion that it had convinced him that few in Australia, including the clergy, had any love or sense of responsibility towards the Aborigines[21] and he returned to the mission in January 1908 to wind up his affairs.

His claim that he was leaving the mission, as he had promised, on a much more solid basis was not unjustified. For one thing, they had at long last a community of nuns and had somehow managed to complete a humble convent. The Aboriginal protector[22] who visited Beagle Bay soon after their arrival had been so impressed with the Sisters that he had persuaded the police to send them the neglected children they so frequently encountered on their patrols. Little ones, mostly half-caste girls, some naked, others wrapped in a policeman's shirt or coat, had since been brought in from all over the Kimberleys and within a few months the mission's count of seven girl children had risen to seventy. This fact alone added tremendously to the importance of the mission and bolstered its claim to government assistance.

A succession of bad seasons and the run-down condition of the stock had reduced the income from cattle to next to nothing, but a wealthy pastorialist, approached by Bishop Gibney, had recently presented the mission with three stud bulls, the effect of which could be expected soon to show results. The great working brother, Henry Krallman, who was to contribute so much to the mission over the years, had

199

begun sinking wells and erecting windmills (purchased on the mission overdraft) and it was hoped that the mission pearling venture, for some time suspended, would soon make a fresh start. The fact that there is no further mention of the debt to the Trappists indicates that it had been by this time either paid off or remitted.

News from the motherhouse was of another strong move, instigated by the Prefect Apostolic of the Cameroons, to have done with the struggling Australian foundation but Father Walter hoped once more to persuade his superiors to carry on. Father Bischoffs' earnest anthropological studies had presumably disinclined him to take on the role of superior, so Father Thomas Bachmair, though rather too gentle and retiring for the position, became superintendent from the time of Father Walter's departure.

Seven months after his return to Germany Father Walter wrote giving the rather contradictory news that the motherhouse, though still 'enthusiastic'[23] about the Australian mission, was now too far committed to the Cameroons to give any further assistance and advised that they must either become independent or close down. He himself, well removed from the day-to-day struggle against adversity, considered that they should now find it easy enough to support themselves and he promised to try for German vocations with which they could start their own novitiate. Perhaps he did so, though no record of his success has come to light. He had by that time retired from active participation in his Society and become chaplain on his family's vineyard near Wuerzburg.

Years later he wrote a book[24] about the Beagle Bay mission, with photographic illustrations of the community symmetrically assembled, all very serious and hardly likely to have attracted anyone either to the Aborigines or the missionaries. What he wrote was factual enough as far as it went, but the true story lay in what he did not tell and that he had probably never understood.

# CHAPTER EIGHTEEN

## 1908

THERE can be no doubt that the arrival of the nuns had had a decidedly tonic effect on the community and that the atmosphere at Beagle Bay was now more hopeful and relaxed. For one thing, the constant strain of trying to get people to come to the mission had been relieved. Natives, curious to see for themselves the reputedly 'nuzzer kind' of human beings who had manifested themselves in the form of angels, began drifting in of their own accord and most decided to stay. Father Nicholas, when about to accompany the Benedictines to Drysdale River, as told later, brought a number of families from his base at Cygnet Bay and, most significant of all, the acknowledged half-caste children of lonely station owners and managers from as far away as Booroloola, in the Northern Territory, began arriving in the care of the police.[1] Their fathers, trapped in an isolated land where white women were almost non-existent, were mostly robust pioneers of good family and by no means without conscience towards the children of their Aboriginal consorts. Previously, however, they had simply not known what to do with them. To have sent them to schools in the south would have meant almost certainly condemning them to outcast misery, while leaving them to grow up in the native camps was a far from happy alternative. With the arrival of the nuns the mission was seen as a God-sent solution and most of the fathers concerned were only too pleased to pay for their children's education as at an ordinary boarding school.

Although most of the missionaries saw the main purpose

of their work as the conversion of the tribal-living Abo
rigines, it was the half-castes who, lacking the comfort and
security of any culture of their own, stood in the greater
need of their direction. It was these young people who were
to become the backbone of the mission, their development
into good self-supporting citizens perhaps its greatest
achievement.

This rapid rise in the mission population was a tremendous encouragement but the establishment was still patheti-
cally poor and the food situation was often desperate. Since
so much depended on the sale of cattle, beef figured spar-
ingly on the mission menu. Bread, too, was always short for
flour was expensive and had to be carefully rationed. When
a cyclone early in 1908 sank the mission lugger, *Jessie*, with
a cargo of precious provisions the community was faced
with near starvation. Brother Kasparek struggled into
Broome with the bullock wagon, hoping to get an extension
of credit to replace the basic necessities of life. Everyone in
the port, however, had been likewise hard hit by the
cyclone which had sprung on Roebuck Bay with terrible
force.

At least fifty bodies of Asiatic crews had been recovered
and others were still being washed up among the mangroves
at the mouth of Dampier Creek. The foreshore was littered
with wrecked luggers, houses were blown down and the
marsh and scrub for miles around strewn with the debris of
the town. No one had time to listen to a hard luck story
about Beagle Bay. The stores refused to extend credit until
outstanding debts were paid and Brother Kasparek was
forced to return empty-handed to the waiting community.
There was nothing for it but to live 'off the country' until a
donation from a southern parish enabled them to pay off a
part of their debt.

The nuns soon became adept in the art of improvisation
and the cooking of 'bush tucker'. They kept no private
stores, for Mother Antonio, who, although of a comparatively well-to-do family, had like most Irish in 'the
troubles' been frugally reared, saw no reason why the

202

missionaries should live any better than those they were pledged to serve. When times were bad even the occasional glass of wine seemed to her an unwarranted indulgence on the part of the German religious. Little luxuries, such as eggs or fruit, she insisted should be kept for the expectant mothers and the sick, and the importunate brother who once protested at these precious items being 'wasted on the blacks' discovered that there was another side to the gentle tongue of the mother superior.

She never talked of the missionaries' goodness to the Aborigines, only of the people's great kindness to them and of the gratitude owed them on that account.

'Remember,' she told her sisters, 'the natives did not ask us to come. We are here of our own choice and we can remain only by their goodwill and the grace of God.'[2]

None the less personal relations between the Irish sisters and the German Pallottines were extremely amicable. The nuns appreciated the culture and courtesy of the priests, the humble dedication and efficiency of the brothers. They accepted, even cherished their foibles, excused their failings and often helped resolve their differences. Still the fact remained that no financial agreement had been arrived at between them and it did not seem to have occurred to the male religious that nun's clothing became worn out like their own or that they might require pin money for small personal items. The sisters, well aware of the financial situation and too sensitive to mention their modest needs, had intended from the beginning to divide their forces between the mission and a school in the port by which they would become financially independent.

Within a year of her arrival, therefore, Mother Antonio, having established a smooth-running system at Beagle Bay, set out by lugger with one of her sisters. It was a journey with which the nuns were to become all too familiar over the years and one that even Mother Antonio was prepared to admit was something of an ordeal. The lugger, in turns becalmed and buffeted by headwinds, took over a week to cover the hundred miles between Beagle Bay and the port, the sisters meanwhile desperately seasick and embarrassed by the lack of cabin accommodation or any kind of privacy.

They arrived at night, unknown, unannounced, penniless and weak with hunger. Father Verlin, the secular priest, formerly of Roebourne, who had taken over the Broome parish, was out of town and his presbytery was locked, so the nuns were forced to take what sleep they could in a lean-to outside the church. Early next morning they were directed to the home of a Filipino pearler named Gonzalez, whose wife, overcome with shyness and awe, placed before them tea, bread and a dish containing a dozen boiled eggs, then rushed off to spread the news of their arrival.

Filipino and Irish residents eagerly offered hospitality but Mother Antonio insisted that they were adequately accommodated in the church premises until they found a little place of their own. Some brief notes supplied by one of the pioneer sisters describe the place that became their first home in Broome:

Mother Antonio and Sister Mary Benedict slept in the lean-to outside the church until a kind pearler named Mr. Tommy Clarke said it was high time they had a decent place to live in. Mother Antonio said it was easy enough to talk but that there were no places available in Broome and anyway they had no money. 'If that's the case,' Tommy said, 'I'll make you a present of a fine mansion' and he took the two sisters to a cottage about forty yards from the church, unlocked the door and revealed a room about 12ft. square. It had been a black fellow's camp and they had left in it some human bones and skeletons[3] and had made fires in the middle of the floor. The walls and roof were blackened with soot and spiders had spun their webs everywhere. The place was strewn with fish bones, kangaroo skins and all sorts of other rubbish but Tommy said the sisters could have it for the cleaning out of the place if it was any use to them.

Humble though it was, the two were very grateful for the cottage and soon had it livable. A third sister[4] joined them from the south, bringing with her a piano which they set in a corner and began teaching music. They cooked and dined in the room and at night spread their mattresses on the floor. At first they taught children in the church but the people were liberal and often pressed a few pound notes or a cheque into Mother Antonio's hand when they came to visit her. By this means, little by little, Mother was able to add to the cottage and to teach on the verandah. The number of school children soon increased and a secular lady graciously helped with the teaching until Mother had enough sisters to carry on.[5]

A State school had been opened some time before but the teacher being then away most parents, including Irish policemen, Japanese and Chinese business people, a Jewish solicitor, and an Italian barmaid, sent their children to the nuns. Their little school was overcrowded until the return of Mr. Goodridge, the government teacher who, far from resenting them as rivals, became their staunch and helpful friend.

Bishop Kelly, anxious to divide the administration of the remote and contentious northern section of his diocese between the Benedictines and the Pallottines, visited the Kimberleys in 1908.[6] The nuns in Broome greeted him with happy accounts of their progress but he was appalled by their poverty. He wrote Bishop Gibney deploring their dependence on the Pallottines, from whom he considered they had received 'neither help nor sympathy',[7] though he did not blame the acting superior, Father Thomas whom he described as 'a holy and timid man who would not move a finger without an order from his superior'. He reported that the nuns were obviously well thought of in the town and that two leading residents had guaranteed them an overdraft of £200. There were then thirty-nine children attending their school but at the rate of 2s a week (for those who could afford it) they were earning the merest pittance.[8]

Mother Antonio had been persuaded to confess her financial situation only on the assurance that they were not to be withdrawn. Although Father Nicholas, on a brief visit from Kalumburu, had warned her that Broome was 'the mouth of hell', she and her nuns had in fact grown as attached to the town as the town to them and had found admirable qualities even in the derelict. Some of the greatest scoundrels in the district they saw as 'kind men', 'lovely men' and these, while in their company, no doubt believed it of themselves.

Had the nuns been less reluctant to admit their lack of financial support they would probably have received more local assistance, for many residents were grateful for their school and most were prosperous.

Pearling, then employing over 2,500 men and 400 luggers, was netting about £200,000 a year and a rich, unestimated harvest of pearls. Less of a free for all than in earlier years, the industry was now considered *respectable*, and the port had sorted itself out into a complicated social pattern in which the white pearlers were the aristocracy, the Japanese and Chinese the brains, the Asiatic crews the serfs and the Aborigines the scavengers. Within these main categories spun wheels within wheels of minor distinctions, rivalries, partnerships and dependencies. The white master pearlers and business people lived in well-appointed bungalows, and, with coloured servants to wait on them, in much the style of their prototypes in eastern outposts of empire. The Filipinos now had an organization of their own and a paid secretary to look after their interests. The Japanese had a powerful club at the foot of Sheba Lane, the Chinese their joss houses and gambling dens behind shops stacked with luxury goods from the Orient, while the Asiatic crews, on three-year terms of indenture, collected in the foreshore shacks.

Despite the exclusive nature of these various groups, however, much of the life of the town was generally shared and enjoyed. Festivals were frequent and cosmopolitan, Christian and pagan eager to impress each other with their different traditions.

At New Year luggers and schooners, gaily flag-bedecked, gathered to race for the Pearlers' Cup on Roebuck Bay. Everyone dressed up for the event, European men in starched white suits and topees, their wives in Edwardian finery, big, beflowered hats, gossamer veils and parasols, Asiatics in bright national dress, the divers in long white coats buttoned with sovereigns to the neck.

At Easter, Christmas and other religious feasts throughout the year the Filipinos went in gaily dressed troupes about the town, serenading friends and business associates to the accompaniment of palm-leaf instruments.

Each year the Chinese smartened up their section of the cemetery and invited the townspeople to a memorial feast spread out on the gravestones, the Malays went gay with a procession of grotesque masks and bright banners for the feast of Ramadan; but the Japanese *Bon Marsuni* – their Feast of Lanterns for the dead – outdid all the rest. For this occasion everyone gathered on the beach where mourners knelt in the sand and kimono-ed women swayed to the tinkle of praying bells and the plucking of lutes. Then came the ceremonial launching of the miniature lugger fleet, bearing gifts of flowers and food to comfort the souls of divers who had been lost at sea. Afterwards lanterns were lit among the rough-hewn Japanese headstones in the cemetery and food was piled on the graves, to be later salvaged, with fearful glee, by the natives and children of the town.

But the colour and delight of carnival could not entirely camouflage the grimmer underside of the pearling industry. Every day across the sunny pageant of life fell the shadow of death. The divers had not yet mastered the art of 'staging' their ascent from the sea-bed and hundreds, hauled to the surface too quickly, were stricken with diver's paralysis. Sometimes the victims were brought ashore and nursed to recovery. Often they were dead on reaching the surface or expired on the lugger decks. Wherever the boats gathered to fish a good patch of shell, one after another would be seen to fly its flag half mast. The Filipino divers would cross themselves, Japanese, Chinese and Malay shrug philosophically, before going over the side again and on with the job.

Before long the nuns in Broome began alternating their day's teaching with night duty at the understaffed government hospital. Work in the crowded and ill-equipped wards, at a rate of something under fourpence an hour, was hard and crude, but the sisters welcomed the chance of breaking through the rigid social barriers of the town and of winning the trust and friendship of the humble Asiatics.

The Japanese had a medical centre of their own but as the government hospital was nearer the foreshore emergency cases were usually hurried there from the boats. The nuns had been nursing only a short time when a Japanese patient, suffering from acute paralysis, cut his throat in an effort to end his misery. He bitterly resented the medical intervention that prolonged his agony and for three weeks cursed and struck at the young nun who devoted herself to his care. Other Japanese patients, deeply ashamed, turned their backs on him, insisting that he was not worth saving – a low-class fellow and a disgrace to his country. As his end approached, however, the poor fellow tried to show his gratitude and grasping the sister's crucifix indicated that he wished to accept her faith. He was baptized on the point of death.

Moved by the nun's demonstration of patient charity, a number of young Japanese came soon afterwards to the convent, offering to pay for lessons in English and Christian doctrine. This made yet another avenue of work for the nuns and although they accepted payment for the English lessons only, it helped support them and the other nuns at Beagle Bay. Their leisure time was now whittled almost to nothing, but these evening classes were to prove a rich source of enjoyment and satisfaction to all concerned.

The nuns soon picked up snatches of Japanese vernacular and once, to quieten a hubbub of laughing chatter, a sister rapped out the word 'Chotto!' which, when used by her pupils, had seemed to have a salutary effect. The exclamation however, instead of creating the expected murmurs of happy surprise and congratulation, was followed by a shocked silence. Heads were lowered and the lesson proceeded. Later it was tactfully explained that this was an extremely vulgar word never used by a well-bred woman and quite out of place in the vocabulary of a holy nun!

The sisters found that they must be wary, not only of thus unwittingly scandalizing their admiring students but also of making any chance remark that might suggest their poverty, for the merest hint of want was followed by an embarrassing shower of personal gifts. A nun had only to ask the time of her class to have the greatest difficulty in refusing an assortment of watches. One Japanese, about to sail after the lay-up, left his wrist watch with Mother Antonio to give his teacher after he had gone. The young diver never returned from that appointment with the sea and his watch has been used and cherished in his memory for well over half a century.[9]

Their first dozen converts the nuns called their 'Twelve Apostles' and they were christened accordingly, but few of them lived to practise their new faith for long, or to return with it to their homeland. They are buried in the Broome cemetery where crosses distinguish their graves from those of their Shintoist, Confucian and Buddhist countrymen.

Father Nicholas had kept the title deeds of the block on which he had previously built his school and hostel and this he presented to the nuns. Here they were soon able to build a school for white and coloured pupils, from whom payment depended entirely on circumstances.

Mother Antonio had hoped to release most of her nuns from hospital work for full-time teaching when Sister Mary Immaculate, having completed her nurse's training in Ireland, joined them in 1909. The young sister, however, had no sooner arrived than she was urgently requested to help Dr. Susuki at the Japanese hospital. Here the situation was desperate, for while the number of diving casualties had increased in proportion to the price of shell, the nursing staff and accommodation had not. Mother Antonio and Sister Immaculate had called at the hospital to explain their situation but the plight of the helpless paralytics in the comfortless and overcrowded wards had changed their minds.

Without a word the young sister had pinned back her veil, rolled up her sleeves, and got to work, while Mother Antonio returned to explain to her nuns that 'a temporary emergency' had delayed the possibility of their teaching full-time. Inevitably, however, the capable young nursing sister became indispensable in this as in every other local crisis of that time. At the beginning of 1912 when a smallpox victim was discovered among her Japanese patients, she took charge of him in hastily arranged quarantine quarters and had no sooner nursed him back to health than typhoid broke out in the town. An Australian nurse, when on her way to take over as matron, was drowned when the *Kombana* sank off Port Hedland with all hands on board.[10] Sister Immaculate therefore carried on and fought the epidemic to an end but she was by this time so exhausted that she herself succumbed to the disease and died within a few days.

The beautiful, twenty-five-year-old nun had already become a legend in the community. She had represented an ideal transcending all differences of race, creed and colour that divided the people of the town, and they united at her graveside to mourn their mutual loss. But it was after all the Japanese who claimed the privilege of erecting her monument – a simple stone plinth surmounted by a Celtic cross and inscribed: 'In grateful memory . . .'[11]

The death of this nun, by whose training Mother Antonio had put such store and to whom she no doubt hoped to hand over the office of superior, was a sad blow to the unsupported community. One of the original seven sisters[12] had since gone back to Ireland to train as a nurse but none of those remaining, except their superior, was then qualified in either teaching or nursing. In demand on all sides, they were too few and their training too inadequate to cope with the needs of the young, the old and the sick who were nobody else's responsibility. Mother Antonio appealed for further helpers throughout Australia and New Zealand and seven girls volunteered to join her community. It was precisely the number for which she had prayed and had vowed to dedicate to the seven sorrows of Our Lady.

This pious intention she had put into literal effect, and despite the embarrassed protests of the young sisters and the amusement of others, she permitted no abbreviation. It was only after her death that 'Mother Antonio's Seven Dollars', as they were locally dubbed, were allowed to take less remarkable names in religion than 'Sister Mary of the Flight into Egypt', 'Sister Mary of the Prophecy of the Holy Old Man Simeon' – and the rest.

But there were now sisters enough to enlarge the communities in Broome and at Beagle Bay and to open a new branch convent on the lonely sea-front at Lombadina where Father Nicholas, after a series of adventures to be related in the following chapter, had set up a little mission of his own.

# CHAPTER NINETEEN

## 1906 – 1910

In April 1906 the most Reverend Dom Fulgentius Torres, who had succeeded Bishop Salvado as Abbot of New Norcia, set forth in accordance with the request of the Australian Plenary Council to establish a mission in north-west Kimberley. In Broome he was met by Father Nicholas who, following his final break with the Pallottines, was then preparing to set up a mission base on Cygnet Bay in King Sound. This project he gladly agreed to postpone so that he could put himself and his recently acquired schooner *San Salvador* at the abbot's service.

As the coast was notoriously treacherous they hired for the journey the experienced coastal navigator Captain Johnson and a crew of four Manilamen and on the way north called at Sunday Island mission to ask advice of Syd Hadley who was familiar with coastal conditions from his pearling days. Hadley, apparently on good terms with Father Nicholas, lent them as interpreters two young natives said to have been 'black-birded' from the Drysdale River area as children and who had often expressed a desire to revisit their people.

The coastal charts of the time were still incomplete and inaccurate and steering the *San Salvador* clear of reefs and tidal rips among the island-strewn archipelagos was a perilous adventure. Cyclones struck and buffeted the lugger and although Father Nicholas assured her passengers that she was under the special patronage of their Blessed Mother the abbot later wrote of how he had shrunk with terror from the fury of the seas. 'Only for God,' he declared, 'one may undertake these voyages in this kind of craft.'[1] The natives all but expired from fright and seasickness and when it came to the point were terrified of setting foot on their former tribal territory. 'It is not likely', the abbot wrote, 'that a Christopher Columbus will ever make his appearance among them.'[2]

Having investigated the coast as far as Wyndham they decided that the Drysdale River area, a well watered but rugged terrain which, according to an official report of 1901,[3] showed little promise for the extension of the pastoral industry, offered the best prospects for a mission settlement. The party then returned to Broome, the abbot to continue south to organize for his new foundation. Father Nicholas to set up his mission camp on Cygnet Bay.

The waters of the King Sound area were renowned for their high quality shell and the pearling crews that foregathered there had earned for it the reputation of a trouble spot. The police, called upon to investigate the outcome of drunken carousals and fights over native women, had long since tired of exhuming bodies in an effort to establish whether death had been due to foul play on shore, fouled life-lines on the tumbled sea-bed, diver's paralysis or other hazards of the bay's 'heavy water' and eight-knot tide. Father Nicholas's influence, especially with the natives and Filipinos, was well known to them and they therefore welcomed and did all they could to assist his project.

A good stone well[4] on the site made it possible to begin a garden at once, and with the help of a Filipino named Leandro and his half-caste wife Madeleine the little mission soon took shape.

In September of that year Father Nicholas in a telegram to Bishop Gibney, sent from Derby, announced that his little chapel on the hill overlooking Cygnet Bay had been dedicated to 'Our Lady of the Aborigines' and inscribed with the biblical quotation: *Nigra sum sed formosa* – I am black but beautiful. He added:

The beautiful image of the mother and child crowned as King and Queen of the blacks got black face and seems to ask Your Lordship a little wine for Mass at their altar on Sundays. . . .[5]

This statue of the Madonna ornately dressed and be-gemmed had been brought to him from Manila by Filipino friends. It had been his own inspiration to colour the faces black, thus indicating the universal nature of the Mother of God and her divine Son. As far as the natives were concerned, however, it seems only to have confused them, for who, they asked, were this black woman and her child to set themselves up as King and Queen of Heaven? Later attempts to encourage their devotion to coloured saints were to be received with the same scepticism, as while prepared to accept white saints in good faith they considered it the utmost presumption to attribute similar virtues to any of their own kind.

None the less the new mission soon attracted people who had been with Father Jean Marie, wanderers from Beagle Bay and bush natives who came to the 'doctor' priest to be treated for their diseases and their wounds. The government grant of £80 a year that had been taken out of his hands was again made payable to him and he used it well, but his new establishment, having a bigger native population than Beagle Bay at that time,[6] was inevitably seen by Father Walter as a deliberate challenge to his own work and a further attempt to unsettle the Beagle Bay people. Father Nicholas found his inability to avoid misunderstanding as distressing as his failure to give more than physical succour to the human refuse of the pearling camps. There was seldom a day when he was not called upon to act as mediator in the minor and sometimes major arguments of his multi-racial community. The Malays, amused at the Filipino tendency to histrionic rage, would deliberately taunt them, laughing with glee and darting for cover when knives were drawn. Sometimes, inevitably, the joke went too far, as in the case of one Severo Roca, for whom, when sentenced to death for killing two Malays, Father Nicholas had made a heartfelt but vain appeal.

Surrounded as he was by so much congenital and habitual corruption the priest longed more than ever to work among these in whom the spark of spiritual life had not been extinguished. He realized, however, the impossibility of tackling the wild tribes of north-west Kimberley without the backing of a community and felt bound, at least for the sake of the helpless children, to remain at Cygnet Bay.

It seemed an answer to his most earnest prayer when in June 1908 he received a request to help establish the Benedictine outpost at Drysdale River, together with the news that a community of nuns had at last arrived at Beagle Bay. His confidence renewed in the mission's becoming a true home for the wandering tribes, he took there as many native families as he could persuade to go, abandoned his little mission and set off to meet the Benedictine advance party in Broome. Captain Johnson again agreed to skipper the lugger and they took with them, besides Leandro, his wife and adopted daughter, seven native boys of the Nimanboor and Bard tribes.

They had arranged to meet the abbot, who was travelling with another priest by coastal steamer, near Napier Broome Bay, and as the *Salvador* waited at anchor off the wild shore Father Nicholas watched the glow from the native fires with mounting excitement. The romantic dream that pious Spaniards had cherished from the time of the conquistadores, the ideal that had eluded him in South America and so far in Australia was at last within his reach. Mindful of the possibility of its being the last letter he would ever write, he struggled in his limited English to leave an appropriate message for Bishop Gibney:

... Revd. Father Planas and Brothers with me on bard my schooner *Salvador*. *Bullara* will arrive tomorrow or the 30 with Lord Abbot Torres and Father Alcade. ...

Ow beautiful to see in the night the five or six tremendous fires of the natives around de Bahie! The desire of

215

my heart to work among de wild tribes is accomplish. ...

Revd. Father Planas and staff are full of religious en-
tousiasme. ... For me, pour old sardine, I have one only
recomendation to make to your Lordship, to the Red.
Clergy of this country, to the Rd. Sisters of the convents
and all catholiques:

In case I where burried in the stomack of one of those
strong aboriginals, I humily implore somme prayers for
my poor soul. I shall be very much oblige. ...[7]

Father Nicholas seems to have derived an almost boyish
excitement from the idea of encountering 'cannibals' and
from his writings one might gain the quite erroneous impression that native fires were kept stoked in readiness for
human feasts. None the less their situation was undoubtedly
a perilous one. The tribespeople whose fires blazed on the
shore were by no means the comparatively gentle and submissive people of Dampierland whose contact with civilization, however corrupting, had given the missionaries a
safe entrée to their confidence. During the long dispute of
1892 concerning the treatment of the Aborigines in the
north-west, one of the correspondents had reminded Bishop
Gibney of this fact. He then continued:

If his Lordship would really like to benefit the blacks,
why not go to a district where the whites have not corrupted the pure (?) minds, as he remarks he had noticed
with shame and sorrow at Beagle Bay. There is ample
scope for him in east or north-west Kimberley, for instance, on the Osman River or at the Leopold Ranges. I
have no doubt that if he started a mission there, he would
reap the reward he so richly deserves, especially if he
tempt Divine Providence by going amongst the harmless
(?) blacks protected by the word of God only. ...[8]

This challenge was now about to be taken up, for although the missionaries had arms for securing food and, one
supposes, for ultimate self-protection, they had come, not as
ordinary settlers, to impress upon the natives, by the quick-

216

est means at their disposal, that they intended to use the land. These Spanish religious had come to make known that their interest was not in the country for the sake of their own profit but in the tribespeople themselves, and then not to exploit, but to rescue them. It was a difficult undertaking, especially since there was not, in that region, any suggestion of police authority to support them, and since the natives recognized no need for salvation except from such intruders as themselves.

The coastal vessel *Bullara*, bringing Abbot Torres and Father Inigo Alcade to join the missionary party, was greeted by a welcoming salvo from the schooner's small cannon – a gesture which, however cheering to themselves, was hardly likely to have inspired confidence in the watchful natives! Captain Johnson then trans-shipped to the *Bullara* and the missionary party came ashore where they flew the Australian flag, pitched their tents and set out to explore the savage terrain.

Of this expedition Abbot Torres recorded in his daily journal: 'Today I had experiences enough to satisfy the life-long ambitions of a man.'⁹ But the story of this precarious foundation belongs here only in as far as it concerns Father Nicholas, its beginnings, in summary, a tale of waiting and attrition, of mission camps beseiged, stores raided and hopeful signs of friendship turned to treachery.

The boys they had brought with them understood nothing of the language of these parts and felt no affinity for the country or its wild people, but their fear made them good watchdogs while the mission huts went up and a garden was hewn out of the tropical wilderness.

All the tactics that had gained the trust of the peninsula people were tried here to no avail, for the natives, sought out in the bush, fled their camps at the approach of the strangers.

In November of that year Father Nicholas wrote Bishop Gibney in some excitement of what appears to have been their first contact with the local inhabitants. Though somewhat lengthy this letter reveals so much of his spiritual enthusiasm and 'temporal' problems as to be worth quoting almost in full:

 ... I would have answer your kind letter sooner, but been out of communication with the people of this world, as we are here in exile, we have only the chance to send letters when the mail steamer is due to Wyndham and then with not small trouble and expenses.

As Your Lordship is aware, I am now with the two other Fathers here in this newly founded mission of Drysdale River to work and share with them the hard task they have undertaken of civilizing the wildest tribes and most treacherous cannibals of Australia, task which I had at heart per many many years as Your Lordship well know. We have already experienced their ferocity and treacherousness in the 28 July in our dangerous exploration on foot about 30 miles inland between the Drysdale and Barton Rivers! A whole camp of about 30 cannibals, absolutely naked and painted with white and red colours speared us with spears of stone. We have had endeed *a very narrow scape*, but thank God we remain all safe!

In this occasion God accorded me the gratest favour I could scarcely expect. In one moment I remain in the place, between other Fathers where in the Barton the natives came, I meet them half way calling them. Then they run to me by groups of five or six (about 30) dancing comicaly like monkeys who surrounded me with grate demonstrations of joy. I could embrace them one by one and count with my fingers their *mogodals* or marks in the breast and shoulders. I was perhaps the first Catholique Missionary who could see them tête à tête and who, with the Crucifix in my hands give them the first notion of Chisus Christ our Lord, and our Catholique Religion! I use with them the *memeque* and the words of *Yaoro* and *Niol-Niol*, two of the native dialects.

They been with me by about 25 minutes when other Fathers came attracted by their noise, and joined me in

218

giving them provisions. We talk to them as kindly as Christianity suggests for about one hour, and when we intended to proceed our journey and have turned our shoulders, they ran at once for their spears which they had hidden in the scrub, and started to spear us! I brok in pieces the first spear in my nees, and beging to prepare for die thanking God.

It is ashamed to consider that in the so advanced Australia exist yet so great number of human beings destituted of all civilization!

God may have pity of these unfortunate creatures!

. . .

As a native *Protector* am sending by this mail a *Report* to the aborigines Department in which Your Lordship will found the very interesting *details* about these cannibals here.

\*     \*     \*

P.S. Kind regards to the Fathers. Later on if my life is preserved by the misericorde of God, shall be able to send your Lordship *interesting details* of this strange people here, with their photos and views of the country.

. . . Address: . . . *Derby*. If you put Wyndham never the letters will come to my hands, or I shall receive them with great retard.[10]

The results of this encounter suggest that the wild people may have interpreted the emblem of Christian faith so confidently displayed more as a threat of white brutality than as the promise of eternal salvation. It was six years before the natives made their first voluntary approach to the Benedictine mission, and even then, as was later shown, the missionaries had by no means won the day. Whether they might have made better progress with a different approach it would be hard to say. A knowledge of the language difficult to acquire in the circumstances, would assuredly have been a help, since the Dampierland tongues, especially as interpreted by Father Nicholas, would have been as incomprehensible to them as English. It would seem, however, that the natives distrusted their altruism far more than they would have the forthright self-interest of the pastoral settler which, as was proved elsewhere, they soon enough understood. In other parts of the north, even where they had the option of keeping out of the way, many Aborigines had come quickly and voluntarily to work for the pastoralists. They did not mind selling their bodies and in many cases found in station work a new interest in life. That was, after all, a surface matter, concerned only with the present. What they did mind was anything that threatened the deep inner life of their 'time without time' that held the meaning of their existence, and it is more than likely that they suspected the missionaries, since they did not want their land, of wishing to steal their 'dreaming'.

Father Nicholas's correspondence of this period shows that he had actually little understanding of the untouched tribespeople of his heart's desire. He had been excited to find, at some distance from the mission, the remarkable cave paintings, originally remarked by George Grey in 1838, again by F. S. Brockman in his exploration of 1901 and in later years by a number of anthropologists.[11] Though obviously realizing the resentment of the natives to his encroachment on this most sacred of all their preserves, he made drawing of the bulky, mouthless figures painted in clay, ochre and charcoal on the cave walls.[12] There was no great harm in this. Indeed, from a scientific view his interest was laudable, but it was tactless from the missionary angle and could only have added to the people's suspicions.

Father Nicholas had always been a keen collector of native weapons and other tribal artifacts, which were, at certain times, almost his only source of income, and the Dampierlanders, warming to his interest, had gladly bartered their handiwork for tobacco, sugar and tea. The Drysdale River people, however, did not wait to bargain and the priest seems to have shared the common belief of his day that anything found in their deserted camps was fair spoil for the finder.[13]

About once in six months Father Nicholas took his lugger to Broome on mission business and in this way kept up with the news of the peninsula. He found that the nuns, having begun a new era at Beagle Bay, had also opened a convent in Broome. He learned, too, that Father Walter had returned to his fatherland and that a superior of a very different disposition had taken his place.

In the meantime the Pallottines, finding they had neither the means nor the staff to develop Lombadina, had sold the title deeds and whatever stock was still running on this property to Thomas Puertollano.[14] The hard-working Manilaman had built up his herd as best he could and with the skill passed on to him by Father Jean Marie established a good little garden, the produce of which he sold to the lugger crews. His great difficulty, however, was that being classed as an Asiatic he could not obtain a permit either to employ or exert any authority over the Aborigines. This led to difficulties as Lombadina had always been a central camp of the Bard tribe and the hundred or more natives gathered there expected to be kept in food, clothing and blankets from Puertollano's meagre store. They could not understand that his was neither a mission nor a pearling base and that he was unable to employ even those willing to work for their keep.

A sympathetic policeman advised the Department of Aborigines[15] to declare Lombadina a government feeding depot. This was done, the depot being put in charge of Syd Hadley[16] to run in conjunction with his Sunday Island mission. More natives than ever flocked to the site and Puertollano found that despite the free rations his vegetables were constantly raided and his stock speared, while Hadley refused to impose any discipline whatever. For a time ill-feeling ran high, those in sympathy with Puertollano contending that a good family man, no matter what his nationality, had more right to control a government depot on his property than a white man who was known to cohabit with Aboriginal women. Hadley was soon afterwards convicted of this charge[17] and relieved of his supervision of the Lombadina depot, though not of his mission. This move did no one any good, as the ration station was thereafter closed down and the natives grew more and more resentful of Puertollano for failing to provide for them on the government scale.

This was the dilemma in which Father Nicholas found his Filipino friend when on his way to Broome early in 1910. It was Thomas's suggestion that the priest should leave the Drysdale mission where the people did not seem to want him and return to where he could be of immediate service. He was sure that between them they could run Lombadina as a useful outpost mission to Beagle Bay, such as Disaster Bay had been in its more prosperous times.

As it happened, the relationship between Father Nicolas and the Benedictines was then becoming strained over the Dampierland boys who, with three or four half-caste youths sent there from station properties, had helped to justify the isolated Kalumburu mission in the eyes of a sceptical government. Naturally the monks, having so far attracted no local Aborigines, were anxious to keep them and argued, not without justification, that their educational interests were better served where they were than on the rough and tumble peninsula. The youths, however, had long since grown homesick and their relatives had protested bitterly at their being kept away for so long among alien tribespeople. Father Nicholas's proposal to return them had been seen by the monks as an attempt to sabotage their struggling mission, and it was only when one of the boys became dangerously ill that the priest decided he could delay no longer.[18]

Benedictine sources interpret his decision to leave their mission as being largely actuated by fear of hostility from the local tribespeople. Nor is this to be completely discounted, for however intrepid he may have been at the outset it would not be surprising if the long period of frustrated waiting under constant apprehension of attack had undermined his nerve.

At all events he knew, when he sailed off with the Dampierland youths about May 1910, that he had burned his

222

boats with the Benedictines and that he was not after all to earn a martyr's crown among the 'uncorrupted' tribes of the remoter north. He seems, however, to have had few regrets on this score. He was now hardly less nostalgic for the arid peninsula than the boys themselves and his enthusiasm for moulding the raw material of humanity into Christian shape had been damped. He yearned now towards the muddled, warm-hearted Filipinos who loved him, and the poor, lost, half-way people who so truly needed him.

# CHAPTER TWENTY

## 1910 – 1915

FATHER NICHOLAS'S return from Kalumburu to the peninsula in 1910 had been a real homecoming and he settled into life at Lombadina with more tranquillity of spirit than he had previously shown. Indications are that his experiences with the 'uncontaminated tribes' of north-west Kimberley had helped him to see Dampierland less as a hot-bed of corruption than as a place where the mingling of races was inevitable and the results not necessarily tragic. It was certainly clear that many of the children of mixed blood had grown comely and intelligent, the Asian strain bringing greater adaptability and application to the Aboriginal and the latter tending to improve the height and physique of the Asiatic. The Aborigines, expected soon to disappear from the settled districts, still showed little sign of decrease or even of overall degeneration in the Lombadina area, where there remained, despite all outside influences, the strong core of tribal pride and stamina that is to be found there to this day. Under Father Nicholas's benign influence they quickly curbed their marauding ways and many set to work with a will to help build up the mission, extend the garden and tend the stock.

Puertollano then had about 500 head of cattle, some goats, pigs and poultry, and since he demanded after all no more than a modest living for his family, he shared what he had with the community in a prudent, but truly Christian spirit.

Father Nicholas had something of Syd Hadley's *laissez-faire* attitude to money. He had only his special grant of £80 a year and the *per capita* allowance for children and indigents to which any station was entitled, but he did not apparently complain of receiving no other government subsidy.

That Puertollano's base was a traditional and favoured camping site of the Bard was as advantageous for a mission as it had been unfavourable from a station point of view, for there was no need whatever to encourage the people to come in. Being already on the sea-front they had no need to move to a fishing camp when rations ran out, while the fact that the site was not sheltered enough to have become a lay-up base for the pearling luggers made it much easier to control the native community.

The Filipinos and their half-Aboriginal families, camped in the little coves and along the tidal creeks of the vicinity, soon made the mission the centre of their lives, straggling in to Mass on Sundays and holy days, bringing their children to be baptized, their young people to be married and calling on the priest in sickness and trouble. The Lombadina register of these years gives some impression of the racial mixtures and situations that confronted the missionary priest:

April 14th 1911, is baptized *Joseph Maria* (half the half caste), by Father Nicholas Emo, missionary in charge. Father – Thomas Puertollano (Manilaman and owner of the station where is this mission). Mother – Agnes Bryan Puertollano, daughter of the white man William Bryan. Godfather – Joseph Marcelina of Chile, S. America who is married in Beagle Bay. Godmother – Marie Lamborg, Aboriginal Christian of Disaster Bay.

*Maria Francisca*, about eight years old, half caste, father unknown, mother the Aboriginal *Chaan* of King Sound, married to the Aboriginal Mundy of Melegon. Godfather Damasco Maagina (Manilaman). Godmother Agnes Puertollano.

*Joseph Maria Cambor* about six years old of Cunningham Point, King Sound, half caste. Father, John Andriasin, diver of Manado, Koepang. Mother, the Aboriginal Mary Diu.

*Pablo Maria Chagatab*, half caste, about five years

225

old. Father Severo Acosta, Manilaman, diver of Broome. Mother Nelly Maignor, Aboriginal, deceased.

*Maria Regina*, the Aboriginal child of about five years who has the broken neck and will not live long. . . .

*Maria Pallaware*, Aboriginal of Madana, King Sound, wife of the Aboriginal Rob Roy, baptized in *periculo mortis* before being taken to the Doctor in Derby. Mother of one child by . . . the whiteman of Bulgin.

On the day 4th Sept. 1911, in the afternoon, is dead in my arms, at Madana station, *Maria,* wife of Rob Roy, and was buried by me in that place. R.I.P.

In May 1913 is dead in this camp the very old woman, *Maria Anna Cognongor.* In my absence was buried or deposed according to native customs in the branches of a tree from where was translated and buried by me in the cemetery of this mission.[1]

Other entries in the register are: Theresa Maria, Francis Xavier, Maria, Benedict, Sebastian, Dorotea, Antonio . . . and occasionally, baptized in *periculo* or in *articulu mortis*, drifting natives for whose naming the missionaries were obviously not responsible – Frypan, Combo, Kangaroo . . .

The ancient tribal marriage system had made no provision for miscegenation and the white side was not taken into account when working out tribal marriages. This meant that half-caste half brothers and sisters could still be reckoned 'straight' marriage partners in native law, which not only defeated its original purpose of preventing the marriage of close relatives but made the untangling of genealogies a task for the specialist. The Aborigines themselves were never confused by this, but for the missionaries, anxious lest they should bless incestuous marriages, it was a nightmare. Father Nicholas struggled with such problems in a mixture of French, English, Spanish and numerals, quite impossible to follow. Father John Herold, who took over his task at Lombadina many years later, made a tidier job of it, as shown in an example here quoted in abbreviated form and (for discretion's sake) with the substitution of letters for proper names:

The Aboriginal woman X was living with:

(1) ... (the Londoner) and got one son – A.
(2) ... (the Frenchman) and got one son – B.
(3) ... (the Aboriginal) and got one son – C.

    Her half-caste son A was first married to the Aboriginal daughter of Z, who when living with ... (the Londoner) got a daughter, D, who married B who was the half-caste son of X and the Frenchman.[2]

There were always a few who, ill-disposed to any missionary activities, or prejudiced against a Catholic establishment, perpetuated the sort of rumours that had sabotaged much of Father Nicholas's work in Broome, but the corrosive antagonism and distrust of his fellow missionaries had now disappeared. The Pallottines appreciated the advantage of having a Catholic base as a buffer between their own and the Protestant mission at Sunday Island and although unable to help Lombadina financially were willing to co-operate by sending a priest or brother to assist from time to time.

It would seem, however, that Beagle Bay had the best of the bargain for the schooner *San Salvador*, which Father Nicholas could now navigate himself, was constantly at its disposal. The Pallottines, in order to meet a financial crisis had, some time before, been forced to sell the pearling lugger *Leo*, while in April 1912 the *Pio* had been wrecked in the hurricane which had sunk the *Koombana* and scuttled the north-west pearling fleet. This had left Beagle Bay without any independent transport pending the building of a new lugger, and but for Father Nicholas's readiness to carry their cargo, passengers and hospital patients to and from Broome, they would have been at a great loss.

Mother Antonio had been eager to help Father Nicholas since he began the Lombadina mission in 1910.[3] She saw in the Spanish priest a devotion to the cause of the outcast and helpless that had been acknowledged more readily by the ordinary residents of Broome than by his missionary associates. Rumours of his engaging in 'money making' activities for his own enrichment she had found to be groundless. In

227

fact she realized that he was living at a subsistence level that had seriously undermined his health. Since discarding his Trappist habit he had kept, for his visits to Broome, a shabby black alpaca suit, one shirt and a pair of boots that he wore without socks. A kindly pearler's wife had once offered him a good tropical outfit from her husband's wardrobe, but this he had declined with thanks and the long cherished comment: 'I am one priest, not one dandy!'[4]

Gossip that he was the father of a part-Filipino child in whom he was known to take a particularly affectionate interest had also reached the nun's ears. The story, although not unlikely in the environment, she had never believed but it was only after his death that proof of his innocence emerged. It appears that the man responsible had been a mentally disturbed Trappist novice who, when leaving the Order, had begged the priest to see that his child did not want. This he had done, while guarding the secret faithfully at the risk of his own reputation.

The nuns looked forward to Father Nicholas's visits to Broome, even though their superior sometimes insisted on a younger sister's washing his feet as an act of mortification! At that time they often nursed patients in their own homes and the priest, on his night rounds, would frequently take a weary nun's place so that she could get a few hours' sleep. He had, he said, formed a Trappist habit of wakefulness and liked to find tasks to help him pass the night hours.

Typical also of the kindnesses recalled of him was his concern for an Aboriginal Christian woman who, suspected of being a leper, had been isolated in a wire enclosure wherein she was subjected to the nightly molestations of the lugger crews. Moved by her pitiful condition he had looked after her until he succeeded in making better arrangements for her accommodation.

It was not, however, until after the arrival of new recruits in 1913 that the nuns could be spared for Lombadina, their three pioneers in this centre including Sister Mary Bernardine Greene, who, owing to Mother Antonio's failing health, had been that year elected superioress of the missionary community in Kimberley.

The Puertollano family vacated their little home for the sisters until a convent was built for them, and the Aborigines flocked around with words of welcome and gifts of food.

Conditions were even rougher and more primitive than the nuns had found on their arrival at Beagle Bay but they were by this time well versed in the arts of makeshift and invention. Paperbark huts served as school and 'dining hall', the skins of goats, donkeys and kangaroos as bed coverings for the girls' dormitory, and sugar-bags, stuffed with dried seaweed and chaff, as pillows and mattresses.

Despite its poverty there was from the beginning an atmosphere of peace and harmony about the remote little mission spread out within sound of the sea in the shelter of the high, white dunes. There were no working facilities, not even a vehicle with which to cart building materials from the bush or stores from the landing stage three miles away. The natives, however, accepted the carrying process as a kind of game, to be played in their own time, at their own pace and to the accompaniment of a great deal of laughter and buffoonery.

The community had also acquired the whole-hearted cooperation of a Filipino-Japanese youth named Martin Sibasado[5] who years before had been picked up by Captain Owen as a neglected waif and later taken to Beagle Bay. He had come to Lombadina soon after the opening of the mission, where, married to a Disaster Bay half-caste named Eriberta Idon, he was to make his life and rear his vigorous family.

News of the outbreak of war in 1914 made little impression on the Lombadina but since the movements of the German Pallottines were thereby restricted, Father Nicholas's services were more than ever indispensable to them. Being now so often at sea he tried to make up for lost time on his return to the mission, though he was in no fit state of health for strenuous work.

It was an occasion of grave anxiety to the nuns when he set out, during that year, at the request of the government, to investigate a report, made by the captain of a coastal

229

steamer, that the Benedictine mission had been burned down and its occupants apparently massacred by the blacks. The priest and his Filipino crew found the rumour to have been false, as a place where the natives had left a number of smouldering fires had been mistaken for the mission site.

The missionaries, however, had been twice attacked during the previous few months, once by over one hundred armed tribesmen who had wounded Father Alcade with a spear and others with clubs. A rifle fired by a half-caste boy named Fulgentius Fraser had dispersed the natives and the injured men had since recovered.[6]

He returned to Lombadina more than ever emaciated and racked with a distressing cough but even then he would not consent to rest, insisting that if indeed his time was running out, he had none to waste.

On the morning of 5th March 1915, Father Drostë of Beagle Bay, though not long back from a three-monthly visit to Lombadina, had felt an unaccountable impulse to return and saddling up his mule set out once more on the lonely fifty-mile ride. He found Father Nicholas at the point of death, having not long before suffered a severe stroke.

A brief entry in the *Liber Defunctorum* of Lombadina mission registers, on a quiet note, the end of its founder's strange and turbulent life:

On the 8th of March 1915 at 3.40 a.m. died Rev. Father Nicholas Maria Emo, born 6th July 1849, Villa Flames, in the Provence of Castellon (Spain), son of Vincent Emo and Mary (born Conception). The burial took place the same day, Rev. Father Drostë assisting him in his last moments.[7]

Father Nicholas had requested that the sheet-iron coffin in which he had slept during the latter years of his life should be used after his death as a press for the sacristy and that he be buried wrapped in a blanket like the humble people he had tried to serve, a wish that was respected as in keeping with the Trappist ideals of austerity he had never abandoned. This manner of burial was interpreted, in some quarters, as a gesture of contempt on the part of his fellow religious but there was no misunderstanding among those who gathered at his Requiem. Not only the simple people of the Bard and the Nimanboor but the Filipinos and people of mixed blood whom he had befriended over the years were to honour his camps and anchorages as long as they lived, while some believe to this day that he wrought a miracle involving the *San Salvador* a few weeks after his death.

The schooner had not long before been declared un-seaworthy and lay beached awaiting repairs when an out-of-season cyclone took the pearling fleets by surprise. The weather was still rough when three exhausted Koepangers staggered into the mission to tell how the schooner *Alice* had been driven on to Brué reef in the nearby Lacepedes. They had managed to detach a small whaler from the wreck and, leaving the skipper and the rest of the crew clinging to the rigging, had struggled ashore to seek help.

Thomas Puertollano explained that since their lugger was out of commission they were powerless to assist and he appealed to the nuns to confirm the state of the *San Salvador*. Torn between pity for the seafarers and concern for Thomas they were completely at a loss until Mother Bernardine recalled the dream in which Father Nicholas claimed to have been promised Our Lady's special protection for his ship. The Manilaman, insisting that it meant suicide, then made a few hurried repairs, called for a volunteer crew and ordered the rest of the community into the church to pray for a miracle.

Some hours later a cry from the dunes made known that the *Salvador* had returned with the survivors of the wreck.[8]

While recovering at the mission, the skipper introduced himself as James MacKenzie[9] who had left Queensland in charge of thirty luggers that James Clarke, 'The Pearl King', had decided to transfer to Western Australian waters. The parent vessel *Alice* had lost sight of the remainder of the fleet somewhere south of Timor and had been alone when the cyclone struck off the Lacepedes. The ship had stuck on

231

a submerged reef and while the three Koepangers rowed in for help, the rest of the crew had endured an agonizing wait of five days and four nights, with only a small canvas bag of drinking water between them. Thirteen men who, half crazed with hunger, thirst and cramp, had insisted on swimming to an exposed part of the reef in search of shellfish had been swept away by the returning rip tide and the others had almost given up hope of rescue when the mission schooner was seen fighting towards them through the heavy swell.

Years later, when the drifting dunes threatened to obliterate all signs of his grave, the bones of the mission's founder priest were removed to the centre of the present Lombadina cemetery. Here, under a cross erected to his memory, lies all that remains of one of the most controversial figures ever to find his way to the multi-racial peninsula of pearls. In his time both revered and despised, his actions sometimes honoured, often twisted and misconstrued, he was a priest of true fervour, a man of practical deeds and romantic illusions. He had come to Australia for the 'secret attraction'[10] he had felt towards a type of innocent savage that existed only in his imagination and had here worked out his destiny among people such as he need hardly have travelled so far from Patagonia to find. . . .

It was many years before his brave little schooner *San Salvador* was finally beached at Beagle Bay, worn out with long service, but never defeated by the sea.

# CHAPTER TWENTY-ONE

## 1914 – 1918

THE outbreak of war in 1914, while placing the German missionaries in a very difficult position, at least put an end to the Pallottine conflict that had for so long discouraged enthusiasm and impeded enterprise in the Australian foundation. Ever since 1902 this argument had no sooner been 'settled' than it had cropped up again with such renewed vigour and bitterness that one can only pity the superiors concerned, faced as they were, not with a simple decision between right and wrong, but between two righteous causes.

In 1909, a visit of several months to Beagle Bay by the Limburg Provincial, Father Vincent Kopf, seemed for good and all to have confirmed the issue in favour of the mission. His stimulating report resulted in the decision to send further recruits and brothers to Beagle Bay and was probably a factor in persuading the Western Australian government to raise the mission's annual grant to £500 from that year. It was not long, however, before the matter of dissolution was mooted once again[1], this time in view of the threatening political situation and its possible repercussions on the German missionaries in this remote British outpost. Again the move was defeated, no doubt largely due to the urgent appeal of Father Droste, who had come from Limburg with Father Kopf in 1909 and who at once took over much of the practical administration of the mission.

A big man with a warm heart and a practical head, Father Droste, who had been a miner in Rhineland-Westphalia before entering the seminary, threw himself into the development of the mission with the vigour so often noted in a

233

new arrival. His was a case, however, in which, despite more than his share of trials and tribulations, enthusiasm did not flag, and in which the people's appreciation of his qualities was to increase with the years. He lost no time in providing better living conditions for the nuns and in obtaining further bores and windmills and replacement of the stud bulls and stock horses that had died in the previous year.[2]

The effects of these improvements, together with Brother Henry Krallman's ability as a stockman and an increase in the price of beef, meant that by 1912 the mission's prospect of becoming self-supporting looked brighter than at any previous stage. The institution could of course afford no luxuries but it was now relieved of the need for severe rationing that had reduced the numbers of dependants and hence the *per capita* government allowance.

As usual, however, just as the situation began to seem promising, fate had another blow in store, this time in an especially literal sense when the hurricane of that year caused the wreck of the *Pio*, an incident still vividly recalled by the mission people. The lugger, with a few religious and a number of natives, had been returning from Broome and had already entered Beagle Bay when the storm struck. The boat broke anchor and drifted for two days in tempestuous seas towards the Lacepedes, to be cast up at last on a reef in Carnot Bay about thirty-five miles from the mission, her passengers, apart from being badly shaken and cut about on the sharp rocks, none the worse. To the missionaries, the loss of the lugger and its precious cargo was a heartbreak, but the natives, once out of danger, regarded the incident as a tremendous joke, always, when repeating the story, reminding each other of further ludicrous details:

'What about Father Traub baptizing the two old men – the waves breaking over us and him with a pannikin trying to pour water on their heads?'

'What about that cripple girl Carmel saying "Thank God we don't have far to walk home", and we had to carry her over thirty miles?'

'And what about Brother James, sitting on the rocks singing out over and over: "Oh, Mother, what do we do? Oh, Mother, what do we do now?" ' . . .³

What they did was, as usual, to inform Bishop Gibney who although retired from office in 1910 applied at once, in moving terms, for a government 'grant in aid' of £500. His appeal was successful and work began at once on a new lugger to be called the *Namban*.

The natives, of whom the missionaries had frequently despaired, were now making real progress in a variety of trades. The men, while learning the use of tools, had helped erect a number of solid buildings that gave the mission the appearance of a sizable village. The women were showing similar progress in domestic arts, making their own and their families' clothes and producing some fine embroidery. All the younger people could read and write, were well-spoken and gently mannered, while the influence of the nuns had also done a good deal to discourage promiscuity.

Since 1903, at the request of Father Walter, a police constable had been stationed at Beagle Bay over the lay-up months to protect the mission natives from the Asiatic crews.⁴ This was a lonely and not very popular job, particularly after complaints were made by the mission of the immoral behaviour of one of the 'protectors'. In 1908, therefore, permanent quarters were erected for a married officer who, as the international situation worsened, was expected to double as a security agent.

After the declaration of war the iron of an unsuspected national fervour entered the normally easy-going Australian and quickened the imagination of the most ordinarily prosaic citizen. When third or fourth generation Australians of known or suspected German origin were shunned as possible enemy agents or sympathizers, when 'foreign-sounding' surnames, towns and streets were being hurriedly changed and even German music was suspect, it was hardly likely that the activities of German nationals on the unwatched and defenceless north-west coast should escape scrutiny. The entry of the Pallottines to the north-west in

235

1901 was seen by some as a factor in the Kaiser's long-range plan for world domination, their 'so-called mission' a screen for the establishment of a strategic military base. This school of thought found sinister evidence in the 'military bearing' of some of the priests and brothers, in Father Walter's disciplinary ways, in his desire to get rid of Father Nicholas and later of Father Jean Marie, not to mention his frequent visits and final return to Germany. Some saw the superior education of the German religious as out of all proportion to the qualifications needed to teach the benighted 'binghis' and even the mission's failure to become self-supporting was cited as proof of its being maintained for a completely different reason.

Authorities arrived at Beagle Bay to take particulars and fingerprints of all non-British residents and it was strongly advised that the mission be closed and the Pallottines interned for the duration. Once more it was Bishop Gibney, now forcefully backed by Archbishop Clune[5] of Perth, Bishop Kelly of Geraldton and other influential friends, who rose to their defence. Apart from dismissing the suspicions of the public as absurd they pointed out the impossibility of the missionaries engaging in subversive activities while there was a police station and a community of Irish and Australian nuns at Beagle Bay and an Irish priest stationed in Broome in the position of Pro-Vicar Apostolic of the Kimberley Vicariate and overall Superior of the Pallottine missions.

Their arguments finally prevailed and all were allowed to remain, with the exception of Father Bischoffs who, always ebullient and outspoken, had apparently continued his polemical observations beyond the point of discretion. He was a loss to the mission, as he was popular both with the natives and his own community and his anthropological research was beginning to assume real significance. At first interned in the camp at Liverpool in New South Wales, he was soon allowed out on parole and found refuge with the Bishop of Armidale until after the war. He was then transferred to South Africa where he died in 1958.

Those were hard years for the exiled missionaries, their

conversation restricted, their correspondence censored, their movements supervised, their only war news derived from British sources. The resident police officer found nothing subversive to report in their behaviour except that the natives, on timber-cutting forays in the bush, were heard to sing something suspiciously resembling *The Watch On The Rhine*. This, it was suggested, might be in preparation for the welcome of an expected invading army, but the nuns, appreciating the missionaries' singleness of purpose and understanding their nostalgia, tactfully dismissed the rumour.

For the Aborigines themselves the war made no sense whatever. That Christians should have killed pagans would have seemed bad enough but for Christians to 'finish' fellow Christians seemed inconsistent with everything they had understood of the Master's teachings. Aware of the hostility of the outside world towards the German religious, now referred to by new names seemingly fraught with sinister significance, they rallied with more loyalty to the mission than they had ever shown before. They were still close enough to the basic principles of tribal life to see in this crisis the chance of demonstrating the gratitude in which they were often thought lacking. As hostilities dragged on and the Pallottines' movements became increasingly restricted, they even showed themselves capable of working together without white supervision. Young Remigius Balgalai (Remi for short), who had been at Beagle Bay since Trappist times, was accepted as head stockman for the duration and the cattle were somehow got to Broome for shipment to Fremantle. Remi's brother Gabriel meanwhile skippered the mission lugger *Namban*, bringing vegetables and fruit for sale in the port and returning faithfully with stores and mail.

It was now that Father Thomas Bachmair saw the chance he had longed for of erecting at Beagle Bay an edifice that, come what might, would stand in testimony of the religious fervour and sincerity of the Pallottine regime in Dampierland. Although he had grown to love the mission as much as anyone who had so far set foot on its reluctant soil, he had made no great mark there up to this time and although officially superior of the mission leant heavily on the support and practical advice of Father Drostë. He was not one to stand up to the forceful and forthright Australian bishops, demanding that the Pallottines do this and that when to have urged the Society for more support might have tipped the delicately balanced scales of opinion definitely against the Australian mission. Now that the war had ruled out for some time at least their recall to Germany and the local issue of their remaining at the mission had been favourably resolved, hè laid before the community the drawings of a church that he had drafted some years before. What did they think?

Everyone agreed that it was beautiful but it fell to Father Drostë to explain that such a plan was well beyond their means. Father Thomas had considered that. Almost all materials required could be locally produced, timber, bricks and mortar, interior decorations. Father Drostë demurred about the time and the labour, reminding the enthusiast that the existence of the mission now depended on themselves alone and that they had hoped to build a factory for the processing of hemp which had been grown successfully at the mission for several years. Father Thomas had an answer for that too. This was no time for commercial enterprise. What better, while the world was rent by hatred and doubt, than to labour on a symbol of love and faith? Besides, when the war was over and, by the Grace of God, a Pallottine elected Vicar-Apostolic of the Kimberleys, the mission would be his seat and the church his cathedral.

The design, a combined effort that was finally passed as practical, was shown to the mission people as something that was to belong to them and of which they could be proud. Perhaps to please the missionaries in their time of trial they began the task with at least a show of interest but, as the building took shape, they worked with genuine enthusiasm and unprecedented constancy. Day after day parties set off into the bush or to the coast to cut timber, cart sand, dig clay and gather tons of broken shells for lime.

238

As the timber structure mounted, 60,000 double bricks were shaped and baked in stone kilns and thousands of live shells, mother of pearl and many other varieties from small cockles, cones and trochus to giant clams and bailers for holy water fonts were gathered in from a wide range of coastal water and tidal reefs.

The church had been about quarter finished when, as already noted, Father Drostë rode to Lombadina in March 1915 on the hunch that all was not well with Father Nicholas, arriving only in time to administer the Last Sacraments. After the Requiem, when Thomas Puertollano set out in the *San Salvador* to convey the sad tidings to the Pro-Vicar in Broome, Father Drostë accompanied him, expecting to be put ashore at Beagle Bay. From his own account of the voyage, as written to the motherhouse, we see that it might well have been his last:

... We pulled out to the *Salvador* in a dinghy and got aboard. The anchor was weighed and the sails set; the wind was against us and presently it blew more strongly and grew to a storm. The waves crashed over the deck and washed away everything that had not been fastened down. I became sick and made a bee line for the little cabin. The ship tossed hither and thither and I rolled about on the floor, the musty smell of the cabin aggravating my nausea until my stomach was empty. For thirty hours I lay there in the most abject misery, not heeding the straining of the masts or the bluster and howling of the wind – I felt as though I should prefer to die. Suddenly I heard a shout: 'Bring out the priest!' Terrified I endeavoured to rise, but was unable to move. At the same time two aborigines came down and dragged me on deck.

The vessel had been driven violently on to the coast and the rocks threatened to smash it to pieces. With their last ounce of strength the dog-tired sailors pushed long oars against the rocks to ward off destruction, and as the gale had by this time abated, in an hour's time we were out of danger. We had been hammered by the storm for

239

two days and had not covered a greater distance than one could walk in a couple of hours.

The crew swam ashore to get some shell-fish and when the tide had run right out and left the ship aground so that she toppled over on her side, I resolved to walk ashore. I tried to clamber down the side of the ship, but I was too weak and Peter, my aboriginal assistant, had to carry me.

There was a pearling boat with a Japanese crew ashore not far from us, and we asked them for drinking water, but they had none.

We lay down on the sand, it having grown dark meanwhile. Peter got some wood and kindled a fire. The other Aborigines (the crew) caught some small fish and crabs and roasted them in the ashes. The sailors decided to refloat the ship and return to Lombadina. I resolved to make for Beagle Bay on foot but had no blankets and as I was wet through I was shivering with cold. Soon afterwards the Japanese diver from the pearler came over with a couple of bottles of water and also lent us a blanket, which probably saved me from an attack of fever.

About 3 a.m. I woke Peter and we made a start, breakfastless, in order to get as far as possible in the cool of the morning, although I was stiff, weak and hungry. A creek impeded our progress for fully half an hour. After that we had stretches of deep sand to trudge through, up hill and down dale. I took my boots off and carried them.

Three hours later the sun rose, and almost immediately it was hot. I had continual recourse to the one bottle of water we had remaining, but Peter refused to take any, and in about eight hours the bottle was empty.

An hour later we had reached the place where we had bored for water a year previously and drew up a little red, muddy liquid which we drank eagerly.

After hours of torment – Peter had to drag me along by the hand – we reached a well and were able to drink our fill. At four o'clock we started again, and before long reached the notorious Pender Bay Creek, which becomes very swollen at high tide. We had to hurry before it got dark. The Aboriginal had a look at the creek and thought we might try it at about five o'clock, we entered the water, Peter in the lead. In a quarter of an hour the water was level with my mouth and I expected to be swept away by the current, but Peter held me up. Presently the water was only up to our knees and we had a spell for a while.

By the time we were half way across the tide began to rise. I was completely worn out – everything looked black, green and yellow to me – but Peter literally dragged me forward and at length we reached the other bank – after a struggle of three and a half hours.

We were safe but famished, so in spite of the darkness we plodded on for the house of a settler⁶ with whom we were acquainted. Ordinarily we could have reached it in an hour, but now at our snails' pace the journey seemed an eternity. The owner happened to be away, but we found some victuals in the house and had a drink of tea.

When I woke at 10 a.m. next morning my body was paralysed with cramp. Just as we were going to start on the five hours' walk to the mission an Aboriginal rode up with a letter for the settler. He lent me his horse on which I rode to Beagle Bay.⁷

Father Drostë was a heavy man and it was no small feat for a lightly built youth to have pulled him out of this predicament. In a story so much concerned with the frustrations and exasperations caused by the outlook and character of the Aborigines, it is as well to remember that without a good deal of such frequently unrecorded devotion on the part of the natives, few of the pioneer missionaries could have survived to tell the tale.

The Irish Redemptorist, Father John Creagh, who soon after the outbreak of war had been appointed Pro-Vicar Apostolic of the Kimberley Vicariate and Superior of the Pallottine Society in that district had already proved himself a good friend to the missionaries and their charges. His position was a delicate one but being a man of good heart and considerable tact, he had remained popular with the townspeople and done much to keep disruptive rumours within bounds.

241

The death of Father Nicholas presented him with the problem of maintaining Lombadina which, since Father Nicholas's small grant had ceased with his death, was now in a critical situation. Father Creagh's repeated appeals for a government subsidy were, for reasons later manifest, to no avail, but from one source and another, confident that at the end of the war all would come right, he managed to keep it going at subsistence level.

He had assumed that this property, having been purchased for that purpose by Bishop Gibney in 1892, was a Pallottine branch mission and it was some time before Thomas Puertollano realized the misunderstanding. Puertollano had, as already told, since purchased the rights to this property and Father Nicholas had formed a mission there at his invitation. This had suited both parties as the lonely priest had thereby found a home and an outlet for his vocation while taking custody of the title deeds to comply with the law. Puertollano's stock and gardens had been at the disposal of the mission while Father Nicholas had helped develop the property and had created for Thomas and his growing family the religious background that was the breath of life to them.

Since he was able neither to hold land nor employ Aborigines, Puertollano had accepted without demur the appointment by Father Creagh of Father Thomas Bachmair in place of his old friend, but as time went on the relationship between them deteriorated. Father Thomas, in bad health, bitterly disappointed at having to leave Beagle Bay at such an interesting stage in the building of 'his' church, and lacking in force and confidence at the best of times, was unable to maintain control of the natives as Father Nicholas had done. Since stores were in short supply they soon reverted to pilfering the gardens and killing stock and before the year was out Puertollano, thoroughly dissatisfied with the situation, left for Broome to put his point of view to Father Creagh.

Puertollano evidently saw no chance in the circumstances of the mission's being carried on any longer. There were several parties interested in buying the property and he proposed to sell out to the highest bidder. Father Creagh was shocked, not only to realize that Puertollano was the actual owner of Lombadina, but that he could be disloyal to the mission he had done so much to develop. Thomas, however, possibly as Father Creagh suggests under the influence of one of his bidders,[8] was determined to make the best bargain possible. He had always loved his Church and had given the best years of his life to helping it to a footing in Dampierland. His two greatest friends, Fathers Jean Marie and Nicholas, had, none the less, received short shrift from the Pallottines at different times and he had not taken kindly to the assumption that they now inherited Lombadina and all that went with it, including the services of himself and his family.

Father Creagh could see no way out than to negotiate for the property himself, a proposal to which Puertollano had no objections so long as he got the price of £1,200. To this end the Pro-Vicar enlisted the help of his brother, Monkton Creagh, then in Broome, to purchase the station in his own name and return it to the Church for, in his own words, 'I was afraid to buy it straight out for Beagle Bay mission . . . on account of the German question and I was also afraid of buying it with mission money on account of Neville[9] and the Aborigines Department.'[10]

This led to yet further trouble, as the Pallottines, who hoped to take over Lombadina after the war, suspected Father Creagh of betraying their interests, while the Creaghs' agent reported that the Lombadina cattle were seventy-eight short of Puertollano's estimate of five hundred head. Father Creagh wrote to Father Thomas Bachmair in exasperated tones:

If ever the devil seemed anxious to destroy any place he seems particularly anxious to ruin Lombadina. I have done all possible to save it but when I seem to have averted one danger another comes. Now the danger comes really from Thomas Puertollano. . . . The real reason I

243

entered into negotiations with him was to rescue the mission. I saw that he would soon have to go and it was impossible for your Society to acquire the mission at present. Later on you will understand for yourselves. . . . It is [my brother's] intention that your Society shall have it as long as they remain in Kimberley. . . .[11]

Puertollano's case was that any cattle short of the number stated by no means made up for the stock that had recently been killed on behalf of the mission or (without authorization) by mission natives, but he finally agreed to cut £100 off his price and the deal was closed. Thereafter all hard feelings were patched up and in the following year Father Creagh wrote of Thomas as 'a man to whom I am under the greatest obligations. He was the former owner of Lombadina and for years he kept the mission there going – I can never repay what I owe him.'

The relationship between Puertollano and the Pallottines also improved as evidenced by Father Creagh's report on his repairing the *San Salvador* on their behalf:

> Thomas said the *Salvador* was quite unfit to go to Drysdale [as requested]. The jib got badly torn and the sails are in very bad condition. He undertook to look after the repairs and got the Manilaman Dorotheo and a Jap carpenter to help him. . . .
>
> Thomas has now bought a fishing place here. . . . I have promised him that he can take all his family and effects away [from Lombadina] in the *Namban* free of charge.[12]

The main problem now lay in finding another superintendent for the mission, for it was becoming clear that Father Thomas could not long maintain this post. He had written to Father Creagh in May 1918 that he was ill and would like to visit a doctor in Broome. The Pro-Vicar had replied that his leaving the mission confines on any pretext would be misinterpreted but that he would arrange for his relief as soon as things improved. 'The bitterness,' he added, 'is very great, particularly now . . .'[13]

Father Thomas was sicker than anyone realized when a few weeks later, overcome with a desire to see the progress of the church, he set out alone for Beagle Bay. Who knows by what effort of will he rode those fifty hot, rough miles of marsh and sand, but as he turned the last bend in the winding track his sufferings were rewarded by the sight that met his eyes. There, almost completed, stood the church of his dreams, an emblem of faith, hope and charity in a time of bitterness and woe. Gleaming white against the dark background of pandanus palms and paperbarks, its tower sharply cut against the sky, so well proportioned as to seem larger than life, it dominated and at the same time unified the scattered mission, making it appear for the first time a composite and attractive settlement.

Soon the people had spied the traveller and helping him from his mule pulled him by the hands to the church door. See now what they had done, everyone working on a part of it until the altar and sanctuary floor glowed with pearly mosaic in which the emblems of the Church mingled with those of the Njul Njul, the Nimanboor and the Bard! See how they had set whole shells around the arches of the windows and doors, and studded the side altars with shining cowries, olives and volutes! See how Brother Henry had so delicately inlaid the tabernacle and altar rails with the lamb, the fish and the shepherd's crook! And the dome and roof, sky blue and beset with gleaming pearl-shell fragments denoting the constellations of the southern hemisphere – who could guess it had been beaten out from kerosene tins, patiently, piece by piece, joined together and shaped with loving care?[14]

'What do you think of it, Father?'

'We must finish it for my Requiem,' he said, and picking up a bucket of whitewash began to slap it over the still unpainted bricks.

The church was completed a week later, not quite in time for his Requiem and with less of his own effort than he would have wished but he was remembered as having been its inspiration. It will always be his monument.

# CHAPTER TWENTY-TWO

## 1918 – 1930

THE land again at peace and the bright seas safe from enemy ships and submarines, the pearlers foresaw a new era of prosperity made possible by the sacrifice of 6,000 Western Australian lives in the War To End War and of some 4,000 Asiatics in establishing modern diving techniques. A ladies' choir, in white dresses and long kid gloves, had sung *Land of Hope and Glory* at the unveiling of a monument to the fallen in the public square and a flag-bedecked fleet had raced in victory festival on Roebuck Bay.

But armistice brought little consolation to the German religious. The bitterness of holocaust continued to find focus on their missions and the movements of priests and brothers were still restricted. Money and men from Germany, hard enough to obtain at the best of times, were now out of the question, and rumours persisted that the government intended taking over the Dampierland native reserve. Then came the post-war epidemic of pneumonic influenza which took heavy toll of the Kimberley Aborigines, including eighteen at Beagle Bay. In a letter to Perth from Broome on 3rd January 1920, Father Creagh writes:

> The influenza has been very prevalent here and in Beagle Bay. I paid a flying visit there as Father Drostë and the sisters are down with it. The poor Blacks have suffered very severely. . . .[1]

Beagle Bay had none the less come through the war years as a more stable institution than at any time before. Sheep had been reintroduced for local consumption and the sale of cattle and garden produce was bringing a steady return. Few besides the mission people and occasional government officials found their way out there along the wagon track that wound through eighty miles of heavy sand, but none who came, however unsympathetic to missionary work, could have failed to catch his breath on emerging, suddenly, from the monotonous pindan to find that neat little farming village encircling the fine, white church. Visitors spoke of the wonders of the garden, of the promising band of Aboriginal and half-caste workers and tradesmen, of the cleanly women, trained in a wide range of domestic arts, of the children, black and brindle, reading, writing, singing, reeling off prayers, poetry, tables, litanies. They described the white-robed Irish and Australian nuns, cheerful, capable, hospitable; the German priests, instilling the importance of a time-table into a timeless people, dinning Latin responses into surpliced altar boys, training choirs; the hard-working brothers, transformed for Mass in the white soutanes and black sashes of their Society.

It was conceded that the Pallottines, by sheer, Teutonic efficiency, and the nuns by devoted care, had shown results at Beagle Bay, but the mission policy was still more often criticized than praised. Some said the natives were being taught too much and given false ideas of their equality with the whites. Others complained that their intellectual development was being neglected and that by directing their education towards manual skills the missionaries had produced a 'peasant type' inconsistent with Australian democracy. One school of thought maintained that the natives should have been left completely alone to pursue their tribal customs and beliefs, another that these should be supplemented by some 'basic but strictly non-sectarian form of Christianity'.[2]

Dr. W. Ramsay Smith had written in 1910:

The problem of what to do with this race, the most interesting at present on earth, the least deserving to be exterminated by us, and the most wronged at our hands, is not a difficult one to solve, were a solution really desired.[3]

It was expecting rather too much that a satisfactory solution could, with all the goodwill in the world, be found to all the facets of this complex problem but it was true enough that the situation had stagnated for want of positive interest and ideas. The few to express real concern deplored the lack of a practical policy but no two were agreed on what direction it should take. Whether scientist or settler, politician or missionary, each saw the question from his own viewpoint, in the light of his own experience and the shadow of his prejudice.

Daisy Bates, generally considered one of the greatest authorities on the subject at that time, had declared it her policy 'to make their [the Aborigines] passing easier and to keep the dreaded half-caste menace from our great continent'.[4] Despite the help she had given to Bishop Gibney's missionary cause she was by this time convinced that as the Aborigines were soon to disappear there was no point in confusing them with ideas that they had no time to absorb. As for the half-castes, believing that they inherited the worst characteristics of two races and were doomed to degeneracy and misery, she saw any attempt to assist or encourage them as completely useless. Far better, by registering one's firm disapproval, to freeze the very idea of miscegenation out of countenance!

Though some of her anthropological statements were later to be held in question, there can be no doubt that she understood the Aboriginal mind and comforted many of the displaced tribespeople who drifted to her desert camps. To these wanderers she was the all-wise Kabbarli, the grandmother who could move and think in two worlds, speak with them and for them and strengthen them in the observation of their own law. On the other hand, anything she might have done to discourage the mingling of races was entirely negligible. The inevitable factor with the mixed-blood people was not so much their degeneration as their multiplication and her attitude only served to increase the prejudice and indifference that had led to the development of an increasing, fringe-dwelling minority that was growing every year harder to integrate.

One man who dared to face this uncomfortable truth was Mr. A. O. Neville, who was appointed to the position of Chief Protector of Aborigines in 1915. He saw that the mixed-blood people, left to breed haphazardly and to grow up in their rubbish-tip camps with little training or education of any sort, would soon become a serious problem, not only to themselves, but to the whole of Australia.[5] Contemptuous of the school of thought that dismissed them as being incapable of improvement, he pointed out that many both in country areas and the far outback, despite their lack of opportunity, were playing an extremely useful role. The fact that some had already been successfully absorbed into the white community, to the extent that no one, ignorant of their history, was aware of their native blood indicated that the Aboriginal strain was not inclined to throw back and that future trouble could quite simply be averted by an upgrading of their education and a forthright programme of assimilation. 'We are,' he declared with cheerful confidence, 'going to merge the native race into our white community.'

The mating of Aboriginal with half-caste, or even half-caste with half-caste, which perpetuated the dark strain, was to be kindly but firmly discouraged. Instead there was to be a progressive breeding out of the Aboriginal by the pairing of half with quarter-caste or preferably with white. Why, after all should the Mendelian law not be applied to the solution of a human problem?

Since Aboriginal women begot children by the white or the mixed blood much more readily than by the black, it seemed expedient to segregate the full-bloods in areas where their racial decline could follow its apparently inexorable course.[6] This did not mean, however, that they were not to be encouraged to maintain their pride of race – a much simpler matter away from the degenerating influences of the closely settled areas. He wanted sterner control over the conditions of native employment on private stations, stricter penalties for 'consorting', and the introduction of a minimum wage for all Aboriginal employees. He also embarked on a campaign for bigger and better native reserves, more stations like Moola Bulla, in East Kimberley, that had been purchased by his department in 1912 to be run for the benefit of the Aborigines. For this purpose he saw an ideal prospect in the Dampierland peninsula, the whole of which area, including Sunday Island, he was anxious to have declared a government native reserve. This proposal entailed making a clean sweep of the three struggling missions and starting afresh on a 'sound economic basis' – a move in which he saw nothing to be lost and much to be gained. It would put an end to sectarian bickering, to complaints about inadequate subsidies, to fear of subversive activities and to the wholesale mixing of part-coloured and full-blood aborigines that was going on in that region.

There were strong indications that the Labour Government then in power would favour the submission[7] put before it by Neville in 1916. This document was confidential, and fortunately so for the Pallottines, who might otherwise have lost heart instead of going on to finish the church that was to become their cathedral.

In July of that year John Scaddan's ministry went out, and with it Neville's proposals that had been still under review, for the Liberal Government was generally more sympathetic to both Church and pastoral interests. It had, moreover, triumphed by too narrow a margin to risk offending the one by closing the missions or the other by introducing a minimum wage for Aboriginal employees.

At the end of 1916, the St. John of God nuns in Broome, whose subsidy had been discontinued by the Labour Government in 1913, were given an annual grant of £125 and soon afterwards all missions in the State were divided into two groups – those which owned land or held free government grants and those which did not. The former were given an annual *per capita* subsidy of £5 and £7 respectively and the latter £14 a year for every native cared for at the request of the department.

Neville, while obliged to administer these changes, was by no means pleased with them and following a tour of the Kimberleys in 1917 he resubmitted his proposal for the

Dampierland peninsula. The new Minister for the north-west[8] was in favour of its implementation but by this time Archbishop Clune who was popular, persuasive and politically astute, had got wind of the move and made strong representations to the then Premier H. P. Colebatch. As a result of his protest the scheme was left in abeyance, to be brought before Cabinet in 1918 and again in 1919 when it was finally thrown out.

Neville's attitude towards the missions is summed up in what he had to say shortly after his retirement in 1940:

> In the course of his official life a Public Servant is occasionally warned off the grass, so to speak, and given more or less direct hints not to proceed in certain directions, however reasonable it may seem to him to do so in the interest of his duty and charges. In the early days of my administration it was 'hands off the missions' and so the work was not strictly supervised or interfered with, neither was it greatly encouraged.[9]

Neville, generally regarded as a meticulous and able administrator, was a kindly man and tried to make his department one to which his charges could come, assured of a sympathetic ear and paternal guidance, with their troubles and grievances.[10] Given more money, more authority, more consistent government support, more help from the public and more co-operation from the natives themselves, he might have gone down in history as a man of vision, as in some ways he was. At a time when the purpose of his department was generally thought of, if at all, as being to cope as quietly as possible with the native question until, in the course of nature, it had ceased to exist, an expression of faith in the future of its charges was a refreshing change. Theoretically, and in contrast to a more usually negative approach to the problem, the assimilation policy sounded uncommonly sensible. In practice it would be found wanting in commonsense understanding of human behaviour; but of that later.

The colour-conscious white residents of Broome suspected

251

it as seeming to bless miscegenation – a thing that everyone knew was inevitable but did not want to see legalized. In certain circumstances 'consorting' might be condoned but who could respect a man who went to the lengths of *marrying* a coloured woman? And who indeed would want anyone belonging to him to do so? They agreed with Neville, however, that Beagle Bay had no right to keep so many trained coloured workers who could be making themselves useful outside. Why should the mission consider it owned these people whose training had been subsidized by the ratepayers?

The proposal that the more reliable workers should be encouraged to take jobs in the town placed Father Drostë now superior of the mission, in a very unhappy position. Though reluctant to antagonize further the community he found it very difficult to reconcile himself to this idea or to the fact that the same people who had often enough accused him of maintaining too little hold on his people were now charging him with exerting too much. Officially he had no power to prevent their leaving if they so wished, but it was true that he could influence them one way or another, and he saw it in their best interests and that of the mission that they remained.

He was justly proud of his spruce band of young tradesmen, for though none had actually attained standard qualifications, a number had shown outstanding ability in various branches of building and carpentry, two or three had learned plumbing, others tailoring, bootmaking, saddling, baking and butchery. It had been the aim of the mission ultimately to equip them for entry into a normally expanding economy, but as the priest knew all too well, local development had come to a standstill with fewer white residents in the Kimberleys than before the war. The fact of the matter was that the mission, having been unable to obtain recruits from Germany since the outbreak of the war, then needed her trained native workers far more than any outside enterprise. Orientals provided all the skilled labour required in Broome and were unlikely to help or encourage native apprentices. The pearlers needed not tradesmen but labourers and domestics, preferably full-blood Aborigines, content to work for keep or pocket money, and whom it was the aim of the department to keep away from the towns.

Father Drostë saw that such a move would militate against the very policy with which Neville accused the missions of failing to co-operate. Interrelated as they were, once a few people left the rest would become unsettled and it would be quite impossible to hold on to the full-bloods and let the others go. What did this dictator think he was dealing with – mice that could be segregated in cages and made to conform to the will of man, or warm-blooded human beings who would fall in love, marry and beget children according to the law of God? One after another, the people the mission had helped a little way up the ladder would all drift into the port where they would fall back again to the bottom. The time would come, please God, when they had gained enough stability to resist prostitution and drink, enough self-confidence to demand ordinary wages and in time even citizenship. As it was they were not yet ready to stand on their own feet.

Sceptics asked at what stage a missionary would admit his charges 'ready' to face the world, and whether continued protection was in fact the best means of developing independence and moral stamina. Such questions, however, could not be put to the test, for the combined pressure of the department and the Broome community succeeded in forcing the issue.

Before long every white family in Broome had acquired a mission-educated 'binghi' couple. Some of these had left their children and old people behind; others had transferred in family groups, sent their children to the convent school in town and settled their elder relatives in nearby camps. Despite frustrating aspects where the mission and the department were concerned, this arrangement worked very well, for a period at least, for the Broome residents and the natives themselves. The white families were delighted with the clean, capable, good-natured people who tended their homes and gardens and doted on their children, while the natives took readily to the life of the port. The shops, the coming and going of ships, Saturday night picture shows, every night 'cobba-cobbas' and big poker schools provided excitement and variety such as they had never known before. They suffered none of the restrictions of Aboriginal station employees, for although they usually adopted their white families for better or worse, if they were for any reason unhappy in one household they could up and go to another. They returned to Beagle Bay or Lombadina for regular holidays, while the interchange of nuns between the town and the missions kept them in touch with friends and relatives 'at home'. Loved and appreciated and with all their needs provided for, the Broome natives of this era, still half way between the white world and their own, but at ease enough in both, could be counted happier than the majority of their descendants today.

Mission-trained stockmen who struck out for jobs on the stations were less successful. In an environment where blacks were expected to speak pidgin English, their superior manner of speech was regarded as an affectation – even an impertinence. If they were seen to read or write a letter they were accused of showing off. Efforts to practise their religion were ridiculed and if they had escaped tribal initiation they were despised by their fellow workers. These, therefore, either returned to the mission, took up with itinerant drovers or became escorts to surveyors and government inspectors. Some accompanied their employers to the cities and worked as gardeners and household servants until 'heart-sickness' for their country and their people drew them back again. Others found employment in such unlikely places as the Sydney power house and the Gippsland timber mills. Two or three took up with the skippers of small cargo ships and got as far afield as China and the Celebes. One full-blood youth married the half-caste daughter of a station owner for whom he acted as storeman and book-keeper, wrote letters and read aloud, tactfully maintaining the fiction that the old man was afflicted with failing sight, though in fact he was illiterate![1]

It is a pity that more is not recorded of this generation of mission-reared Aborigines, for every one of them who remains has a fascinating tale to tell of his adventures and wanderings. Their schooling had of course been limited, but their general knowledge, all-round usefulness, courtesy and reliability gave the lie to the glib assertion that an educated Aboriginal was a spoiled one. No one who had the good fortune to employ them, with the exception of a few station managers, has anything but praise for them.

Meanwhile Beagle Bay and Lombadina missions continued to support about one hundred and fifty people. A few half-castes, such as Martin Sibasado of Lombadina and David Cox of Beagle Bay, remained and worked faithfully with their families, but the exodus of so many of the best workers had thrown back on the religious a heavy physical burden, and priests who had been previously free to teach and administer were now called upon to help in gardens and stock camps. After all their time in Australia, the situation had never looked blacker for the Pallottines.

# CHAPTER TWENTY-THREE

## 1922 – 1929

THE local hierarchy which had given the Pallottines every support in the past seem by this time to have decided that they were no longer serving the best interests of the Church in Kimberley. The Aborigines Department continued to cite national feeling as good enough reason for closing Lombadina and to point out that since the Pallottines were unable to obtain further support from Germany and had now lost most of their best workers, development at Beagle Bay was at a standstill. Anti-German sentiment had prevented the appointment of Father Drostë to his appropriate position as Vicar-Apostolic of the Kimberleys, and Father Creagh, who had held the fort so splendidly over the war period, was now anxious to return to his proper Redemptorist role. This meant that the district would be without an official administrator at a time when strong forces were at work to undermine the already limited enough influence of the Church in that area.

Whether or not prompted by the colonizing spirit of Mussolini's Giovanezza, it was at this juncture that an Italian Society expressed its readiness to enter the Australian missionary field, and early in 1922 an Italian Salesian named Father Ernest Coppo was recalled to Rome from his post in New York to be consecrated Bishop of Kimberley, Western Australia. He arrived soon afterwards to join the five priest and two brothers[1] of his Society who had preceded him to take charge of Lombadina. The astonished Pallottines considered themselves to have been the victims of an act of treachery for although, officially, Bishop Coppo had comto administer the diocese from Broome and his companions to look after the smaller mission until the situation improved, it was obviously their ultimate intention to assume control of Beagle Bay. But hurt and outraged though the pioneer missionaries were, they decided to keep their mouths shut and try to accept the Will of God. The former they appear to have done to some effect, the latter with less resignation.

As far as the public was concerned Bishop Coppo handled the situation quietly and tactfully and no hint of conflict between the two societies reached outside ears. The Italians were well received by the community. The appointment of a man of such culture and dignity as the new bishop seemed a compliment to the country while the priests and brothers were young, strong, vital and full of optimistic but practical-sounding plans for developing Lombadina and teaching its happy-go-lucky and almost entirely full-blood people to conduct their own affairs.

As a first step in his administration the bishop acquired a car – this being considered a very modern and sensible move – and embarked on a tour of the vast and intriguing vicariate that had been represented to his Society as so rich in the promise of pastoral and agricultural development and the prospect of souls.

The further he travelled his 283,000 square-mile-vicariate the more his astonishment grew. So here was what they called 'the Kimberleys' – east and west divisions but of much the same character, remote, rugged and lonely beyond words. In the six hundred hard miles between the crude ports of Derby and Wyndham, he found only one town, Hall's Creek – relic of the brief gold rush of 1886 when it had been slapped together of bush timber and galvanized iron, to be abandoned at the whisper of richer finds elsewhere, leaving a single shanty pub, a store and butchery, the rude shacks of a few persistent prospectors and the unspeakable 'humpies' of the derelict Aborigines. The fenceless sheep and cattle stations, fifty to one hundred miles apart, their boundaries quite unmarked, were so vast that it was possible to drive for a day without seeing a single beast, far less a worker or fellow traveller of any kind or creed.

Few of the scattered homesteads had any pretensions to comfort, even of the simplest kind. The best had creeper-shaded frontages that reduced the glare of the hot plains, but were no protection against dust and flies, their white residents mostly bachelor managers and book-keepers for absentee owners, some of whom had never set foot in Australia, let alone in the north. On the fifteen or so places that lay along his route he met fewer than five white women, their children, except for infants, being at school two thousand miles away.

Living conditions were rough and ready, to say the least. While still unfamiliar with the customs of the country, the visitor, having prepared to take a shower, was startled at finding himself deluged with water poured from above the roofless enclosure by a native woman wreathed in unembarrassed smiles. The staple diet appeared to be salt beef and bread, with the occasional addition of some ill-prepared vegetables, this unattractive fare served by equally unattractive native women who had been summoned for the purpose from their squalid camps. But although incredible to the newcomer, these poor creatures were, he had been given to understand, the consolation of their white employers and some of them the mothers of half-caste children then at Beagle Bay. The subject, however, was not raised, for those concerned, whether for reasons of indifference, embarrassment or stiff-necked Anglo-Saxon pride, had neither inquired for the welfare of their families or asked that messages be conveyed to them.

None the less, evidence of some background culture was not entirely lacking, for some of these strange people, though quite uncommunicative on a personal level, had been prepared to discuss literature with which they had a more than passing acquaintance, while one man had even shown a comprehensive knowledge of grand opera. He and the Italian bishop had sat together, drinking black tea from battered pannikins, while selections from Mozart, Puccini,

Verdi and Wagner, played on an ancient gramophone, rose incongruously against a background of Aboriginal singing from the river bank.

But nowhere had his Lordship found any normal family life, any sign of the land's being cherished or husbanded. It was as though the inhabitants were under a sort of spell, in a state of torpor, of waiting perhaps, but if so, for what? Certainly it was not for the ministrations of the Church, for only a fraction of the population was even nominally Catholic, while the majority made no pretensions to professing any faith at all.

Although photographs had done less than justice to the wild scenery of plains and ranges, rivers and billabongs, to the European it had a forbidding, almost a frightening quality. Its silence, broken only by the anguished shrieks of cockatoos and the boding utterances of the crows, seemed to defy the settler to impose upon it any pattern of domesticity, any sound but the harsh voices of its own wild progeny.

Asked his impressions at the end of his tour, Bishop Coppo replied with guarded courtesy that the country was vast and picturesque beyond his expectations and that it offered to the missionary pioneer an interesting challenge indeed.

One of his first moves was to appeal to the St. John of God missionary nuns to re-form themselves into a branch of his own Society, to be known as the Sisters of Our Lady Help of Christians. In favour of this suggestion was the argument that whereas the Sisters had not, up to this time, been officially recognized or subsidized by their mother-house,[2] the Salesians would provide the support needed to extend their work.

Shortly before this suggestion was made, Mother Antonio O'Brien and Mother Bernardine Greene, who had succeeded her as superior, had died in Broome within the same week.[8] Mother Antonio, having expected to live only long enough to see her sisters established in Kimberley, had after all weathered the sorrows and cyclones of sixteen years, but her going, at the same time as her first successor, when their guiding influence was so badly needed was a sorrowful blow to their community.

To do as the Salesian bishop asked meant breaking with a tradition that was extremely important and dear to them, while to refuse to do so could mean their replacement by nuns with the means to attract the new recruits necessary to extend their work. The majority voted against the change but three young nuns, all Australian born, went to Melbourne, donned the habit of the new sisterhood and embarked on the recruiting and training of postulants.

Discreet silence obscures much of this period of mission history for after the retirement of Bishop Gibney in 1910 there was less exchange of news between the Kimberley missions and the Church leaders in the south, less too, of the lively press correspondence that had thrown so much light on local Catholic activity during his term of office. None the less he had always intervened where possible on behalf of the Pallottines and they felt that his death in 1925 had deprived them of one of their few faithful friends.

This great pioneer priest who had done so much, not only for the Catholic Church and its flock within the State, but for the community as a whole, had been criticized in his latter years for debts incurred in the acquisition of property for the establishment of innumerable Church institutions. Only in time was he to be given the credit for his vision, his enterprise and his energy and the things he stood for fairly assessed:

Bishop Gibney retired when the pioneer days of the colony were ended. . . . He walked the streets, and rode the lonely bush tracks, and voyaged the seas solely for the betterment of his fellow humans; he thought little of himself. His life welded the priesthood of a young country to democracy – he was indeed one of the great democrats of Australia. . . . There have been pastors more able, more gifted, more cultured. There has not been a better priest, or a greater Australian missionary. . . .[4]

There was now no other of his calibre to help the Pallottines, but in their present crisis the country itself, that had so often frustrated them, was to prove their ally. They had grown by this time so accustomed to its harshness, its intractability and its inconsistencies as to derive a certain grim satisfaction from anticipating its next malevolence. It was now the turn of the Salesians to find, as had they and the Trappists before them, that this was no Promised Land of responsive soil in either a pastoral or a spiritual sense.

They smiled in their beards when the Italians announced, with the happy enthusiasm of inexperience, that following their 'discovery' of guano on a nearby island they had produced such a crop of maize and vegetables as would astonish them. So, the newcomers had had success with their first garden. Now let them wait for the frost or the grasshoppers, the out of season 'cockeye' or a treacherous king tide. Let them wait until the kangaroos found an entrance, under or over the enclosure, or someone forgot to shut the gate against the goats. . . . And so, now they were to develop the cattle industry by the introduction of good bulls and stock horses – expensive unimmunized stock, to feed the cattle tick, the buffalo fly and soon to perish from pleuro and horse disease. Now they had the 'new' idea that they would grow tobacco and start in the pearling industry, while instructing the Aborigines to manage such business projects for themselves. They would put a stop to the worst of their customs by giving the people better things to occupy their minds. And there would be a strong new rule – 'No work, no tucker', for how were the people to learn a sincere faith or the dignity of labour if they remained at the mission only to be fed? Just so, but let these good men see who would prove the stronger – the Italians who had been there two or three years, or the people who had occupied this land before the dawn of European history.

And now what was this? They would tell the white people, the pastoralists and the pearlers, that their attitude to the natives was iniquitous. They would tell them that

261

their system of indentured labour – bringing in Asiatics without women of their own – had caused the prostitution, drunkenness and decay of a defenceless people. They would tell them that they had brought in not only diseases of which it was hard to speak, but hookworm[5] which a government inspector had recently found to be rife at Lombadina and Beagle Bay, not to mention leprosy that a doctor[6] had warned was also to be found in Kimberley. So! they would 'talk turkey' like the great leader in Italy to some newly taken colony. They would tell their Australian allies what they thought of them and of their government that be-grudged a miserable subsidy to help the people they had so misused. And they would accuse the Australian prelates of misleading them about the wonderful potential and the eager welcome awaiting them in this vast rich Kimberley vicariate!

As is the way of rival missions, relations between the Pallottine establishment and Sunday Island had hardly been notable for Christian charity but when, in 1923, Hadley, on the death of his elder brother, had inherited the family title and estate in England and was about to leave Australia, he and Father Drostë had parted almost like old comrades in arms.

'Don't worry about those Italians,' Hadley had said. 'They won't last long – they're too keen to make good.'[7]

When the Salesians realized what they were up against in Kimberley they had, unlike those who had previously come to the same conclusion, an acceptable excuse for getting out. It was quietly stated that the experienced missionaries already in the Australian field had now recovered from the effects of the war and were in a position to carry on alone.

Bishop Coppo's departure from Broome in 1928 was marked by a memorable sermon in which he declared that both that port and its industry merited 'the wrath of God'. This and previous forthright criticisms – expressed before a largely coloured congregation – had shocked the white residents who recalled that no German cleric had ever shown such poor taste. Otherwise the Salesian chapter closed quietly with the unobtrusive return of the three sisters from Victoria, clad once again in the familiar white habit of St. John of God.[8]

The bitter memories of war had at last begun to fade and there was no voice raised against the Pallottines assuming jurisdiction over the Kimberley Catholic vicariate.[9] The happy association between Beagle Bay educated natives and the people of Broome had brought about a situation in which hostile outside criticism of the mission was challenged by indignant residents. In November 1925, a traveller named J. C. de Lancourt who was walking round Australia for a wager had published a scathing report of Beagle Bay in which he remarked that the work of the missionaries on behalf of the Aborigines did 'not appear to have gone very much beyond their exploitation for the purpose of profit'.[10] He alleged that money made from what he deemed to be some of the finest country in the north-west and the use of unpaid native labour was being used for the enrichment of the Pallottine Society in Germany but that the missionaries were, at the same time, neglecting the major proportion of their rich reserve which others 'in the district would gladly put to full use'. He added:

The subject of marrying off the half-caste girls controlled by the Society is also one which would bear greater attention. . . . The open disposal of these girls to Japanese, Chinese and Manila boys is no longer possible, but indications point to the way being still open, provided the cash (nominally for the ceremony and usually in the region of £50) is at hand. . . . It seems rather difficult to understand, since such traffic is known to have been carried on, why the mission is still permitted to retain control of these girls. . . . Looking at the whole facts it would appear unreasonable to claim that this 'Pious Society of Missions' is all piety, nor would it seem that the missionary work justifies by its results the retention of control of either the natives or the land. Further, since these stations are obviously run for the profit of the Society there is no

reason why they should receive from Government departments any different treatment to any ordinary pastoral
and trading company.

An Anglican resident signing himself 'Broomite' wrote in
reply:

> ... The Reverend Father Drostë and five lay brothers
> have been at the mission for over twenty-two years with-
> out a holiday for the simple reason that the mission has
> had such a struggle for existence that the necessary funds
> cannot be found for holiday purposes.... The mission
> has never had more than 5,000 head of cattle not because
> they are not wanted but because the land cannot carry any
> more.... The cattle now number about 3,000.
> The land is very poor – in fact so poor that two adjoin-
> ing stations have been up for sale for years and no buyers
> can be found.... Mr. de Lancourt asserts that girls are
> given in marriage for £50. If he can prove one case the
> Rev. Father Drostë will pay £50 for any charity he likes
> to name. ... Some of the half-caste girls marry Manila-
> men who in ninety per cent of cases make good hus-
> bands but as a precaution against any girl being deserted
> and left stranded there is a regulation which compels any
> foreigner to deposit £50 with the Resident Magistrate at
> Broome. ...
> When the critic has given twenty-two years of his life to
> helping bring the outlying parts of Australia within the
> reach of civilization as have the brothers and sisters at
> Beagle Bay he will have done something a thousand times
> more valuable for his country than walking round it for a
> wager.[11]

It was now Father Drostë's turn to tour the district. After
being so long confined to the peninsula the priest found this
an exhilarating experience, and he thanked God that he had
been denied this vast vicariate until suffering and rigorous
experience had made him so much a part of it. Its beauty
and grandeur filled his heart with praise for its Creator and a

love that he had once thought possible to feel only for his native Germany. Despite the hard feelings of the war years he had grown to understand the people of the outback and could meet them now on a basis of their mutual struggle against bad seasons, stock diseases, falling prices and lack of outside interest in their problems. Missionary and pastoralist found a strong bond in their two somewhat contradictory grievances against the government for its neglect on the one hand and its interference on the other. Why should this Aborigines Department be allowed to dictate policies for circumstances it did not understand? Let these officials come and live in the country themselves, under the same conditions, before they gave advice on what must be done and what not done on the mission and station properties. If the government would help in the right place, with financial assistance to develop the land and to encourage closer population, then things could begin to change for the better and the coloured people, too, would benefit.

Men whose children had been sent to Beagle Bay were pleased to hear from this fatherly and understanding pastor of the matches the young people had made – the daughter of one now ageing pioneer married to the son of another, good blood on both sides and beautiful grandchildren coming on. A few were settled at the mission – wonderful couples, steady, loyal and always cheerful. Others had nice little homes in Broome, Derby or Port Hedland, the men in work and making out as well as any others in these hard times.

Father Drostë was accepted by the outback people as a commonsense man of broad-minded humanity and few illusions, while one at least paid him the high compliment of being 'a good practical bushman'.[12] When it was announced in 1929 that he was going home for a holiday it was assumed, without adverse comment, that he would return as the new Vicar-Apostolic, but this was not to be. His years of hard work and tribulation had taken heavy toll of his health and he died, at the age of fifty-nine, soon after returning to his home town. His funeral procession was lit by the lamps of the coal miners with whom he had worked as a youth.

# CHAPTER TWENTY-FOUR

## 1929 – 1938

FATHER DROSTE'S successor was the slim, black-bearded Bavarian Father Otto Raible. The son of a wheelwright, he had ben born in Stuttgart in 1887 and had shown himself from earliest years to be of scholarly and musical bent. In 1905 he entered the Pallottine seminary in Limburg and after his ordination followed his uncle to the Pallottine missionary field in the Cameroons. The effects of malaria fever, aggravated by an allergy to quinine, then the only known remedy to this disease, forced him to return to Europe shortly before the first world war. In 1919, after serving as chaplain in the Kaiser's forces, he was appointed Professor of Philosophy at the Limburg seminary and later established a new foundation in Czechoslovakia. In 1928, when Father Drostë's health began to fail, Father Raible was instructed to proceed to Australia to take his place.

He admitted in later years that nothing he had heard of the difficulties with which his Society was faced in this region had quite prepared him for the shock that awaited his arrival. While expecting certain differences he had more or less equated the task in Australia with that which he had faced in Africa but he found that there was little, if any, comparison to be drawn between the two. In the Cameroons, a relatively small area of two million people, the Pallottine mission had supported 42,000 Christians and some 25,000 catechumens. The Bantus had been eager to learn and to progress and the soil they worked was fertile and responsive to cultivation. What a contrast was this vast land in which a population of about 20,000 included less than a thousand of his own flock, a country which seemed to European eyes the most arid of deserts, its native people simple nomads of whose past little was known and of whose future few offered any hope.

Depression lay like a blight on the land, the price of wool down, bullocks scarcely worth getting away, the demand for pearl shell reduced by a glut on the market. Beagle Bay still ran 4,000 head of cattle and was cultivating some twelve acres of rice but the once famous garden had deteriorated as a result both of bad seasons and shortage of labourers. Departmental regulations had whittled away almost the last remnant of mission authority and there seemed little prospect, after Father Drostë's departure, of ever again training the people in the habits of usefulness and stability.

In such circumstances, especially with 'old hands' on all sides advising him against further waste of time and money in a lost cause, the new superior required a stout heart to carry on. This together with an unshakeable faith in the goodness of Divine Providence, he undoubtedly had, but apart from this, having been given his orders, he had no option, short of abandoning his vows, than to persevere. Fortified with the motto that 'nothing is lost in the household of God', he took courage and soon discovered that the economic cloud was not without its silver lining where the mission was concerned. As the hard times drove more and more unemployed from the cities to the north, the natives, especially those on wages, found it increasingly hard to compete for jobs so that the mission, formerly seen as less attractive than the lively port, now became a place of refuge against a hard world.

This revived the missionaries' hopes and it was decided to try out Father Drostë's unrealized scheme for developing small communal industries at Beagle Bay. The plan was received with enthusiasm and an experimental output of mission-made shirts would have done credit to any factory. The wares were generally admired, the missionaries commended on having encouraged the people in a useful occupation and orders promised well. The catch in this instance was that trade union regulations ruled out the marketing of the goods!

An anthropologist who visited Beagle Bay about this time remarked that he found the mission carrying on through the depression 'with the same air of utter detachment from the world outside that had characterized it from the start'.[1] In the circumstances, however, since enterprise was even more futile than before, there was nothing much better that it could have done. Only a trickle of priests and brothers had been made available to the Kimberley missions since the war and although small contributions from Limburg and the Society for the Propagation of the Faith helped eke out the government subsidy, the financial situation continued, as always, to move from one crisis to another. Father Worms, the missionary anthropologist who arrived in 1930, writes of this period that:

The impression I got when I came and first worked together with Bishop [then Father] Raible was our extreme poverty. Every penny that could be spared went for the benefit of the natives, which meant that our standard of living was much lower than that we were accustomed to in our houses. I was often worried where the next money was to come from, but the bishop only cracked a joke about it and we always kept our heads over the water.

I admired more than I can say our old brothers at Beagle Bay and Lombadina, who never asked for more than their daily bread and even that they were ready to share when the flour was held up by bad weather. The stock had been well looked after and there was always plenty of meat for the people. The bishop was anxious always that they were well fed and had enough of the other needs of life. He never had a thought for himself. You know what a great musician he was – yet in all his time here he never got a piano for himself. When kind people in Melbourne and Perth twice or three times presented him with a piano for his own he gave them to the sisters for their schools. . . .[2]

Though never concerned for himself or his own comfort, Father Raible was not of the school of thought that held that his fellow religious should be called upon to endure inhumanly harsh privations. It grieved him to find that some of his community had had no break from the rigours of the Kimberleys in over twenty years and in 1929 he took the risk of purchasing a wheat farming property at Tardun, in the south of the State, where they could come for an occasional break. This plan, as well as that the farm would serve as a training ground for local part-Aborigines, was to prove a sound one, but drought conditions throughout the State that year imposed a heavier financial burden than he had bargained on. Sensitive as he always was at having 'to come as a beggar to the Catholics of Australia', he was forced to appeal through *The Advocate* in order to provide the 'barest necessities' for his 326 dependants then at Beagle Bay and Lombadina.[8]

The result of this drive was one in accordance with the hard times but in the following year Thomas Clarke, the pearler who had presented the nuns with their first little home in Broome, died, leaving his estate to the Pallottine mission and the St. John of God Sisters. This represented the biggest single windfall the mission had ever received as it included several luggers, a few small houses and some blocks of land in Broome as well as a quantity of recently taken shell and a few pearls. The nett proceeds, stripped of probate, totalled some £6,000.

The mission people themselves admit that they hardly felt the pinch of the depression years but they were not entirely unaware of the behind scenes struggle to make ends meet. They loved and respected their bearded pastors – Father Raible, the patriarchial administrator, Superintendent Father Benedict Puesken at Beagle Bay, Father Augustine Spangenburg at Lombadina. Though inclined to take the missionaries' sacrifices for granted, the people's concern for them in sickness or misfortune was spontaneous and heartfelt. In emergencies, moreover, such as the cyclone of 1935 that laid flat many of the mission buildings and destroyed the gardens, it was seen that they had not lost their capacity for rising to the occasion.[4] In this instance, with the financial assistance of a government grant in aid, they worked with such a will that the damage was repaired and everything back to normal in an astonishingly short time.

But of all the problems that had ever assailed the Kimberley missionaries the greatest was in store. The consequences of long neglect had by this time caught up on the north. The depression, want of rain and lack of government support had all, as the pastoralists said, contributed to the deterioration of the land, but so had their own ignorance of stock control and general husbandry. The attachment of the black people to their squalid camps and the failure of the government to carry out proper health inspections had played their part in the spread of disease, as had also the landholders' failure to encourage better living conditions and their opposition to native education.

Leprosy – a word that had been whispered from time to time – was now on everybody's lips. Thought to have been introduced with the influx of Chinese to the Territory and Kimberley goldfields,[5] the disease had been reported by a medical officer in Darwin in 1894 and not long afterwards by Father Nicholas in Broome. Their diagnoses might in some cases have been mistaken but no one bothered to investigate.

In 1912 the Mayor of Broome wired the Premier in Perth:

BROOME ALARMED CASES OF LEPROSY AND SUGGEST GOVERNMENT SCHOONER VENUS CALLS AT ONCE AND REMOVES INFECTED PEOPLE.[6]

The reply came promptly:

LEPROSY MATTERS RECEIVING CLOSE ATTENTION BY GOVERNMENT.[7]

Presumably the cases mentioned were dealt with, but the situation thereafter drifted until 1923 when both the matron and a native orderly of the Broome hospital were quietly removed to a leper station near Cossack.

In 1924, Dr. Cecil Cook, Commonwealth medical officer in Darwin, advised a systematic investigation, but his suggestion was ignored. In the same year the Chief Protector of Aborigines replied to Broome residents, who had appealed for a leper survey: 'There appears to be nothing whatever in the condition of the natives in Broome or Derby to cause any alarm.'[8] But it was not, strictly speaking, the protector's business since Aboriginal lepers 'came under the Public Health Department'.[9]

The inertia seems hard to credit today, but government action had not yet been really hard pressed. The population directly concerned was small and the pastoralists were by no means anxious to stir up one of the intermittent inquiries into the condition of the Aborigines. Their traditional self-protective resentment of outside interference carried over into a situation where they would have been well advised, if for selfish reasons alone, to co-operate with the medical authorities. Times were admittedly hard, but the attempts of some to side-track medical fees for Aboriginal employees was to cost the country dear. Station owners, having so far successfully resisted the introduction of wages for native workers, saw nothing illogical in claiming that these people were entitled to the same treatment in government hospitals as whites whose incomes were too low to pay hospital tax, and when a submission to this effect was defeated some went so far as to discharge their sick or injured native employees and to disclaim any responsibility for their hospital expenses.[10] It was not until 1933, after members of the Board of Health in Derby had resigned in protest, that an investigation was organized and a team sent out to inspect all main station and bush encampments.

A hurried survey returned with eighty-five suspect cases to Derby, where they were huddled in wretched, unventilated huts in the native hospital compound awaiting further orders. Another thirty cases, some found on the missions, some in Broome, others in the bush, were rounded up in the Dampierland area and ordered to be held at Beagle Bay.[11] A number of these were found to be suffering from other diseases for which they were treated and discharged, but the incidence was alarming and more thoroughgoing 'leper hunts' were quickly organized.

On station after station lepers were discovered among native stockmen, house and kitchen helps and *de facto* wives. Soon, realizing the price of discovery, they tried to conceal symptoms of what they termed 'the big sick' and many took to the bush when suspecting a medical survey. 'Checking up on lepers here,' a distracted doctor reported, 'is like a game of chess – your move, then their move!'[12]

The fears of the white population also mounted. Conditions for contagion were unknown and although theories abounded, none, except that full-blood and caste natives were more susceptible than Europeans, could be long sustained. Station camps, though ideal to the spread of disease, were not a necessary factor, for a number of clean-living townspeople – mostly coloured – were among those affected. It was clear, too, that despite efforts to raise the standard of hygiene on the missions, their people had not escaped the consequences of association with the Asiatic crews.

Reels of red tape had meanwhile been unwinding between government departments. Leprosy, it seemed, came 'under Commonwealth', which meant that patients from Western Australia could be sent to the leprosarium near Darwin, but it was some months before a surprise influx on this scale could be accommodated. The 13-ton lugger, *W. S. Rolland* was then hired and the captain instructed to take as many cases as possible from Beagle Bay. The leave-taking of the twelve who were packed on board was one of the most pathetic incidents in the mission's history. The more advanced half-caste and part-Filipinos among them, hoping to encourage the terrified full-blood victims, made brave attempts to be merry, as though setting off on a holiday cruise. One had an accordion and played a jaunty air, but as the lugger pushed out to sea a high-pitched keening of tribal lament went up from both the ship and the shore, and even

272

the captain,[13] a hardened old sea-dog, could not restrain his emotion.[14]

The St. John of God nuns appealed to the Health Department to allow them to open a leprosarium near Derby where victims could be cared for in their own country, but their offer was turned down. Official bungling continued and with it the mounting sum of human misery. Lepers in the Derby native hospital, so far patient and uncomplaining, hearing that they were to be shipped to the Territory, demanded to see their local protector. They begged that they might be isolated somewhere within their tribal territory, preferably on the coast, where they undertook to live by their own resources until pronounced cured or dead. Leprosy, however, still came 'under Commonwealth' and orders stood that cases were to be removed to Darwin as accommodation became available. The two main spokesmen among these lepers, both natives of known integrity, were kept in chains until the lugger arrived to take them away.

After their departure, six lepers broke out of the compound of the native hospital and made for the bush, but being too weak and sick to travel far were all brought back except one who was presumed to have been drowned.[15]

Publicity could no longer be avoided and as expected it again drew attention to the Aboriginal question. The matter was raised at a meeting of the British Commonwealth League in London and a letter sent to the Lieutenant-Governor. Was it true that conditions of 'virtual slavery' still existed in Western Australia and that natives, riddled with disease, were being rounded up like criminals and herded into an enclosure without proper medical attention or indeed even beds?

In 1934 a commission of investigation was put into the hands of Magistrate H. D. Moseley whose report, submitted early in 1935, was realistically in keeping with a depression budget and a relief to the local public. The inquiry had ascertained that the natives were being nowhere exploited and that the alleged 'virtual slavery' was nothing more or less than a mutually satisfactory business arrangement. He found that reports of the ill-treatment of sick natives had been grossly exaggerated, but strongly advised further medical surveys and the setting up of a hospital centre in West Kimberley and concluded that:

> With the exception of improved medical conditions there is little, I think, of importance which should be done to better the condition of the Kimberley natives. . . . They are well fed and clothed, and the huts in which they live made of bush material – bags and sometimes flattened petrol tins – are suitable to their needs; anything more elaborate would not be appreciated by them – indeed would not be used. . . . The number of blacks employed on stations in the Kimberleys cannot be far short of 2,000, on 70 or 80 different stations. . . . I do not say that in the years to come these people will not become ready subjects for advanced training. In the missions it can now be observed that the people provide good material on which to work. . . . My point is that while the natives are on the pastoral stations any scheme for bringing them under our code of civilization will react to their disadvantage. . . .[15]

The commissioner found that certain natives in the Murchison district, to whom pastoralists were voluntarily paying wages, had shown an improvement in appearance and general behaviour and did not, as predicted, appear to be gambling their money. He was much in doubt, however, that a wage system would benefit native workers in Kimberley since these had no understanding of money!

Of the half-castes he observed that 'at the present rate of increase the time is not far distant when [they], or a great majority of them, will become a positive menace to the community, the men useless and vicious, the women a tribe of harlots'. He made no comment on what the missions had done, by moral and manual training, to remedy this state of affairs, seeming rather to have agreed with Neville that these establishments tended only to confuse the native mind. The chief protector's evidence to the effect that the Aborigines could not but impute immoral undertones to the relationship between male and female religious, dismissed the Catholic institutions – by implication – as totally ineffectual. Native psychology, he insisted, rendered it 'imperative that missionaries be married people living together'[16] – a likely sounding observation, unsubstantiated, curiously enough, by a shred of evidence.

Having summed up the supposed outlook of the natives, the commissioner went on:

> ... Are these people then suitable subjects from whom to expect a ready response to Christian teaching? Is there not some preliminary work to be done before the Christianizing process begins? ... Is it not necessary that he should first, and for some considerable time, be trained in the habits of civilization more universal than the habit of going to church – first and foremost in the habit of work? ... He has no cultivated relation or understanding of worship. Fear of evil spirits is to him the only restraining influence....
>
> The opinion is often heard from the pastoralists: 'I would not have a mission trained boy on the place.' These people have nothing against the mission; their objection is to the method adopted with the native. One fundamental principle of Christianity is 'brotherhood'. The danger of adopting that principle with the native is that by familiarity he will be spoilt. The native does not appear to understand that attitude. He regards it as a weakness on the part of the white. All he looks for is fairness. ...[17]

In view of the high level of scholarship then being brought to bear on Aboriginal culture and psychology – in a number of cases by men of missionary or clerical background[18] – these rather naïve statements read more like a parody on the contemporary outlook than a serious assessment of the facts.

Mr. Moseley's assignment was, however, even more

275

difficult than that of Dr. Roth thirty years previously, for complications, like the mixed-blood people, had increased with every year and the evidence given was correspondingly more confusing. Recommendations would have been simpler to arrive at had there been a clearer case against the missions or in favour of the Aborigines Department, but whereas the former had at least achieved something, the government-run stations and feeding depots were obviously mismanaged, rundown and uninspired. One particularly authoritative and objective witness[19] stated that the general attitude of the Aborigines themselves was that they were being 'not protected but persecuted' by the department. He thought that missionaries in general should show more respect for native law and have at least some nursing experience, but he thought the Catholics were held in high regard by the Aborigines, for whom celibacy, when properly explained, had 'a particular occult significance'.

Paul Hasluck, who accompanied the commissioner as reporter for *The West Australian*, gave a rather better summing up of the situation than the official report itself. He told of the earnest efforts of the six Christian missions in Kimberley[20] to develop their properties and improve the native people, and of the prejudice against them 'in the workaday world of the north'.

In general [he observed] Christianity, like alcoholic drinks and wages, is considered to be allowable for whites but bad for blacks. A satirist might find something to tickle his fancy in that. ... But criticism does not pretend to consider the relation of the Christian black to God ... only [whether] the mission boy makes an obedient stockman, willing to work and not given to trickery or answering back, and above all, not presuming in any degree on the brotherhood of man that Christianity teaches. ...[21]

Of Beagle Bay he wrote with some feeling:

... The garden in the waste land, the pure beauty of the altar in the church raised by devoted hands are the glories

276

of the place. Somehow the making of these two things appears as a manifestation of something more lasting and more vital than the other work accomplished. Even if all the rest were failure, there is in these the expression of an idea that is enduring. ... The substance that is the witness of faith. . . .[22]

It was somehow in the tradition of the Pallottines' experience in Australia that such a highlight as the consecration of one of their Society as Vicar-Apostolic of Kimberley was overshadowed by so much trouble and anxiety. Father Raible had gone to the provincial house at Limburg for this great event, the materials chosen for his episcopal ring – a Broome pearl and a nugget from the heart of the Kimberleys – being symbolic to him of the country to which he had given his heart.

He returned to Australia with four Pallottine priests, including the famous Father Herman Nekes, Professor of Linguistics and Ethnology at the Berlin University, two brothers and a husband and wife team of two doctors, experienced in tropical medicine, to help fight the spread of disease in his diocese.

He at once suggested that the government act on the recommendation of the Moseley report that a medical centre be set up by establishing a clinic at Moola Bulla to be run by Doctors Betz and Betz-Kortez with the help of the St. John of God nursing sisters. This proposal was declined[23] and the two doctors[24] thereafter concentrated their efforts on Beagle Bay, which mission, having been used as a dumping ground for all leper suspects in the Dampierland area, was now being damned by the department as a 'nest' of leprosy and venereal disease.

Following the commissioner's visit all lepers at the Derby native hospital had been put in charge of Mr. and Mrs. Luyer, the latter a trained nurse. This couple worked enthusiastically for over a year, when they resigned because of differences with local medical authorities.[25] The lepers, who had in the meantime been moved to a compound fourteen miles out of Derby, were then left to look after themselves. The nuns again volunteered to step in but were once more rejected. This time, however, their proposal had the support of the District Medical Officer, Dr. Musso, and the local Member J. J. Holmes, whose bleak report on the situation brought the departments to their senses.

The announcement, in 1937, that their offer had at last been sanctioned was received with great joy at the convent in Broome and the three younger sisters of the late Mother Mary Bernardine Greene, Sisters Mary Gertrude, Mary Gabriel and Mary Bridget, soon to be joined by Sister Alphonsus Daly, then studying tropical diseases in Perth, embarked at once on their new task.

They came to chaos, desolation and despair. The Beagle Bay half-caste boy, Willy Wright, being of superior education to the majority of his fellow patients, had assumed a measure of responsibility and was bravely trying to cope with an influx of from twenty to thirty sick natives a week. At the time of the nuns' arrival there were 340 patients in the enclosure of whom about half, found to be suffering from other complaints, were removed for treatment in the native hospital and thence allowed to go home. This assuaged the worst fears of the Aborigines both inside and outside the reserve, who had regarded being picked up by a medical survey as amounting to a sentence of death, but there was still no escaping the fact that far too many were the victims of a terrible disease for which there was no known cure.

The resident doctor advised the nuns to try everything, not overlooking the possibility of finding a local herb with curative properties. The patients were questioned and plants of reputedly medicinal value sought out and tested, but to no avail.[26] Meanwhile the place was cleaned up, buildings and modern equipment provided by the government, trees, lawns and gardens planted, until soon the dreaded 'lep' had taken on the aspect of an attractive community centre.

Whatever might have been feared from the entry of a

religious body into this field, the arrival of the cheerful, proficient nuns lifted a heavy burden of anxiety from the people of Kimberley and saved the faces of government departments that had come under fire for muddling and incompetence. To the lepers themselves it had brought not only devoted nursing skill but new hope and encouragement in what had been an outpost of despair.

# CHAPTER TWENTY-FIVE

## 1930–1939

WHEN Father Ernest Worms was appointed parish priest of Broome in 1931 the townspeople knew nothing of his background, either as a scientist or as a soldier who had won the Kaiser's Iron Cross in the 1914–18 war. With his fresh complexion, wide blue eyes and gentle manner, he appeared to them younger than his years and certainly no match for the guile of the Aborigines and half-caste people who made up the greater part of his congregation.

A story is told in Broome of how a resident, in search of shells on an early morning ebb tide, was drawn by the sound of chanting to a 'ring place' where an Aboriginal man-making ceremony was in progress. Watching from the outskirts he was amused to notice among the participants a number of supposedly faithful Catholics and he had wondered whether he should inform their no doubt deluded pastor. Peering more closely, however, he had discerned, squatting in the outer circle of elders and busily taking notes, none other than the parish priest himself.

Father Worms who was born in 1891 at Borchum, Westphalia, had entered the Pallottine Society two years before the outbreak of the first world war. Conscripted into the army he served his country with distinction, was severely wounded and decorated and eventually returned to the seminary, where he was ordained in 1920. During and after this time he had studied ethnology and linguistics under the Pallottine missionary priest, Professor Herman Nekes, a master he greatly revered and with whom he was later to collaborate in Australia.

He had arrived in Kimberley at what was probably the most important time for Australian anthropology since Darwin's hypothesis of the previous century had aroused curiosity about the place of the Aborigines in the evolutionary scale. The establishment of a Department of Anthropology at the Sydney University in 1925 had been a great stimulus to scientific research and students had since penetrated to the last strongholds of tribal life in the Northern Territory and Kimberley. Time was running out and the workers were all too few to gather what remained of the vanishing culture, but by 1930 the accumulated data had greatly increased the status of the Aboriginal in the evolutionary scale and established his society as infinitely more complex and ordered than had previously been supposed. He was now seen, not as a living fossil preserved in a cradle of the human race, but as himself an immigrant and an amazing example of intelligent adaptation to environment. Theories of racial origins could now be put to the objective test of new archaeological techniques, and Australia had launched its own ethnological publication, *Oceania*, in which many of Father Worm's articles were soon to see the light.

The priest found that all study of native law and languages, together with the use of prayers and hymns in the local tongues, had come to a stop on the missions after the departure of Father Bischoffs in 1914. This had been due less to a change of policy than to preoccupation with what seemed more vital aspects of missionary work and to the overshadowing of the Aborigines by the rapidly increasing people of mixed blood.

A number of his fellow missionaries regarded Father Worms's absorption in things of the mythological past as so much waste of time. The scientist priest, on the other hand, while not discrediting what had been achieved by sheer Christian compassion, commonsense and hard work, saw in much missionary teaching a failure to face psychological realities. It had not taken him long to discover how few of the mission-educated natives, for all their outward conformity to Christian teaching, had actually abandoned their native beliefs and practices. Far from deploring what some considered backsliding and duplicity, however, he appreciated the natural ease with which so many managed to balance 'a faith on either shoulder'. He saw as immeasurably precious the phenomena of *faith itself* and the Aboriginal's belief in his 'dreaming' as a flame of spiritual vitality that once extinguished could not be rekindled from another source. Confident that the natives would themselves come to adapt their beliefs to Christianity (as many had adapted an ancient ritual time-table to the working schedules of industry) he eschewed any evangelistic tendency to destroy or devaluate the faith quality of tribal law.

It was this approach – one in accordance with the ancient tradition, if not always with the practice of the Church – that had been taken by Spanish Jesuits in Mexico in the seventeenth century and had led to one of the few examples of successful 'acculturation' in modern history. There were no 'lost generations' among the Pueblo Indians fortunate enough to have received their introduction to European civilization in this enlightened way. They have kept their pride of race and practise many of their ancient rites to this day, the patron saints of their different villages presiding over the enactment of their ancient corn festivals, the birth of the Christ Child and the Resurrection, hailed with Christian hymns and Indian drums, while deer impersonators leap about the church.[2]

On this theme Father Worms was to write in the later years of his life:

The missionary should first consider the strange and wonderful history of mankind, the background from which he himself has emerged and the many influences that shaped his own complex culture. . . .

As a farmer must know the soil for his seed if he desires a good harvest, so the missionary must know at least something of the attitude (religious, social and economic) of the people he would influence. Otherwise he talks strange words against a wall. He will commit many grave mistakes and will not only destroy their confidence but will offend the people and he will therefore work in a vacuum.

Every faint candle of his research will reflect the *nobility* of the human creature wherever he is found, the *unity* of the human race with its immense intellectual capacity and points of contact, its slow but persevering progress in the face of great difficulties. All science must come to reverence the universal natural law of the Maker before which the student bends in deeper homage with every new discovery. This he should try to bring systematically to the knowledge, not only of his serious colleagues, but to the understanding of all men. . . .[3]

Father Worms was equally intrigued by the universal aspects of religious impulse and the particular differences between basic Aboriginal and European concepts. He paralleled the pre-Lenten Christian carnivals with many of the seemingly demonic Aboriginal ceremonies – the wearing in both cases of fantastic masks, benign or satanic, manifesting an impulse common to all mankind towards identification with supernatural and all-powerful beings. On the other hand he pointed out that a too facile acceptance of logic as operating in the same way for Aboriginal and European prevented many would-be teachers from ever coming to grips with the essential native mind. A case in point was the way in which the Aborigines, like the American Indians or for that matter the patriarchs of Judaic scripture, accepted their dream visions as real and true and acted on the revelations and instructions received from their tribal spirits while in this state, whatever the consequences involved. Of this he wrote:

. . . As a rule dreams project previous patterns of myths, songs and ceremonies and are not revolutionary. They remain within the limits of tradition and sometimes revive rites and beliefs gone out of custom. As dreamed phantasms are not produced by rational recognition, the

283

Aborigines are not disturbed by logical contradictions which are allowed to co-exist with other 'truths' serenely and undisturbed. In this way it is possible for the supernatural being to have sons without a mother, to be revered and yet be killed without loss of respect, to withdraw to the stars and yet remain in its previously earthly abode by its presence within its *tjuringa* wherever these may be carried. A young man may well be conscious of his personal power of procreation and, though still unmarried, see his future children without recognizing any problems in the mysterious functions of the spirit child which exists before it is born.[4]

The importance attached to the dream life and the impulses received therefrom also explained why it was not the individual but the clan as a whole that either accepted the credit or was called to account for his behaviour – a state of affairs that had proved so exasperating to missionaries, not to say station managers. Father Worms believed, however, that while tactfully discouraging the 'sponsored irresponsibility'[5] entailed, the strong clan spirit of the people stressing the importance of giving and sharing, co-operation rather than competition, was a thing to cherish and use to good effect.

He considered it both dangerous and futile to interfere with marriage taboos and (at least in the earlier stages of contact) with those aspects of initiation that were regarded as indispensable to the development of manly character and tribal status. He had found the tribal elders were in most instances ready enough to admit that some aspects of ritual, including the more harmful practices of mutilation and disease-spreading blood rites, were of comparatively recent origin and not essential or basic elements of their law[6] but that a too adamant missionary attitude served only to intensify their zeal for every embellishment. This problem of initiation was certainly the subtlest of all, some missionaries justifying the forthright prohibition of its every aspect on the grounds that youths emerged from the attendant ceremonies if not less tractable, certainly less teachable. This was probably true, for in the words of W. E. H. Stanner, referring to the effects of initiation:

> ... Responses to given stimuli have become so deeply settled that an aboriginal feels true interest, spiritual ease, and intellectual satisfaction only in that system of life which the stimuli connote. Initiated men may learn to live with Europeanism and even to manipulate it skilfully, but I have met none – except those whose transitional world has utterly collapsed – who are happy with it. It is not difficult to see why. . . .[7]

On the other hand, much of the apathy found, especially among the unitiated, was attributed to such natives having lost their 'dreaming', and hence any direction in life, by the cutting of the sacred cord that bound them to their spirit world.[8]

The natives themselves were quick to appreciate the priest's interest in their dual lives and to recognize him as a man in whom they could confide. The Yaoro people, indigenous to the Broome area, had by that time dwindled to less than fifty, and, delighted to find that Father Worms could record their vanishing language and locality myths, they took him from place to place, following in the footsteps of their ancient heroes, sometimes far afield, sometimes within the town itself where buildings covered their ancient landmarks. They showed him the quartzite boulder where a malignant spirit had imprisoned the souls of men caught 'dream-walking' at night;[9] the spring where a mythological trickster had been destroyed by his own magic; the island to which a young giant had swum to claim the daughter of the towering Emu-Man who now resides in the Southern Cross; the spot where their hero Miriny saw their first *tjuringeas* fall from the sky. The site then covered by the Broome picture show (which the remaining Yaoro none the less patronized) was where the great spirits Gagamura and Gonbaren had given them their lore of good and evil magic. . . .

Their songs and legends trailed off on the wind like the long beards of the dream heroes:

> At the place of Gonbaren, lightning,
> Lightning,
> Camps and shadow,
> Shadow.[10]

As time went on the Dampierland people came to address the priest as Ibala – learned elder of the tribes – by which title he was to become known throughout the north. It was no merely formal gesture, like the 'tribal brotherhood' bestowed as a tribute of friendship and goodwill, and it was of much more significance to the people than Syd Hadley's ritual initiation. The latter had never become proficient even in the tongue of the Bard tribe whereas Father Worms's study of linguistics and ethnology ranged from the surviving languages and laws of the north-west, the Kimberleys and the Northern Territory to those of Tasmania that were long since extinct. Although fluent in only a few of the many Australian tongues, his knowledge of their basic principles, root words and grammatical structure gave him ready entrée to any tribe he encountered. In the Kimberleys at least he was accepted as a greater authority on the law than the elders themselves and as such he was not only highly respected but sometimes feared.

In such a period of transition, confusion was inevitable, and there was a tendency for natives of higher tribal status to take advantage of those less advanced in or ignorant of the law by inventing 'tribal rights' to suit their own purposes. Natives suspicious of having been 'put upon' came to Ibala as the one man they could trust and if their case was valid the deceiver was quickly brought to heel. The Broome police records bear witness to the occasions on which the priest was called upon to give evidence in cases where native offenders claimed to have acted in accordance with tribal law. Sometimes his testimony vindicated the prisoner, while those who had given false information had usually only to see him in court to admit their guilt.

There was now almost no place in Dampierland where ritual objects were safe, not only from the risk of desecration but, in the native view, from causing serious harm to the finder, some emblems being considered so dangerous that even the elders feared to handle them unless they were bound at either end to prevent the escape of indwelling magic. The old men, faced with the inevitable disappearance of their law, brought their problem to the priest, who was able both to fulfil their trust and to serve the cause of science by depositing them in the Anthropological Museum at the Pallottine House of Studies in Kew, Victoria.

While his scientist's mind was preoccupied with the collection of anthropological data, his missionary mind searched for aspects of Aboriginal belief through which Christianity might be introduced or made better understood. The idea was by no means new, but his equipment for the task was probably superior to that of any other missionary in the Australian field. The results of his search may have had little effect, one way or another, on the outlook of the Aborigines he encountered, but, as an insight into the *'nosce teipsum* – the God-given and unquenchable urge of modern and primordial man alike into the Where-from and Where-to of existence'[11] it provided the inspiration for his last great work: *The Religion Of The Australian Aborigines.*[12]

Not content with existing interpretations, he sought a precision of definition for the many facets covered in the all-embracing term – 'the dreaming'. What exactly were the Aboriginal conceptions of death, the soul and the life hereafter, of a Supreme Being in relation to the many other spirits of creation? In seeking answers to these questions he collaborated with anthropologists in different parts of Australia, awaiting their private letters or published papers with all the excitement of a schoolboy following the instalments of a thrilling serial.[13] In simplest summary the general trend of their findings was that while belief in a realm of the dead was common to most tribes, ideas concerning the fate of the spirit varied considerably. Some conceived the hereafter as an island where spirits passed their time much as on earth, but free from all pain and anxiety; others to whom death was 'the last great catastrophe'[14] and who held that souls – perhaps after a period of shadowy island existence – were finally destroyed by lightning, 'their remains rain-swept under the roots of the tree of death'.[15]

Some image of an All Father was also common to most tribes but this spirit had become isolated among the distant stars, leaving earthly affairs to innumerable secondary ancestor and creator beings with whom man could unite himself in spirit by the enactment of ritual and the proper use of his sacred implements.

The idea of Father, Son and Holy Ghost – *Go Go baba ... ba ba Nimandjara* – appealed to the natives as within their own conception of one great spirit divided into many,[16] but as other Catholic missionaries had suspected, there was no parallel in mythical law to the concept of Mary, Virgin and loving Mother of God and of all mankind. Their fertility mother and many other powerful female spirits were so far from being virginal that their matings and the prodigious fruits thereof were the themes for many an amazing myth.

The priest sought similes (with what success he could not say) within the environment – the boab tree, stark and grotesque, burgeoning into foliage and blossom before the coming of the life-saving rain; flood waters, like the blessings of divine grace, filling the parched river beds. He also tried to introduce the Christian teaching of union with God through grace and redemption through the natives' own desire to be united with their tribal spirits in the realm of the dead – their Bang-aranjara, located in the Milky Way.

The Pallottine Father Herman Nekes, Professor of Linguistic and Ethnological Studies at the Berlin University, had meanwhile become so interested in the work of his former student in Australia that in 1935 he came out to join him at Beagle Bay. They at once began their combined study of tribal languages[17] which they believed held the key to the mystery of Aboriginal origins. On this monumental task Professor Nekes worked on in Dampierland while Father Worms followed the ancient highway of tribal migration and cultural exchange, along the Mary and Fitzroy Rivers to the Indian Ocean. He also re-explored the caves of the great Wondjina spirit hidden deep among the tumbled hills and fertile springs of north-west Kimberley and found pictorial and linguistic evidence of a previous pygmoid race – 'the little people' or *Guridid* of north-west legend.[18] He would return from these expeditions sunburnt, almost inarticulate with excitement and in his own words 'stripped as far as decency would allow', most of his clothing having been given away in token of thanks to his native guides.

At La Grange, about 120 miles south of Broome, then a government ration station and by tradition an intertribal meeting ground, the priest met members and studied languages of nomad groups from the vast desert areas to the west. He then joined Father Francis Huegel, who had come to Kimberley at the same time as himself and was then Superintendent of a small station known as Rockhole near Hall's Creek which Bishop Raible had purchased in 1934.[19] This he had intended to provide a buffer or stepping stage to civilization for the desert people who were steadily drifting to the settlement in search of the abundant hunting ground rumoured to lie to the north of their arid frontiers. In earlier times such wanderers had been obliged to pay for the white man's fare in station work, whereas now they could find everything provided at government feeding depots without any effort at all. The former conditions had left much to be desired but they were infinitely more realistic and less destructive than the latter. It was the bishop's wish, therefore, to provide some healthy compromise, a place of refuge and training for civilization that could also be made self-supporting by the sale of cattle, wool and vegetables. The purchase of the property had been a private transaction between the Pallottines and the former owner but it was not a move likely to have found favour in the eyes of the department. Mr. Neville clearly regarded this encroachment of his least favoured missionary body into the heart of the Kimberleys as a further setback to his plans for greater control of the situation. It also represented what he saw as a threat to the proper working out of the assimilation policy that had been given formal sanction in 1936 and to which he was as devoted as the missionaries to their different ideal.

By 1937 the future of Rockhole was obviously in jeopardy but for Father Worms it provided a place of contact with the sort of people to whom, like so many missionaries before him, he especially yearned. In his case, however, it was with a much more realistic idea, not only of what he was up against, but of what was required. He realized that it would have been entirely futile to enter the country of the still tribal-living Gogadga people without a knowledge of their language and distinctive laws and before having won the sponsorship of several tribal elders. It is suggested that tribes encountered in open country were generally found to be less suspicious and aggressive than those inhabiting rugged, heavily timbered or mountainous terrain, but even so, how different might have been the early history of Drysdale River mission had such an approach been possible!

When Father Worms set out at last, equipped with a thin swag, water-bag, billy-can, pannikin, camera and notebook and a few iron rations, he was accompanied by two already devoted members of the tribe, and had no more fears for his safety than had he been embarking on a holiday hike in his native Germany. None the less, it was no small undertaking for the only indication of white penetration to this area was the Canning stock route, the longest and loneliest track in the world, that ran for 870 miles between Hall's Creek and the railhead at Wiluna.[20] A few white stockmen had been speared in the vicinity but such incidents were thought to have been the result of foolishness or inadvertence on the part of the travellers. Many of the desert people had never set eyes on a whiteman and it was these who most interested the scholar priest. As Ibala, his reputation was already something of a legend among these wandering hunter-foragers and he was welcomed to their camp fires as an honoured guest. Their food – snakes and lizards, bush rats, frogs, insects, wild honey, eucalyptus leaves, desert roots and berries – and their primitive methods of preparing them were all of great interest to him but his attempts to share them were sometimes disconcerting. On one occasion, presented, as a special delicacy, with what looked like a type of nut, he had no sooner put the kernel in his mouth than it disintegrated into a mass of wriggling maggots. The 'nut' was a hardened exudation of sap from a tree strung by some astute insect to form a hatchery for its eggs!

In 1938 his field work was interrupted by his appointment as rector to the newly established Pallottine House of Studies in Kew, Victoria, in the purchase of which Bishop Raible had been generously assisted by his friend Archbishop Mannix of Melbourne. Professor Nekes accompanied Father Worms to this centre in order to continue their collaboration on Aboriginal languages.

Meanwhile, plans for the development of the Rockhole property as a primary producing, educational and medical centre had been frustrated, and Bishop Raible, on the advice of Father Worms, had applied for a lease of about 1,000,000 acres on the table and adjacent to the Canning stock route.[21] This had seemed to the priest, in the course of his wanderings, an ideal area for the formation of a true frontier mission, and early in 1939, when the Under-Secretary for Lands advised that the application had been approved, he lost no time in joining the bishop in search of a site.

The choice of area, dependent on its water and its suitability as a tribal gathering place, could be merely tentative, but having sold the Rockhole property, Bishop Raible organized the removal of stock and equipment to a location about seventeen miles south of Gregory's Great Salt Sea and some fifty south of Billuna. The little missionary band, in charge of Father Alphonsus Bleischwitz, then began sinking bores and moving stock in search of water and agistment, like the nomad shepherds of ancient times.

Father Worms returned to Melbourne happy that a start had been made where the forbidding nature of the land had preserved the richness of primitive tradition. With the depression at an end and the Minister for the North-West[22] in support of their plans, there seemed reason to hope for a new era of missionary inspiration in the north. Even the declaration of war, disturbing though it was to the German religious, seemed hardly likely to affect their work. But as a precaution Bishop Raible, on hearing the news over the Rockhole Station radio, wrote to Archbishop Prendiville requesting that he act as their protector should the necessity arise. 'Rev. Father Albert Scherzinger and myself are naturalized British subjects,' he wrote, 'but nevertheless it may be necessary to have somebody in a high position to hold a protecting hand over our work.'[23]

The Archbishop replied assuring his support at all times and advising that the German missionaries avoid all foreign correspondence. He also suggested that their letters within Australia be written in English 'because of the necessity of avoiding the limelight'.[24] To this the bishop replied in unruffled agreement: 'The only thing we want is to go quietly on with our work as we have done for the last thirty-nine years. We are not interested in politics in any shape or form.'[25]

# CHAPTER TWENTY-SIX

## 1939 – 1945

'THANKS be to God, so far the position is not dangerous to our work or to ourselves,' ran the mission chronicle when news of the outbreak of war reached Beagle Bay. After all, the 1914–18 war, despite its many sorrows and tribulations, had brought out the best qualities in the mission people. The threat from without had served to consolidate the spirit within and there seemed no reason why it should not be the same again.

As it happened, the threat during the ensuing years was to come not only from without but also from within, although over the period of the so-called 'phoney war' everything continued normally enough. Cattle and garden produce were still marketed and the German missionaries, apart from being fingerprinted and required to fill in alien registration forms, were left alone. Professor Nekes returned from Melbourne to continue his work on the languages of the Dampierland tribes and Bishop Raible embarked on plans for the proper celebration of the mission's Golden Jubilee in June 1940.

A usual prelude to major setbacks in the mission's chequered history was the fact that prospects seemed particularly bright. The depression had lifted, stock prices had picked up and the panic over the spread of leprosy had subsided as control measures had improved. Mr. Neville, after a long, hard and by no means one-sided battle for authority, had retired, and Beagle Bay had come out on the right side of a heated dispute concerning the treatment of natives on missions throughout the State.

This argument arose from the gazetting, in 1938, of a number of additional regulations, including a clause to the effect that all missionaries must qualify for licences from the Department, of which the married state was one requisite – a move that had been strongly attacked by church authorities of various denominations as an unwarranted interference with religious freedom. Parliamentary Chief Secretary W. H. Kitson, had received from the Aborigines Department, in answer to his inquiries, allegations against the missions the like of which had never been levelled at pastoral employers of native labour even by their severest critics. In justification of the campaign for stricter control, departmental officers accused missionaries not only of sexual licence and perversion but of the flogging, shooting and solitary confinement of natives, of enforced marriages, curtailment of freedom and lack of medical care. The story made headlines at home and abroad, *The West Australian* lamenting that:

> At a time when decent Britons are seething with indignation over German treatment of the Jews it is humiliating that in W.A., at institutions which are supposed to be looking after the natives' spiritual and physical welfare such things . . . have been alleged. . . .

Leading churchmen throughout the State rose in defence of their own establishments and demanded an investigation. Bishop Raible wrote to Archbishop Prendiville in Perth[1] requesting that Mr. Kitson be asked publicly to declare his missions free from implication in the shocking allegations that had besmirched the reputation of all missionary work within the State. Old grievances against official antagonism were at the same time brought to light, attention being called to correspondence showing the department's consistent lack of co-operation or goodwill and the high-handed way in which individuals had been moved about at the will of the chief protector. What was now required, the bishop declared, was a proper investigation into the separate rights of Church and State.[2] Members of Parliament expressed varying degrees of concern and indignation, one, in an attempt at moderation, exemplifying the old guard attitude that had prevailed since the middle of the last century:

We must not forget [he said] that the Australian native is of an extremely low type. To suggest that he is not is futile. He cannot be treated like a whiteman . . . in spite of the fact that they live in dirt and squalor and inbreed and have intercourse with whites, they always appear to be happy and laughing and apparently in good health. . . . I cannot help thinking that it is not in their nature to be unhappy at all. . . . Eating, smoking, etc. represent the apex of their emotions. However, as Christians, as I suppose we all are, we must care for these natives, whose country we have taken. . . .[8]

Why, it was asked, if such allegations were true, had the matter not been properly aired during the recent Royal Commission? The answer to this pertinent question was that the instances quoted had occurred on the isolated establishments of one or two minor sects and that those responsible for misconduct had been summarily dealt with some years before the date of the commission. This was not to say that such things could not occur again and that constant vigilance was unnecessary, but the case was weakened by the fact that similar abuses were found to be currently prevalent on the government-run stations and reserves such as it was the department's aim to substitute for religious institutions.

In the meantime Bishop Raible had established his position in the community and become a familiar and well respected figure throughout his diocese. His friendly interest in the people of the country, his sympathy with local problems, his musical gifts and droll humour had made him a welcome guest on his annual visits to the scattered station homesteads.[4] His repertoire of stories, many of these against himself, included one concerning his first trip outback when he inquired of a team of drovers (in an accent that later became more acclimatized) whether there were any Catholics in that area. The man in charge, mistaking the casually dressed cleric for a stock inspector, nodded dolefully.

'Thousands of them,' he said. 'Anyone who says cattle tick is no longer a problem in this country is a b— liar!'

The aspect of his work that gave him the greatest pleasure was his establishment, some years before, of a novitiate at Beagle Bay for seven or eight part-Aboriginal girls who had shown a desire to enter the religious life. It had always been his dearest wish to see the formation of an indigenous missionary community equipped to help their own people and to fill the thinning ranks of the Pallottines and the pioneer nuns, and as the mission's jubilee drew near plans were made for the official reception of the four who had persevered.

Mounting tension after the fall of Paris to the Nazis may have accounted for the fact that so few of the general public turned up for the special day of festivities arranged for them. The clergy, however, responded warmly to the invitation to see what had been achieved in fifty years of missionary endeavour in the remote Kimberleys. No less than eight members of the hierarchy, including the Apostolic Delegate and the Archbishop of Perth, arrived with their retinues and expressed delight at the mission that had grown up in the face of prevailing poverty, recurrent disaster, public indifference and often damaging prejudice and indeed that it had succeeded even so far in equipping primitive nomads and outcast part-Aborigines to take their place in the new economy was a far greater achievement than met the eye.

The highlight of the celebrations was the reception of the first four postulants to the native sisterhood that had been the long cherished dream of their Vicar-Apostolic. Archbishop Prendiville of Perth referred to these girls of the Queen of Apostles novitiate as 'the most notable fruit of fifty years' hard work'. Nor did he exaggerate, for whether or not they could live up to their ideal it was undoubtedly remarkable that any young people of that turbulent peninsula should have aspired to the difficult and disciplined life of religious service. Their dedication on this day was a reminder of the many children of part-native blood, some saved from death by the Trappist monks, others from prostitution in native camps throughout the Kimberleys and given into the care of nuns. A number of these, since grown to womanhood, married and rearing healthy families, had come from as far afield as Carnarvon, Port Hedland and Derby to join in what was described in the mission journal as 'a splendid resurgence of hope and gratitude'.

The war continued to seem of little relevance to mission life until October of that year, when police arrived at Beagle Bay with a warrant for the arrest of all non-naturalized German priests and brothers. A brief entry in the Beagle Bay journal bespeaks the shock and dismay of the community:

> Days of disaster for the mission ... all are to leave except old Brother Mathias Wollseifer ... practically that the station is destituted of its whole staff of missionaries, so that unless other priests and lay brothers come to its immediate aid not only great damage will be caused but the mission is gravely endangered. ... The sergeant and two policemen have come to take us off and another has gone to get Father John Herold from Lombadina.[5]

A last Mass said, the people exhorted to faithfulness and endurance, the six Pallottine priests and seven brothers were escorted to Broome. News that they were being held in the local jail pending their removal to internment camps in the south caused a sensation in the port. Japan had not yet entered the war and residents, having then little thought of invasion or possible German intrigue, reacted with helpful sympathy. Comfortable bedding, special food and other amenities brought to the prison not only contributed to the wellbeing of the distressed religious but relieved the embarrassment of their jailers. The response of the white residents, however, was considerably quieter than that of the coloured

297

people who flocked to the prison loudly protesting their sorrow, indignation and bewilderment and bringing a touching miscellany of gifts and tokens.

Bishop Raible, who, as a naturalized Australian citizen, was not arrested with the others, wrote and telegraphed in all directions, and friends, including the Apostolic Delegate, Archbishop Prendiville of Perth, Archbishop Mannix of Melbourne, the Very Reverend Father P. F. Lyons, Administrator of St. Patrick's Cathedral, Melbourne, and the Minister for the North-West rallied to their defence. Only Fathers John Herold, Leo Hornung and George Vill, being the most recent arrivals from Germany, were held in Broome and later sent to serve in Melbourne parishes for the duration. The rest, after ten days' detention, were allowed to return with the bishop to Beagle Bay. The mission chronicle, broken with the arrest of the religious, was resumed to record their jubilant homecoming: 'The excitement and joy of the sisters and people was beyond description. They tore us nearly to pieces then all joined in singing a heartfelt *Te Deum*.'

News of Pearl Harbour and Japan's declaration of war at the close of the year brought immediate rumours of German missionary collaboration. 'Mysterious Lights' were reported to have been seen flashing from the beach at Lombadina and both Dampierland missions were rumoured to be equipped with elaborate transmitting apparatus capable of sending morse messages over a thousand-mile radius. A surprise search revealed nothing more sinister than two standard Traegar Flying Doctor transmitting sets, neither equipped for morse messages, but rumours persisted and grew in magnitude with the bitter realities of war. Bishop Raible met the threat to his Society with a forthright report denying in the first place that he or any other Pallottine had as was alleged opposed the enlistment of mission-educated half-castes in the Australian forces. Of this he wrote:

One needs to know the way in which tales are made up and how the blacks and half-castes answer to questions.

298

They have a certain sense by which they feel what answer is expected from them and they will give it. . . .

In September last I preached a sermon in Broome in accordance with the request of His Majesty the King for prayers for a just peace. In order to impress upon the people the urgency of this matter, I told them that in Broome we had no real experience of what war actually means. 'We read the papers, hear the wireless news and see our men training in the cricket grounds.' This was the sole reference to Broome in that sermon. After Mass was over, a half-caste woman, known to be highly hysterical . . . went to the police and told them that I had said that our half-caste boys should not go into training for military service. The police made inquiries among other churchgoers, who, of course, replied that I had made no such statement. . . . But . . . that lie has come to stay in Broome and I have heard it repeated in Darwin. . . .

One regrets to be obliged to state that a 'war mentality' has blinded a certain portion of our Broome people so that they cannot see facts which are obvious to any unbiassed observer.

The facts are these. In the past fifty years the mission has spent approximately £250,000 on buildings, maintenance, provisions etc., for the benefit of the natives. . . . By doing so the mission has saved the Government the same amount which it would have had to find for the maintenance of a native settlement. All that money has, therefore, remained in the pockets of the W.A. taxpayer. . . . All monetary help from Germany was used for the purchase of Australian goods. . . .

As far as a German invasion is concerned and the possibility of establishing a Nazi regime in Australia, I wish to say that, apart from the fact that this is very remote, the German missionaries in Kimberley have just as little desire to see this happening as any Australian-born citizen. Only people who are ignorant of Nazi ideology could credit such a strange accusation. . . . The missionaries in the Kimberleys are fully aware that their work is infinitely more safe under British control than it would be under Nazi regime. To surmise that German missionaries would hail the advent of Nazi rule is just as reasonable as to say that a man would cultivate a particular friendship with his own executioner. . . . It is true that they love their country for what it has been and more for what it could be . . . but they feel no affection for Germany in her present state. . . .

We have no reason to look forward with anything but apprehension to an attack by Japan or any other power at war with Britain. The Japanese are in any case generally hostile to 'foreign missions'. . . . But if this danger is so imminent, why concentrate exclusively on potential 'fifth columnists' among a handful of German missionaries while a potential 'first column' in the form of dozens of Japanese divers is and has been exploring the waters along the north west coast for many years. These divers are employed and paid by the very same people who are dismayed that a few harmless Germans are still at large.

. . . In every country where a clash between European culture and native culture is experienced the role of the missionary is made exceedingly difficult. . . . In many cases he stands in the way where unscrupulous exploitation and immorality want a free hand. . . . The opposing attitudes of the missionary and the trader to the black and half-caste population inevitably create an unsatisfactory situation.

Since all the causes of friction must be accentuated by war . . . I would renew the suggestion made previously that for the duration . . . the Government should appoint a public official to reside permanently at Beagle Bay Mission as during the previous war. . . . His responsibility would be to watch the actions of the missionaries, thereby safeguarding us from malicious rumours. It would enable us to continue our work for the natives without further interruption and at the same time make sure that nothing in the way of subversive activities could possibly be undertaken. . . .

I cannot bring myself to believe that the British sense

of justice would fail these men who are sacrificing their lives in the cause of native improvement and do so gladly without asking any earthly reward.[6]

Archbishop Prendiville, the staunch friend who had defended and encouraged the missionaries through many vicissitudes, who had provided legal advice and guaranteed money for their enterprise in central Kimberley, now used his tactful influence with State and military authorities on their behalf. A police officer (an institution that had been dropped during the 1920s) was re-established at Beagle Bay and the missionaries were granted permission to remain. The removal of a possible 'fifth column' from the pearling industry was, however, rendered unnecessary by the Japanese themselves who, on hearing of their country's entry into the war, had gone at once to the Broome police station and sadly given themselves up. Broome was soon afterwards declared a military base and all luggers requisitioned for defence.

But it was not until the fall of Singapore in January 1942, that the people of the north were fully alerted to the danger of invasion. In 1941 the war still seemed so far away that the nuns had opened an institution in the port for the children of native mothers by indentured Asiatics or drifting unemployed whites of the depressed decade – neglected waifs whose numbers had outgrown the capacity of the convent where they had been cared for previously.

The bright little orphanage was the culmination of many years of hard work and careful budgeting and when orders were issued early in 1942 for the evacuation of all white women in the north, the nuns were understandably reluctant to abandon it. They refused to be panicked about the possibility of Japanese invasion, for their estimate of that race was based on the representatives whom they had long counted as among their most loved and loyal friends. They at last gained permission to remain pending further developments but after the Japanese air raid on Darwin in February they were again ordered to leave.

The nuns at the Derby leprosarium, appalled at the

prospect of abandoning their helpless patients, sat tight and played for time. Some of the sisters in Broome had already gone to Beagle Bay with the orphanage children when the order came for them to return, bringing all the half-caste girls who were to be flown with them and the rest of the nuns to Perth.

Meanwhile Mother Mary Margaret Carmody, one of the pioneer band, who was then superior of the Kimberley community, had been effectively pulling strings from Broome. Her Irish wit and charm won her case with the authorities and she and her sisters were permitted to remain at their own risk. Those still in Broome, however, were firmly ordered to Beagle Bay and advised to take with them their bank savings and as many belongings as possible. The mother superior, out of the world since leaving County Cork in 1906, when asked how she would like her money, disconcerted the harassed stand-in banker by replying, 'In gold, please.'

She and her few remaining helpers were still packing up when, on the morning of 3rd March, ten Japanese bombers swooped on Broome from a clear sky. Military planes assembled on the airstrip went up in a blaze of machine-gun fire. Twelve flying boats packed with Dutch refugees from Java, awaiting take-off on Roebuck Bay, also provided a sitting target and those who endeavoured to escape from the blazing planes were burned by escaping fuel set alight by incendiary bullets. When the enemy aircraft dispersed, the survivors were brought ashore and some seventy bodies recovered and buried in the pioneer cemetery on the waterfront.[7] Pallottine Father Albert Scherzinger read the burial service and the nuns gave what help they could to the wounded refugees before the departure of the latter by plane for Perth. Shocked and grieved by the sufferings of the helpless victims of the raid, the nuns could only conclude that the Japanese had mistaken the flying boats for military planes, nor did they fail to point out that the convent, church and orphanage were among the few buildings to escape machine-gun fire.

302

Four days later a native brought word to Beagle Bay that a Dutch plane, shot down by the Japanese fighters when on their way to attack Broome, had made a forced landing on the beach near Carnot Bay. Mule carts were at once dispatched to pick up the survivors but two of the crew who had gone in search of help had in the meantime encountered some natives and been escorted to the mission. Cruelly sunburnt and weak with hunger and privation they told how their Douglas DC3 aircraft, piloted by Captain Ivan Smirnoff, one of the great pioneer fliers of K.L.M. Airlines, had left Bandoeng with eleven passengers, including a woman and child. The pilot, who with three other occupants of the plane had been wounded by Japanese machine-guns within sixty miles of Broome, managed a perfect pancake landing on the beach with the machine nose-on into the surf to extinguish the flames from the engine. A second attack had wounded a fourth passenger and in the following days the woman, her baby and two of the injured men died as a result of their injuries and were buried on the beach. The remaining eight had managed to survive by distilling sea water in empty tins, until help arrived.

In a biography of Ivan Smirnoff,[*] published after his death in 1956, the story is told of how, after being located by the native scout, they had been brought to the mission by Warrant Officer F. G. Clinch of the Australian Intelligence Corps and Brother Richard Besenfelder.

The missionaries were Germans who had been working among the Aborigines for years. . . . Their mission was in charge of the Rev. Father Francis Huegel, and he and Brother Richard and a motherly woman, Sister Alphonsus, did all they could for the wanderers. . . .

When sufficiently recuperated they bade a grateful good-bye to the missionaries and set off by truck for Broome. Strange, he reflected, jogging along the track which nobody but the driver recognized as a road, he had counted Germans his enemies in two world wars. Yet here he was, rescued alive because Germans had established a charitable mission and taught the savages to do good.

It made the senselessness of war more apparent than ever. And what was the matter with the Germans that they worshipped a man like Hitler, when they had men like Father Francis and Brother Richard to follow?[9]

A cryptic entry, made by Father Francis in the mission journal, reminded us that there was more to the story of the wrecked aircraft than had yet been told.

April 8. A director of the firm of the lost Dutch plane came from Sydney to inspect once more the wreck. It seems he was not so much looking at the condition of the plane but rather the lost treasure it was carrying, valued at £2,000,000.

The 'treasure' referred to was a box full of diamonds (the actual value being probably nearer £500,000 than £2,000,000) salvaged from the Dutch bank in Java, that had been thrust into Captain Smirnoff's hands by a bank official as his plane was about to leave Bandoeng, with the brief information that it would be collected at the other end. He had no idea what the package contained and in the anxious days that followed his forced landing at Carnot Bay he had not given it another thought. A search of the beach had later brought to light the empty package and soon afterwards a beachcomber came up with a few diamonds which he said he had found in the sand around the wreck. When natives began proffering diamonds in payment for articles in Broome shops the story got about that the beachcomber had actually pocketed all the diamonds but had later got drunk and distributed them around, like sweets in a paper bag, to his Aboriginal friends. Charged and tried for theft, he was acquitted on the grounds that he had after all done nothing more reprehensible than pick up something he had found.

What became of the rest of the diamonds is likely to remain a mystery, but a Broome Aboriginal later confessed that a few had come his way as a gift from his tribal father-in-law. Evacuated shortly afterwards to Beagle Bay, with all other natives in the Broome area, he claims to have secretly buried his treasure in a secluded corner of the mission but that on returning to dig them up at the end of the war he found they had been replaced by a few common pebbles. He is still wondering whether someone discovered his hiding place, or whether the substitution was a cautionary miracle![10]

Old Thomas Puertollano, who had been evacuated from Broome with the rest of the coloured population, died two weeks after the Japanese raid. After leaving Lombadina in 1918 he had started a bakery business in Broome where he and his wife Agnes had been both respected and loved. His last years, however, had been overshadowed with tragedy, for of his large and promising family only he and his eldest son escaped the curse of leprosy. The sorrowing community was gathered around his open grave when Japanese fighters roaring overhead for a second attack on Broome brought home the still imminent threat of invasion.

In any event, it seemed that the death of the fine old Manilaman who had been so much a part of local history might well mark the end of life as the mission people remembered it. The peaceful, family atmosphere of Beagle Bay had been shattered by the arrival of over two hundred and fifty outside evacuees, many of whom gambled or otherwise idled their time away in open defiance of authority and scorn of those who respected it. Under the circumstances it was difficult to convince the people that the old slogan of 'no work, no pay' still held good. The sudden doubling of the normal mission population made severe inroads on the cattle and as the morale of the people declined and one after another of the fine old pioneer brothers died under the strain, the garden again deteriorated and buildings fell into disrepair.

Just as in the previous war bitterness mounted as hostilities progressed, and rumours spread that the government intended removing the German priests and brothers and closing their establishments for good and all. Bishop Raible, his beard now white on his chest, was no longer able to hide his anxiety, but in September 1942 his negotiations for the preservation of the missions resulted in the arrival of three chaplains of the Australian Missionary Society of the Sacred Heart to be stationed at Broome, Lombadina and Beagle Bay. In the words of the mission journal: 'Their main interest is to save us from further machinations of our enemies who under pretext of patriotism try to harm and even abolish the missions.'

The bishop's greatest hope for the future lay in the perseverence of the native sisters, now six in number, who, under the guidance of a devoted mistress of novices, had stood up to the cynicism of the worldly and the blandishments of the weak. It had begun to seem possible that they might soon assist with the development of the primitive tribespeople at the struggling desert mission, which project was causing his Lordship deep concern. After sinking bore after bore the first two sites selected had been abandoned for lack of water, and in 1943 a new site was chosen in an area known as Balgo Hills. This seemed more promising but wartime restrictions made progress impossible. Firearms and ammunition having been forbidden them they were unable to eke out their meagre rations by shooting wild game or kangaroos, but what they found hardest of all was the refusal of suspicious neighbours to sell them beef at any price, and the sabotage of their stockyards and shelters.

Tormented as they were by flies and other pests, in a temperature often over 115 degrees, rationed to two cups of water each a day, their situation would have seemed hopeless indeed but for the attitude of the Aborigines themselves who, as in the early days on Dampierland, bestowed on the religious their sympathetic if erratic patronage. Occasionally a headman would wander in with the gift of a lizard, a snake or a kangaroo. He would introduce a bashful wife, indicate but not press her availability, push forward a timid but fascinated child. The only ones who remained for any length of time, however, were a few old people who were only too glad to find a place where they could sit down quietly and be fed. Though these were long past any possibility of conversion, Superintendent Father Alphonsus Bleischwitz bore patiently with their querulous complaints and endless impositions in the hope of baptizing them before death. But even this satisfaction was denied him for one wet season they went off to attend a tribal ceremony, caught influenza from a group of station Aborigines, and 'died like beasts in the field'.[11] 'God knows why these things happen,' his successor wrote when relating the incident. 'He does not ask us to have success. He only asks us to go out and work for Him.'[12]

In spite of having toiled 'in great sorrows'[13] Father Alphonsus was able to record at the end of the war that he felt their labours to have been already blessed.

# CHAPTER TWENTY-SEVEN

## 1946 – 1953

POSTWAR reconstruction was to mean more this time than memorials to the heroic dead and a resumption of normal life from where it had been interrupted by the call to arms. The white race, no longer confident of its ascendancy, looked at the backward peoples of the world with a new humility, and at the Declaration of Human Rights as something more than a talking point.

In Australia the whiteman, embarrassed for the first time about how his Aboriginal situation appeared from the outside, wondered not so much why the black man had failed to progress and integrate as where he had been failed. Many would, for one reason and another, continue to oppose citizen rights for the indigenous people, but the reformer was no longer a voice crying in the wilderness. The man who talked of standard education, improved living conditions and a regular wage scale for Aboriginal workers was no longer a 'crank'.

The suggestion had been made by Chief Protector F. I. Bray, who succeeded Neville in 1940, that all half-castes be given the right to vote subject to a certificate from a magistrate that they were intelligent and had severed all tribal connections. Despite an objection from the Member for the North-West on the grounds that controversial legislation should be shelved for the duration, a Bill[1] to this effect, hailed as 'a most modern piece' of legislation, went through with little opposition in 1944. It turned out to be, in many respects, a modern piece of impracticability but it marked the beginning of the end for restrictive Aboriginal legislation.

The change in outlook can be clearly seen by comparing the 1935 report of Magistrate H. D. Moseley with that of Magistrate F. E. A. Bateman of 1948. Moseley's statement that: 'With the exception of improved medical services there is little, I think, of importance which should be done to better the condition of the Kimberley natives'[2] was received with much the same general agreement as Bateman's conservative enough opinion of only twelve years later that:

The fact that the Kimberley native still has no idea of the value of money is really an indictment against ourselves. . . . It is obvious that unless some steps are taken to educate these people not only in money values but in other matters also then assuming that they do not die out in the meantime, the state of affairs which exists today will be exactly the same in fifty years' time. A start must be made in the advancement of these northern natives and the sooner the better. . . . It may well be that before the process has been completed the full-blood may be extinct, on the other hand the adoption of different methods in their treatment and training may arrest the present decline in the race, but in any event there can be no justification for a policy which allows them to drift into extinction without any serious attempt to uplift them. . . .[3]

Whereas Moseley gathered bad reports of missions and mission-educated natives, Bateman expressed surprise that he heard so little against them of any account. He considered that a mission native seeking station work was justified in objecting to squalid camp conditions he had been taught to shun, and he thought it only just that missions complying with government policy should be provided with all necessary facilities.

Living standards that Moseley had considered adequate for station Aborigines, Bateman deplored and thought contributory to the high incidence of disease. He anticipated the many problems that would attend the introduction of wages to native employees and suggested that the transit.on period begin with small credit payments, the people meanwhile being fed and clothed as before: 'Surely this is not too much to ask for a race of people upon whom the pastoral industry is entirely dependent.[4]

That the Kimberley pastoralists were by this time ready enough to embark on a change of policy was due partly to an improvement in their financial position, partly also to an increasing awareness that conditions hitherto defended as suitable to the circumstances were a threat to the health of the entire community. But perhaps an even stronger incentive was the apprehension caused by an obscure bush worker named Don McLeod under whose hypnotic influence six hundred Aborigines had struck for wages on sheep stations in the neighbouring Pilbarra district in 1946.[5]

For the north-west wool growers this had meant little more than a temporary dislocation of station work, and many of those whose natives did not return soon found that they could get on well enough without them. For McLeod's followers it meant the exchange of secure employment, with pocket money and keep for themselves and their dependants, for a precarious co-operative mining venture at a subsistence level such as few of them had known before. It gave them, on the other hand, a new concept of collective effort, a future to strive for and the determination that their children should have the education that they themselves had lacked the confidence and initiative to seek. In the early stages of the co-operative, the children were taught by a young half-caste – the only literate member of the group besides McLeod – who had rejected the 'opium of the people' by which he had become convinced that the 'tools of capitalist imperialism' at Beagle Bay mission had contrived to enslave his mother's race.

The fact that McLeod's scheme represented for a while a rallying point for communism within the State was, as he came himself to realize, no help to it. Like most innovators, he was to see the failure or perversion of his fondest hopes. His dream was to elude him and his proselytes to fail him but he had stirred a pot that had for too long stagnated. Fear of his influence penetrating to cattle stations in the Kimberleys, where a walk-out of Aboriginal workers would have caused far more serious disruption than on the north-west sheep properties, accelerated changes that had been overdue for half a century.

At a meeting of Kimberley pastoralists held in July 1950 agreement was reached on a standard payment of £1 a month for native stockmen. It was put on record, however, that the pressure groups agitating for this decision were 'for the most part entirely misinformed' and that the pastoralists themselves were still of the opinion that the existing system of payment in kind was the best suited for the natives' needs.[6]

Mr. S. G. Middleton, appointed Commissioner for Native Welfare in 1948, entered the field at a much more auspicious time than any previous protector-in-chief and was to prove the most progressive influence so far to occupy that position. Mr. Neville, although a thorn in the side of all missionaries except a few of the more amenable, had worked hard for what he considered to be in the best interests of his wards and between 1932 and 1940, the year of his death, had doubled the expenditure of his department on their behalf. His cherished assimilation plan, however, though an honest attempt to avoid the growth of an apartheid situation, was obstructed by what he saw as an unreasonable lack of co-operation and by what most others, including the natives themselves, thought its sheer absurdity. The 'special schools' that were to have upgraded the education of the mixed-blood people would first have had to condition their pupils not only to avoid their darker relatives but their own opposite numbers. Even had this been possible and had most of the girls been able to find white mates, it meant that the majority of coloured men were virtually condemned to a life of celibacy. In fact, short of resorting to methods that only a Hitler would have considered, the proposition was totally unrealistic.

Neville's successor, F. I. Bray, though a less formidable

opponent to missionary activity, had no more faith in its efficacy. His main objective was to upgrade the status of half- and quarter-castes but, restricted by wartime conditions, he seldom left his office in Perth.

Mr. Middleton, who had gained experience in native administration in Papua-New Guinea, although a man of strong democratic principles had a humbler attitude to his task than the two former chief protectors. Less dogmatic, none too proud to admit mistakes, he was prepared to listen to every point of view before formulating a regulation, but where native rights were concerned he took a firm stand from the beginning. He told a convention of State and Commonwealth Ministers in Canberra in 1951 that the time had come to repeal all legislation discriminatory to Aborigines and although the conference was a failure in this regard he returned more than ever determined to work towards this end.

Using to effect his journalistic training, he launched an unrelenting campaign for Aboriginal rights to social service allowances and civic privileges, tackled the knotty problem of native housing and assisted the introduction of the wage system for station workers. He cast a cold eye over his legacy of disgracefully run government settlements and reserves and reversed the view of his immediate predecessor that missions were of no benefit to the natives. In short, he considered it better that welfare institutions should be run by dedicated altruists, even if lacking in formal qualifications, than by the succession of too often self-seeking civil servants who had brought the government establishments into public disrepute. 'I regard missions,' he said, 'as being valuable and important administrative adjuncts to this department and missionaries as being vitally necessary to the welfare of the native race.'[7] He also noted that the success of religious institutions in Papua-New Guinea had been due not only to better conditions for land cultivation but to the generous support of the Australian public that had so little regard for its own Aborigines.

The commissioner's struggle for social service allowances, grants-in-aid and an increased welfare subsidy soon raised the general living standard for natives throughout the State, including those employed in the pastoral industry. This was indeed an important turning point but not, as was soon to be seen, an unqualified success.

In an effort to provide incentive to improvement, missions were graded into three classes according to the standards of living and education provided, the weekly child subsidy varying accordingly from 12s 6d to 9s. An 'A' grade subsidy required modern ablution and sanitary arrangements, contemporary State school standards of education, farm workshops, technical training and recreational facilities, including a gymnasium.

None of the Pallottine, or any other Kimberley missions at that time, qualified for this award. Owing to chronic lack of finance and acute shortage of labour and materials during the war years, both Dampierland establishments were in poor shape and the desert mission still entirely primitive. The bishop's visit to Limburg to procure new recruits soon after the armistice had been a sadly disappointing one. Most of the older priests and brothers at the motherhouse had died of hunger and cold during the war. All the novices had been conscripted and many had been killed or dispersed to Russian territory. He returned to Kimberley with only two brothers to replace the many who had died there in missionary service and a few who, disillusioned by the natives' increasing tendency to take for granted the duty of the religious to work for them, had gone back to secular life.

Few of the nuns were trained teachers and indeed up to this time they had been given little enough encouragement in schooling the natives at all. The technical training that had once been the pride of Beagle Bay had languished, not only for lack of staff but because the natives had so little chance, in a stagnant economic situation, of being employed as tradesmen.

Kimberley missionaries of various denominations saw the system of grading as both unrealistic and unjust, for it was

313

obvious that establishments nearer the urban areas had a greater chance of achieving the required standards than those more remotely situated. The scheme, in effect, provided the greatest assistance and encouragement to those in the least urgent need.

When brought to see the validity of their argument, the commissioner with typical fair-mindedness introduced a more equitable plan whereby the subsidy provided for all adult natives was 10s and for children 22s 6d weekly, together with the provision of blankets and clothing.

But missionaries and departmental officials were uneasy allies at the best of times. Where previously the begrudging issue of government subsidies and the deliberate lack of interest had, for reasons of self-preservation, justified the mission's equally determined lack of co-operation with the department it was now more difficult to uphold an independent stand. The principal point of dissension however, namely that of authority over the natives, was if anything accentuated. The modern trend towards encouraging the people in the management of their own affairs often led to complications in which the natives, past masters as they were at playing parties off against each other, would seek help from both missionaries and local welfare officers (an innovation of the new regime), sometimes complaining to each side of the other's injustice or misunderstanding. Government officers saw it as their duty, in the new era of equal rights, to maintain constant vigilance for any suggestion of unfair pressure of a sectarian or self-interested nature and they sometimes gave a decision that the missionaries, from close association with background facts involving several generations of family ties, obligations and vendettas, saw as leading inevitably to further trouble. There were times, indeed, when the sudden quickening of social conscience, political interest and departmental zeal in native affairs caused those long dedicated to a forlorn cause to wonder whether they had not been better off in the bad old days when they had struggled along largely on their own resources and initiative. As things now stood, for what they

314

had gained in financial security they had lost in the control of their own affairs. Official inspections became increasingly frequent and exacting, demands for complete and regular reports more insistent, but most irksome of all was the insinuation of the department, backed by the Bateman report, that the missions were lacking in policy. This was no more or less true of the missions than of the department itself but a clear sense of direction was hardly to be expected of either in what was now, in many respects, a completely new situation.

# CHAPTER TWENTY-EIGHT

## 1954–1959

QUITE suddenly the problem could no longer be seen as one of a disappearing primitive race and an insignificant part-Aboriginal minority. It was now clear that the latter were multiplying out of all proportion to the white and perpetuating their dark strain and gypsy ways by breeding among themselves while the death wish of the displaced full-bloods had apparently vanished overnight. Babies were being born in station camps that had not known an Aboriginal child in twenty years and every woman of child-bearing age in and around the ports and towns had a baby in her arms. After all the weighty dissertations on the reasons for sterility and the common practice of abortion and infanticide, had the remedy been as simple as the bestowal of social service benefits with no strings attached? Or had their advent coincided with the moment in history when the people, for so long stunned from the impact of civilization, regained their racial consciousness? Had the torpor of several generations provided the breather for a fresh start, a renewal of interest in life and a belief in their power to adapt to what had previously seemed a totally incompatible culture?

Whatever the answer, the sudden, welcome beneficence soon brought on a crop of new and complex difficulties. To a people used to living from day to day, with no social status to keep up or conception of money as providing a means to an end, this weekly government gratuity was literally money for jam. It was also money for grog, ice-creams, confectionery, taxi rides and any pieces of merchandise that might attract the passing fancy. It meant an end to the old rule of 'no work, no tucker' and enticed increasing numbers of Aborigines to the ports and towns. The diet of natives under white supervision on stations and missions undoubtedly improved as a result of the benefit allowances, but children in the growing outskirt camps, indulged with sweets, ice-creams and soft drinks, suffered more from malnutrition than ever before.

There was now some inhibition about the use of the word 'assimilation', which savoured too much for contemporary sociologists of enforced cultural change. The term 'integration', as suggesting a more enlightened acceptance of racial identity, perhaps even the possibility of a less one-sided merging of cultures, was thought preferable, but the difference was mainly theoretical. Whether desirable or not the one-way process of assimilation was as irreversible as that going on among the indigenous people of America, New Zealand and Papua.[1] There was much we might, but little we were likely to learn from the Aborigines, except perhaps a somewhat better understanding of ourselves.

Every innovation seen as just and progressive was fraught with similar contradictions. Now that the terms 'exploitation' and 'neglect' were no longer applicable to either individuals or government, the popular word of opprobrium had become 'paternalism'. The increasing number of outsiders demanding complete freedom of choice and action for the Aborigines did not, however, always appreciate the anxious dilemma of the authorities, while many had no experience whatever of the outlook and character of the people they sought to befriend. The granting of full Aboriginal franchise, now a popular cause in Australian cities, seemed to those in closer touch with the realities of the situation, including some of the native people themselves, to be too precipitous a step. There were still too few capable of understanding the responsibilities of citizenship status, even fewer of managing their own affairs, and it was feared that legal access to alcohol, already easily enough obtained and often abused, might prove disastrous. Some, including Catholic missionaries, also opposed the measure at this stage in a somewhat exaggerated fear of communist influence and its power to exploit the native vote.

The prudent-seeming policy of a graded and gradual bestowal of rights was, however, resented more by the native people than had been their denial to the race as a whole. A sense of responsibility was not necessarily graded to colour and that quarter-castes enjoy a status superior to that of their often more deserving darker relatives led to no end of trouble. Bitter indeed were the complaints of husbands forced to remain outside while their wives, with the blessing of the law, breasted a hotel bar. Almost equally unpopular was the granting of rights on application to any Aborigines who conformed to the required standards, a concession that many of the prouder and more self-respecting native people considered to be their birthright and refused to accept.

It was an era of troubled social experiment in which, although it was at last generally acceded that the Aborigines must be educated, no one could say to what end. Despite boom prices for wool, cattle and pearl shell, outlets for native employment were if anything more restricted than ever. Some Aborigines had served in the forces; others had filled positions vacated by white service recruits throughout the back country. A number of half-and quarter-castes and a few full-bloods had become head stockmen, boss drovers, truck drivers, even caretaker station managers and storekeepers, and had done extremely well. One white drover[2] who helped keep the supply lines open by taking cattle from the Kimberleys and the Territory into Queensland and Central Australia employed what he described as the most trouble-free team in his experience, consisting of five Beagle Bay boys who left him only after the war when he gave up droving for station management.

But as the white workers drifted back to the north the majority of their coloured backstops sank again into obscurity. Those born and bred in Dampierland had hoped to see a change of the old order in which they had played second fiddle to indentured Asiatics, not only in their parent industry, but in competition for their women. The Broome-born, strongly attached to their polyglot town, had helped with real enthusiasm to adjust the ravages of army occupation. Derelict buildings were put to rights, roads, neglected for the duration, repaired, mountains of rusting junk cleared from among the rank grass and weeds of vacant blocks, a litter of tangled aircraft gathered from the sea front and the surrounding marsh, the encroaching scrub pushed back.

When the pearlers returned to salvage their property and replace the fleet that lay in ruins around the beaches of the peninsula, something of the old atmosphere crept back, but wartime establishments – a meat works, a meteorological station and a civil aviation centre – had come to stay. Seasonal workers and civil servants on three-year terms now confused the clear-cut strata laid down by the pearling aristocracy and it was obvious that Broome, for better or worse, would never be the same again. For the coloured people, alas, it was largely for the worse.

Immediately after the war some were taken on as divers and crew but for the most part only until indentured labour could be procured to replace them. Few, in truth, had much aptitude for diving under modern conditions and most, lacking the discipline of the Asiatic, grew restless over long periods at sea. Pearling was after all a business and it had been long since proved that Asiatics, particularly Japanese, who were permitted to return in 1954, were the most efficient tools for the job.

In the long run the drift of the mission people to the port, begun in the early '20s, had proved as unfortunate as Father Drostë had feared and far from breaking down segregation had done much to encourage it. The generation that had promised so well for the future of their race had produced town-bred children lacking in their parents' background and stamina and whose irresponsible behaviour served too often to widen the gap between the coloured people and any but the least desirable type of white. Most of the girls married their own men in time, but seldom before they had begotten children by short-term Asiatics and drifting whites – the so-called 'orphans' taken over by the nuns under circumstances in which it was almost impossible to prevent their going the same way.[8]

Hitherto those who had encouraged the local people to stick out for better jobs at award rates and dared to accuse the pearlers of neglecting the hybrid people their industry had brought into being had been accused, sometimes rightly, of communist affiliations. There were now, however, some newcomers to the town, who with no political axe to grind saw the situation as grossly unfair and made individual efforts to raise the social level and confidence of the people by the introduction of adult education lectures, sporting activities and youth clubs. These public-spirited citizens included a succession of young English doctors, imbued with the spirit of the welfare state, an occasional secular nurse, teacher, police or welfare officer, and, most forceful of all, the young Pallottine parish priest, Father Kevin McKelson, who was later to take over the new mission at La Grange. Their efforts were by no means abortive but they lacked the whole-hearted support of either the white or the coloured community. Many of the latter were as sceptical as the whites of the new enthusiasm for motivating them to seek a status they did not envy and jobs that did not exist, the girls especially seeing no reason why they should indulge in wholesome communal activities while there were white meat-workers and indentured Asiatics vying for their favours and only too willing to pay for them.

By and large the best type of full-blood Aborigines were now to be found on outback stations and on the more isolated missions where they had been subjected to the strongest 'paternalistic' influence. At Lombadina, where the people were mostly full-blood, secure on their own tribal territory and in many of their tribal traditions, the essential Aboriginal character remained, but at Beagle Bay the influence of the outsiders during the second world war had destroyed much of the people's traditionally affectionate and generous spirit. Both the religious and the older natives who had been the backbone of the mission were shocked and puzzled by behaviour that they could only explain as being a reflection of a world-wide juvenile trend. Actually it was due less to this than to a confusion, that had grown up in the disruption of the war years, between the personal and gratuitous services of the missionaries and the government social services that were now accepted as the right of black and white alike. The misunderstanding was a blow not only to missionaries and earnest social workers, but to the splendid principle of native law that imposed so strong a sense of reciprocal obligation that no verbal expression of thanks was necessary. This period was probably the first in the mission history where the reason given for his resignation by more than one missionary recruit was the selfishness and ingratitude of the people for whom he had been prepared to give his all.

Grieved by evidence of character deterioration in the settled areas, it is little wonder that the bishop saw in the simple desert nomads at the Balgo base his most promising material. The nuns had been so far unable to obtain the consent of their Mother General in Ireland to work at this mission but in 1947 it had been decided to try the metal of the five native sisters who had persevered into the seventh year of their religious life. They set out brave-heartedly into the wilderness, but for the first time without the backing of experienced nuns. Unused though they were to luxury, they found conditions harder than anything they had imagined. The little mud-brick houses on the stony plain were hot as ovens in the summer months, freezing cold in the mid-year winter when the bleak winds whistled across the gibber plains. But used as these young people were to the homely brightness of communal life, much worse than physical discomfort was the oppressive isolation and the eerie silence of the desert wilderness. The natives themselves, who would appear at the mission, spindly as their native vegetation, covered at best with no more than a ceremonial pattern of

321

down and ochre, reeking of dried blood, rancid kangaroo and lizard fat, were a shock to them. Such primitives had long since disappeared from Dampierland and these civilized, part-white girls whom the bishop had hoped to fire with zeal towards 'their own people' felt not the remotest affinity with them. Perhaps it was the very suggestion of such a relationship that drove them to seek reassurance in the company of the few lay helpers, white or coloured, who came their way. In any event, within fourteen months not even the folds of the religious habit could conceal the fact that earthly romance had, where most were concerned, proved stronger than the spiritual romanticism of the religious life. One or two said they were prepared to persevere but the truth could no longer be denied. The time and conditions had not been ripe or the young people yet strong and secure enough for the grand experiment by which the bishop had set such store. The little native sisterhood was quietly dissolved but none who had entered expressed regret for their years in religion. The time, they said, had been a satisfying and happy one and it had equipped them very well to establish stable homes and families.

Sister Alice Evans, a secular nurse, thereafter undertook and held this tough assignment until 1956 when the Mother General on a visit to Kimberley saw that Balgo, with a regular plane service, was less cut off than she had feared, and on the bishop's promise to build her sisters a comfortable convent and chapel, consented to their working in that field.

This was to give the precarious desert station a real chance of success for it was clear that every project the nuns undertook they infused with new hope and vigour. Their work at the leprosarium near Derby had been especially praised by Magistrate Bateman in his report of 1948. 'I cannot', he wrote, 'speak too highly of it. It would be impossible to express adequately the admiration one feels for the devoted and self-sacrificing nursing staff who uncomplainingly give their services without reward in the interests of the natives.'[4]

Leprosy, or Hansen's disease, was still, as it remains today, the greatest and most dreaded scourge of the north where its incidence still compares with the highest endemic areas in the world, but the nuns had reduced as far as was possible the physical and psychological horrors of the disease. The native lepers' fear of detection disappeared almost completely after the discovery in 1947 of a positive remedy, when patients were discharged to spread accounts of the once dreaded 'lep' as a centre of warm community spirit and high level entertainment provided by Mother Aphonsus's amazing therapeutic orchestra.

Kimberley people of all denominations had united in congratulation when, in 1955, the two splendid pioneer nurses, Mothers Gertrude Greene[5] and Alphonsus Daly, who began work there during the 1930s, were honoured by the Queen with the Order of the British Empire.

A project long cherished by Bishop Raible and Father Worms had been the foundation of a mission at La Grange Bay, 120 miles south of Broome. On the home ground of the Garajeri people, this was by tradition neutral territory for the many tribes that foregathered there to exchange songs and rituals, hold councils and ceremonies, and to conduct intertribal barter. The country, taken up for pastoral occupation in the '80s, had always been a problem to the landholder, for not only was the pasture inferior but the natives who insisted on congregating there also persisted in spearing sheep and cattle. In 1931 the focal meeting place of some 450 acres on the Ninety Mile Beach was gazetted as a native reserve and a government rationing station was then set up at the telegraph station that had operated there since 1889.

The tribal significance of the site had since been used to the advantage of unscrupulous whites and La Grange had become notorious for drinking, fighting and prostitution.[6] The swing of departmental policy from State-run institutions and hand-out depots favoured the Pallottine proposition to establish a mission on this site, and in 1954 Father Worms came from Melbourne to make the initial approach to the tribal elders. Assured of a sympathetic hearing from their esteemed Ibala they confided in him their concern for the younger generation that while quickly acquiring the worst habits of the whiteman showed increasingly little respect for the disciplines of the old law. They saw advantages in the establishment of a mission on their inter-tribal ground and in the following year, when Father Worms returned to his duties in Kew, Father Francis Huegel came to take charge.

Father Francis had little finance and for some time no assistance, but his twenty-five years of missionary experience in the Kimberleys and keen interest in tribal customs and languages soon won him the acceptance and respect of the elders. His gentle humour and great love of children attracted the younger people and when joined by the two secular nurses, Sister Evans (released from Balgo by the arrival of the nuns) and Sister Hough, he was able to provide a little school and hospital. When the mission was officially blessed and declared open by Bishop Raible in 1958, buildings made possible by a grant from the department had already begun to take shape.

But by this time the bishop's days as an active missionary were drawing to an end. His health had begun to fail and he knew that he must ask for a successor to take over the problems of his sprawling vicariate.[7] He realized too, that for all his efforts and all his dreams he was leaving a situation more complicated and difficult than the one he had found on his arrival nearly thirty years before.[8] Along with his 283,000 square-mile vicariate, the new bishop would inherit the outcome of past neglect and ignorance in a time of doubt and perilous experiment.

# EPILOGUE

## 1959 – 1967

SINCE the ensuing years have yet to assume the perspective of history it is possible only to present them in the merest summary and to release a few straws in the steadily rising but inevitably wayward winds of change.

Bishop Raible's policy of encouraging local Pallottines into administrative positions had suggested that his successor might be an Australian priest. The man chosen to replace him, however, was Father John Jobst, a tall, scholarly Bavarian, not yet in his forties, whose studies for the priesthood at the Pallottine motherhouse in Limburg had been interrupted by the outbreak of the war. Conscripted into the army, he had been wounded at the Stalingrad front and narrowly escaped deportation to Russian territory at the end of the war. He soon afterwards returned to the seminary, was ordained in 1948 and two years later came to Beagle Bay. Here he had acted as superintendent until posted to the house of studies of his Society in Victoria. In 1959, in the presence of his venerable predecessor, who returned soon afterwards to Germany, he was consecrated Titular Bishop of Titanae and Vicar-Apostolic of the Kimberleys.

When taking stock of his vicariate on an overland tour from Broome to Wyndham he had found that the long talked of 'potential of the north' was being tapped by schemes to control its prodigal rivers and that teams of experts were investigating everything from soil and stock deficiencies to the harnessing of tidal power and the 'seeding' of elusive rain clouds. The bright new township of

325

Kununurra had sprung up on the site of a diversion dam (pilot project for a larger catchment area) on the Ord River and farmers were moving in on irrigated 600-acre blocks with talk of cotton plantations and long awaited closer settlement.

Rough bush tracks and perilous river crossings were being replaced by sealed roads and cement causeways, tempting the ordinary tourist on routes that only the experienced or the venturesome had previously essayed. Cattle trucks had almost displaced the old-time drovers, and air transport had brought the 'never-never' within easy reach of the cities. Refrigeration had replaced the open meathouses, 'Coolgardie safes' and canvas water-bags; electric light banished the hurricane lantern and kerosene lamp; electric fans and sometimes air-conditioning tempered the tropical heat; fly wire frustrated man-hungry legions of insect life.

Pastoralists talked improvements where once they had talked ruin, though some, suspicious of a new regime and sceptical of sustained prosperity, were selling out at boom prices to a wave of neo-discoverers, mostly American.

The pearlers, as used to the ebb and flow of fortune as they were to their time-table tides, now saw that the advent of the plastic button had been no passing reverse. Pearl shell, once among the State's most lucrative industries was no longer a necessity but a luxury item on the world market and the demand was fast becoming limited to the top quality product. One by one the old style pearling masters were dropping out or going into the production of culture pearls.

There was little place for coloured workers in any of the current development schemes. Kimberley's irrigable land was after all of pocket handkerchief proportions to her whole area, and only selected families with a solid backing of capital and experience could gain entry to the Ord River farming blocks. The Aborigines were not, as has been seen, natural agriculturalists and there was as yet nothing to encourage their training to become land owners, or, in a time of increasing mechanization, even farm labourers.

Trade union and other factors had hitherto prevented all but a few from obtaining jobs in the meatworks at Wyndham and Broome. The few men now required in the pearling industry were still imported from Asia and the production of culture pearls required little other than highly specialized labour supplied by Japanese. Prospects for the development of new industries were hampered by the small and widely scattered nature of the population, water shortage, the high cost of transport and the lack of cheap power.

Kimberley's major industry seemed likely to remain, as before, the production of beef cattle on large leasehold properties, but here again the chances for Aboriginal employment were dwindling. The dependable, simple-hearted 'black fellows' who had been the backbone of the pastoral industry, identifying themselves closely with station work and the lives of their employers, were being replaced by a younger generation of wage earners who went 'walkabout' to the towns in trucks and utilities and were increasingly restless, demanding and unreliable.

As everywhere else in Australia, the material needs of the Aboriginals were now being considered as never before. On the majority of stations they had already exchanged their humpies of bags, boughs, scrap iron, and sanitary arrangements that were nobody's business but their own, for angle-iron houses attached to community ablution blocks equipped with showers, laundry facilities and septic systems. Child endowment and pensions provided them with previously unheard-of luxuries such as fruit, preserved milk, vitamin compound and cases of soft drinks shipped or air-freighted from the south. Station stores had become virtually shopping centres in which money paid out in wages at one counter were spent at another. This helped, certainly, to avert the ruin that many pastoralists had anticipated on the introduction of wages for their native workers, but the new system entailed the formidable task of pricing, serving and book-keeping.

Regular medical and welfare inspections and surveys of every conceivable kind had by this time not only convinced the native that he was now, for some reason, important to

327

the government but that the same government was infinitely exploitable. He knew that he could command the full medical facilities of the district, including Flying Doctor transport and hospital accommodation for complaints requiring no more than simple home remedies. This was an improvement on a time when a sick native was considered of less importance than a sick white but many were of the opinion that the position was now reversed and that rather than being served by native labour the white 'boss' and his family lived mainly to serve it. A growing lack of respect for white authority was further hastening the end of the old community system in which entire families had been retained for a few valuable workers. It was foreseen that once Aboriginal stockmen could command full award rates all except those who were as good or better than white workers would be dispensed with. Some would continue to hold their own but the defeated majority would tend to congregate more and more in the sort of segregated groups that the department had been trying to avoid for over thirty years.

Post-war Australian policy, in a precipitate effort to prove its social conscience to the world, had so far done little more for the natives of the north than to deprive them of the few important things they had clung to in their subjection. They had acquired a sense of importance without incentive or self-respect, freedom with nowhere to go, a living without a way of life.

In 1958 a special committee had tried to formulate an 'integration policy' aimed at equalizing the opportunities and conditions for native and white workers and by which the coloured people were to be encouraged to increase their productivity, to develop leaders and to spend their wages in a 'prudent and beneficial' manner. The weakness with these reasonably democratic recommendations was the lack of any concrete parallel plan to provide opportunities for the people whose expectations had been thus raised. As matters stood, the so-called 'empty land' to which the State government hoped to attract population had far more indigenous people than anyone knew what to do with, and to proceed on the airy assumption that employment would be created in the 'normal process of development' was a somewhat dangerous gamble. So far Kimberley had never developed 'normally' and despite the various schemes afoot and the prospects for mineral discoveries, the chances of her doing so in the foreseeable future were still problematical. It was a situation to which the warning of a United States writer to that infinitely richer country might aptly have been applied:

> ... the goal of equality becomes a mockery unless there is some means of attaining it. ... A country must have this endowment [the necessary physical resources and human resourcefulness] to start with or it is certain to suffer intensely from the social waste that results from giving training which cannot be utilized and from the psychological damage that results when a competition has an excess of participants and a paucity of rewards. ...[1]

Even were the most sanguine expectations for northern development to be some day realized the economic time lag was a serious threat, for with every year that the people were subjected to the corrosive idleness of fringe camps and compounds they were becoming harder to integrate. In this situation mission settlements, once generally regarded as charitable institutions of doubtful benefit, were now seen as supplying an important national service and a broadening of outlook on the part of both missionaries and government authorities was narrowing the gulf that had for so long divided them. In this respect Bishop Jobst faced a healthier situation than any of his predecessors but from other angles the outlook was less encouraging.

The population of his vast ecclesiastical territory comprised about 6,000 whites and 5,000 Aborigines, excluding the uncounted nomads beyond the fringes of settlement. Of the total an estimated 1,550 were Catholic. The Pallottine establishments at Broome, Derby, Beagle Bay, Lombadina, Balgo and La Grange, served by nine priests, thirty-one nuns, and seven brothers were educating about 300, mostly native children.[2] The little weatherboard and iron schools, hospitals and living quarters that had compared favourably with earlier standards in a makeshift land, looked primitive and dilapidated in the post-war era. In fact the bishop's overall impression was of a missionary field on which a brave but losing battle had been waged.

Where previously the Catholic Church had had little or no formidable competition, the situation, largely as a result of increased and inter-denominational interest in the Aborigines, had changed. Protestant missionaries from communist Asia and representatives of non-conformist Churches, well endowed with finance for modern facilities and rapidly expanding in Australia, had now entered the Kimberleys. From the point of view of a department anxious to push native advancement by every means available, a competitive situation had definite advantages, but for a Catholic bishop whose Society had been for so long almost alone in the field, the advent of these generally better-supported rival bodies was hardly encouraging. Its worst aspect was the threat of a situation common enough in other missionary regions, where sectarian differences added bewilderment to an already confused people; its brighter side, so long as goodwill could be maintained, that it might stimulate progressive experiment and induce Catholics to support their own institutions.

The bishop realized that the consideration of the missionary, never so simple as one of pure evangelism, must be more than ever directed to the social and economic problems that prevented the development of stable Christian life. It was, however, impossible to begin the tremendous task of reconstruction without the assurance of the financial and moral support of both Church and government. In 1962 he announced in the Catholic press that the situation in the Kimberleys was such that the Church must decide whether they were to build up in that area or get out. The response to this appeal, if by no means adequate to meet the magnitude of the task, was generous in comparison to those of previous years. It indicated that the people of Australia were no longer as indifferent to native welfare as in the past and also encouraged the government in granting financial co-operation.

A simultaneous campaign to recruit lay helpers to supplement the thinning ranks of religious for a year or more of their lives brought sufficient volunteers to staff the growing mission at La Grange, and with several vigorous young Australian Pallottines now in the field, the work of the Society took on a more indigenous aspect.

Priests were stationed for the first time in Wyndham and Hall's Creek and in 1963 a convent school was opened by two Sisters of St. Joseph in the former port. On the earlier missionary fronts the hardy remnant of pioneer nuns was joined by a few fully qualified nursing and teaching religious whose employment by the government assisted their Order, for a time, to establish a novitiate in the developing port of Derby.

The function of the Dampierland missions in the post-war era needed reassessment. No one was any longer under the illusion that either was likely to become self-supporting. The fertility, even of the limited areas of natural springs, had been reduced by a gradual seepage of salt and although the introduction of buffel grass had done something to improve the natural pasture nothing could apparently prevent the spread of 'Gallon's curse' or greatly increase the stock-carrying capacity of the pindan. The definition of a clear policy for their use as educational and community centres was hampered by the social and economic situation already outlined and some, even in the Catholic community, were of the opinion that Beagle Bay had served its purpose. A visitor to the mission at this period wrote:

Years ago the bullock-drawn wagon from Beagle Bay supplied the town of Broome with fresh fruit and vegetables. Today the people of Broome receive (subsidized air freight) boxes of fruit and vegetables from Perth – 1,400 miles away. Why has the produce from the lush spring-encircled mission ceased to come into its natural

331

market in Broome? Any fruit which I saw the children eating at the mission was the same as one sees everywhere in the north – apples and oranges damp with dew from a big freezer . . .

Where are the happy, healthy homes, envisioned by the early missionaries that, built with native hands, were to rise in ever increasing numbers as farmland extended until the colony would rival the size of Broome and set a shining example to that wicked place of how God's benison rests on the faithful?

Where are the skilled tradesmen and artisans that, mission-trained, were to sell their skills throughout the country? . . . What happened? What went wrong? Why did the whole idea collapse?[3]

The answer to these questions may be found in this history and perhaps, too, an understanding of the circumstances that prevented the healthy growth of the little Christian communities envisaged by the Trappist monks. The fault lay not in the ideal or in the work and aspirations of the missionaries but in the lack of anything of the sort outside. What others counted as 'progress' was not after all the missionaries' main concern, for whether the community was growing, static or dying, its material support adequate or otherwise, where there remained some vestige of forlorn and forsaken humanity, or indeed life at all, their duty remained and they would continue, regardless of failure, frustration or what the world might think.[4]

As it happened there were still many Aboriginal and coloured people in Dampierland as much, if not more, in need of a place of refuge as ever in the past. Many children growing up in and around Broome lacked a stable home background and it was becoming clear that the orphanage was badly situated in the port.

A basis for renewed effort was laid down at both Beagle Bay and Lombadina in the building of new schools, dormitories, and hospitals, much of the equipment being supplied by the Lotteries Commission, which assistance Catholic institutions accepted without inhibition.

A feeler towards the establishment of home industries, dear to the hearts of Father Drostë and Bishop Raible, was extended in the opening of a co-operative soft drink factory at Beagle Bay, which soon found a ready market for its products in the port.

Another service this mission, with its bright new facilities, could now provide was a nursing home for children born in the leprosarium and native hospital in Derby. Previously such little ones had been taken care of by foster parents, often on the assumption that their chances of being reclaimed were very slight. As cures had increased, however, so had the disputes and psychological problems and it was a relief both to the parents and the nuns when an alternative was found. These improvements have encouraged native people to think of Beagle Bay in the light of a boarding school and young people from station properties have begun to avail themselves of the education it offers.[5]

Lombadina, a happy and peaceful little mission, presented special problems. Its people, still close to their own traditions, had little wish to leave the cherished sites of their tribal heroes and the equally cherished memories of Fathers Nicholas, Auguste Spangenberg, John Herold and others to whose voluntary exile they owed the protection of their hereditary ground. The young people too showed little of the restlessness of those at Beagle Bay but in keeping with departmental policy were now sent at school leaving age to the technical training centre in Derby.[6]

Pallottine hostels have been established both in this port and also Riverton, close to the State capital of Perth. These are not regarded as institutions, orphanages or boarding houses but as training centres for coloured boys and girls who are themselves anxious to do better in life and who, having completed their primary schooling, have been recommended for high school education. The numbers as yet able or ambitious enough to avail themselves of their new opportunities, though naturally still limited, are showing an encouragingly steady increase and it is significant that the majority of these are from families that owe their start in life to their Beagle Bay background.[7]

The Pallottine base at La Grange was enlarged in 1960 by the bishop's purchase of the neighbouring half-million-acre cattle station where young Aborigines are being trained as stockmen, mechanics and general handymen. This mission, under the vigorous direction of Father Kevin McKelson and nine young lay helpers, has provided an obvious, if by no means total, solution to the special native problems of this area. Here as elsewhere bright new buildings have gone up and educational and social experiments are being tackled with enthusiasm.[8]

In 1963 it was found that the frontier mission at Balgo Hills encroached on the leasehold of its northerly neighbour and it was moved in the following year to a new place on a more assured artesian water supply. A modern establishment in the tribal stronghold of the primitive Gogodja, the mission is the centre of a promising horse-breeding property which Superintendent Father John McGuire is confident of being made self-supporting while providing a training centre for the young and a refuge for the old. The understanding groundwork of pioneer Pallottines such as Fathers Worms, Huegel, Bleischwitz and Puesken, Brothers Henry Krallman, Stephen Contempré and Franz Hanke is reflected in the co-operative attitude to the mission of the adult people. Though many continue their nomadic habits they have accepted the fact that tribal life in the traditional sense is drawing to an end and that their children should be left at school to learn the ways of the strange world that is closing in on their desert frontiers.[9]

Not long before his death in 1963, Father Worms submitted, on the bishop's request, some notes on the approach he considered advisable for future missionary work among the Aborigines. Believing as he did that these people were entitled to and worthy of the best Australia could provide for them, the qualifications he prescribed for their would-be teachers were so high as to discourage any but the most determined and erudite scholars. In this he was perhaps somewhat unrealistic, for the scholastic approach was not the only one that had borne fruit or might do so in future.

As an ideal, however, his requirements are worthy of respect.

First and foremost the missionary should be equipped with a good knowledge of history and of classical and modern languages, the former to impress him with the complication and recentness of his own cultural background, the latter to give him adroitness in the handling of native tongues. . . .

He needs a solid metaphysical outlook enabling him to apprehend quickly the essential and accidental in the philosophy and religious beliefs of the people he meets in the mission field.

He needs a fundamental knowledge of anthropology, otherwise he will feel lost in strange surroundings and be blind to the exuberance of human life around him. This science will enable him to avoid a false impression that all he observes is unique and extraordinary and will give him the support in his task of other anthropologists and educated missionaries.

His religious convictions should be such as to intensify his moral qualities and to provide a great tolerance towards native customs and a perception of what should remain untouched or even fostered, understanding that Christianity, by its own dynamism, will segregate what is incompatible to it in the course of time.

Ideally he should be a member of a religious body so that he will be backed by the discipline and co-operation of his Society and will have the satisfaction of knowing that his work will be continued by sober men of the same ideals and principles. . . .

The missionary should be a wise and practical teacher, a man of restraint and untiring perseverance, a psychologist who understands the impossibility of changing the life style of the nomad within one generation. . . .

Finally he must be prepared to leave the field of activity after twenty or thirty years of hard work without seeing that successful adaptation which he visualized in his younger years. He should find satisfaction with the *little* he achieved, consolation in the fact that some at least without his guidance must have toppled over into disgrace and destruction on the fringe of townships and settlements. . . .[10]

Father Worms' appreciative but not uncritical analysis of missionary activity was one he shared with his friend and fellow anthropologist, T. G. H. Strehlow who summed up his long experience in this way:

> . . . Let me repeat here what I have often said at the end of long arguments about the merits and about the failings of missionary work, that, but for the ministrations of those missions that can fairly be claimed to have been successful even when judged on purely non-Christian considerations, there would probably be no full-blooded Aborigines at all left in the majority of those Australian areas where they are still surviving. . . . As a University man I have the highest regard for what trained University men have done both in anthropological research work and in influencing popular opinion – and Church opinion too – towards a finer appreciation of the Aboriginal mind and more enlightened regard for Aboriginal culture. But the missions were the only agency that held up the complete physical annihilation of the Aboriginal race in this country from the beginnings of white settlement till the time when more enlightened Government policies were instituted in Australia. . . .[11]

The effect of missionary influence in this regard applied nowhere more strikingly than on the Dampierland peninsula where the precipitate entry of thousands of indentured Asiatic divers was an even greater threat to their survival than the gradual encroachment of pastoral occupation. Fifty years ago it was predicted that another generation would see the last of the full-blood Aborigines of this district. Instead, from an estimated 1,500 in the last century (possibly exaggerated as most early estimates are now thought to have been), their decline to approximately 900, with a rising birth rate today, must be comparable to that of tribespeople in parts of the continent least affected by white settlement. The purpose served by the missions in this region has never been fully assessed in humanitarian terms, for the inhabitants of both full and mixed Aboriginal blood undoubtedly regarded them as places of refuge and the missionaries as their only trustworthy protectors.

The last few years have witnessed such a great change of attitude towards the Aboriginal people that some in close touch with the situation fear that the pace is now being pushed too fast – that from expecting too little of the Aborigines we might now be expecting too much too soon. The patient and sensitive approach to acculturation, of allowing a people to grow into a way of life rather than pushing them into it in a single generation, is no doubt the ideal, though history seldom, if ever, awaits the working out of sensible, long-term policies. We must count ourselves fortunate that it has at least given white Australians long enough to develop a more mature approach towards our indigenous people.

The changing attitude might be said to reflect the need for improving Australia's image overseas or of our realization of how the unsolved colour problems of today portend the race conflicts of tomorrow, but however one chooses to explain it there can be no doubt that the tide has at last turned and that the culture and outlook of the Aborigines is now far better appreciated and understood.

Since they are no longer assumed to be a dying race the necessity for their education and development is obvious to all. For the first time in history both the government and public of Australia are concerned to understand and solve the problems formerly regarded as the responsibility of those idealistic or unrealistic enough to espouse a hopeless cause. Gone the days when the Aborigines were considered congenitally incapable of attaining the general European standard of education or of assuming the responsibilities of citizenship. Many problems and contradictions remain but the old defeatist attitude is quickly disappearing and with it the last vestiges of legislation suggestive of racial discrimination or restriction.[12] The Aboriginal people are now seen, not as a small problem peculiar to Australia, but as a cultural minority for whom the process of integration among the Red Indians, the Eskimos and Maoris,[13] the people of Africa, Papua and New Guinea has a direct application. Australian sociologists, educationalists and welfare workers, studying the needs of our indigenous and mixed-blood people on a world range observe how societies elsewhere are learning to live with and often to enjoy the cultural diversities in their midst, no longer seeing it as necessary, or even desirable, to turn native people into submissive counterparts of themselves.[14] The aim today is rather to assist them to understand their own culture in relation to our own and to equip them to play their part as Aborigines, side by side with white Australians in the fulfilment of a common destiny.

Within the broader concept of national responsibility Christian missions in Australia for so long begrudged the humblest government subsidy today receive between them a grant of over two and a quarter million dollars a year. This indicates that their work is now seen in a new light, but perhaps even more significant is the fact that their role is also being reassessed from within. Little remains today of the narrow concept of evangelism that sought to kindle the flame of a new faith on the lifeless ashes of the old and that counted success in terms of baptized heads and passive submission to an often meaningless routine. Most missionaries are themselves vitally aware that the enclosed aspect of their establishments must give place to one increasingly conducive to the development of independence and initiative, that they must come to be regarded, not as charitable institutions or forts resisting change, but as lively community centres that can compete against the attractions of the towns, staging places on the road to successful integration.

Although in many respects the task is no less a pioneering one than when Father McNab set up his lonely camp among the Nimanboor on the shores of King Sound, it therefore requires no stretch of the imagination to conclude on a note of hope and confidence. In this new era of conscientious reassessment however, it would be sad indeed if the question of Aboriginal development were to be reduced to terms of purely material and psychological needs. Who could presume to negate the value of an ideal that drew men from the far ends of the earth to serve the weak and dispossessed in an arid wilderness? It could not have been expected that all entering the missionary field would persevere in the same dauntless spirit, for although one and all had come prepared to face physical hardships of every kind none could have imagined the spiritual dilemmas that were to prove their worst affliction. The wonder is, not that some lost heart and a few perhaps the broader vision of Christian charity but that the majority maintained a dedicated unity of purpose and an abandonment of self to which even the sceptic must concede an awful respect. Whereas they had hoped their missions to prosper in both a spiritual and a material sense, what was required of them was after all not success but that they should stake a claim for the word of God in a babel of conflicting interests. The voices of white trader, tribal elder, missionary and government authority all had their moments of ascendancy but only one voice among them struck a note of hope for the bewildered and derelict people, and who can say that, despite all conceptual differences, its message was not recognized by those in greatest need?

The missionaries could hardly have been asked to provide a final answer to a problem on which others turned their backs, nor could they be held responsible for what the environment and contemporary policy failed to provide or the Aborigines to find in our egocentric and fiercely competitive society. The light they lived by is no anachronism in what we like to think a more progressive age but one as essential and new today as when it was first enkindled in the hearts of men. Only with its continued influence can Australia hope to avoid the greater colour problems of other lands and to approach a true understanding of racial harmony.

# References

*Abbreviations*

ACAP – Archives of the Catholic Archdiocese of Perth.
ADB – Archives of the Diocese of Broome.
Reilly – J. T. Reilly, *Reminiscences Of Fifty Years' Residence In Western Australia.*

CHAPTER ONE

1. At the beginning of settlement in 1788 the Aboriginal population is believed to have been approximately 300,000. Numbers declined consistently until recent years. The 1921 estimate of 58,867 had fallen to 26,363 by 1954 (this figure excluding Aborigines outside the confines of settlement). According to the census of 1966 the number classed as full-blood Aborigines (having more than 50 per cent Aboriginal blood) had risen by about 6,000 in a five-year period to 46,356. Of this total the highest number, 11,542, are in Western Australia.

2. ACAP. From Bishop John Brady, Perth, Vicar-Apostolic of W.A., to Earl Grey, Secretary of State for the Colonies, London, 16th July 1848. The plan to which he referred was as follows:

> *1st.* Large portions of land to be selected in the most convenient parts of the Colony, to be held in trust for the natives with an extensive territory in order to form probationary farms for the different tribes and families who are to be drawn gradually from their wandering habits to settle down and form small native villages in their respective localities. ...
>
> In consequence of the frequent evil communications which take place between the natives and some unfortunate shepherds and stockmen, the efforts and labours of the missionaries have been paralysed by a foul and loathsome disease,

resulting from this evil intercourse, is now widely spread among the natives and if care and remedies are not promptly and effectually applied the native population of Western Australia will soon become extinct. . . .

*2nd.* That the natives thus withdrawn from an intercourse with such people their minds will be directed to settled habits of industry and to the acquirement of some useful employment.

*3rd.* That this comprehensive system will require and shall include a special education and training of the native children on which we build all our hopes and to which the attention of our good missionaries will be chiefly directed.

This plan of civilizing the Aborigines is chiefly intended for the male portion. The education and civilization of the female portion will be placed under the care and management of the Ladies of Mercy.

3. F. T. Gregory and party sailed from Fremantle to Nickol Bay in 1861 and explored inland around the Ashburton, Fortescue, De Grey and Oakover Rivers. His reports began the first confident expansion to the north-west.

4. Originally a free colony, labour problems forced the settlers to request convicts after transportation had ceased in other Australian colonies. Almost 10,000 convicts were sent to Western Australia between 1850 and 1868.

5. Extracts from W.A. Historical Society – Journal and Proceedings – III. Paper by Mr. I. T. Birtwhistle from information supplied by Mr. C. W. Coppin of Mundaring and Mr. H. W. Baker. p. 40.

[The natives] were the white settler's best friends and those of us who were there in the '70s and '80s appreciated their worth and treated them accordingly. They shepherded sheep, fenced in the paddocks, did all the shearing for thirty or forty years and did it well. They tackled all kinds of station work, they were reliable bullock drovers and horse teamsters and they worked cheerfully and solidly. At the De Grey in my time there were 400 natives. They sheared between 50,000 and 60,000 sheep each year and scoured all the wool. Our job in those times would have been more back-breaking and more heart-breaking than most men could endure but for the black man.

6. Extract from W.A. Historical Society – Journal and Proceedings III. Paper prepared by A. C. Angelo. p. 44.

Natives diving in 'bare pelt' as it was called, i.e. naked without diving dress, displayed the possession of some physical attribute that as far as I know is not shared by any other people. . . . I have seen natives brought in from the interior who had never seen a sheet of water bigger than a river pool . . . taken on board a pearling schooner and straightaway they would go down three to four fathoms of water and bring up shell. They have been known to go down six to seven fathoms (thirty-six to forty-two feet) and to have worked successfully in depths up to five fathoms. The procedure was for a couple of white men, armed, to take four to six natives from the schooner in a dinghy and when over the banks where there was known to be shell, the natives would simply step out and go down feet first . . . walking about on the bottom in a bent attitude searching for shell. After what seemed an interminable time they would come up, hand in any shell they had secured, and after hanging on to the gunwale for a few minutes' rest, let go and disappear into the depths again.

7. 'Let the Government have their resident magistrates and such police as they can afford in each district, but the pioneers and outside settlers must and will be the people to fight and subdue the natives. . . . The question is are we or the natives to be masters? . . .' Mr. Walter Padbury, respected pioneer of north-west settlement, reported during heated native controversy of the 1880s.
8. '. . . Governor Weld was, as some of his best friends admitted, "a little mad on the native question".' Letter of Charles Harper to *The West Australian*, October 1892, quoted in *Reminiscences Of Fifty Years' Residence In Western Australia*, J. T. Reilly, Perth, 1903, p. 324.
9. *Black Australians*, Paul Hasluck, Melb. Univ. Press, 1942, p. 166.

Chapter Two
1. Bishop Gibney to *The West Australian*, October 1892, quoted in Reilly, p. 341.
2. Letter to *The West Australian*, quoted in Reilly, p. 318.
3. Paul Hasluck's *Black Australians* and S. R. Marks' 'Mission

Policy in Western Australia' (in *University Studies in Western Australian History*, Vol. III, No. 4, 1960).

4. Article, *W.A. Catholic Record*, December 1879.

5. Archives, Benedictine Abbey, New Norcia. From Father Duncan McNab to Bishop Salvado, 1870.

6. Report of Father McNab, *W.A. Catholic Record*, 10/4/79.

7. ACAP. Report of Father McNab to Bishop Griver, 1885.

8. Paul Hasluck in *Black Australians*, p. 86.

9. From Father Duncan McNab, Rottnest Island, to the W.A. Legislative Council, 11/5/83.

10. George Grey, Vol. II, pp. 373–388.

11. Report of the Aboriginal Commission, 1883.

12. Bishop Griver, Father Gibney, to the Colonial Secretary, Perth, re proposal to undertake a mission to the Aborigines in the north-west, 1883.

13. Report of the Aboriginal Commission, 1883.

14. ibid.

CHAPTER THREE

1. ACAP. Letter from Father McNab to Father Gibney from Cossack, 3/11/83.

2. ACAP. Letter from Father McNab to Father Gibney from Derby, 3/3/84.

3. *Western Australia, Its History And Progress*, A. F. Calvert, 1894; *The Golden Quest*, A. C. V. Bligh.

4. *Pindan* is a rare example of an Aboriginal word that has been adopted for general local use. Common to most Dampierland tribes and variously rendered pindan, bindan, bindana and bindai, it means wild, arid or waterless country. *Binghi*, locally synonymous with Aboriginal, probably derives from the natives' describing themselves as being 'bindai' or 'pindai' meaning 'belonging to the bush or wild country'.

5. Notes taken by the author from early pearlers, B. Bardwell, C. Hawkes, D. MacDaniel. Information from coloured residents of the Dampierland peninsula, including Willie Reed and Robin Hunter.

6. ACAP. Father McNab to Bishop Griver from Derby, 1/3/85.

7. ibid.

8. ibid.

9. ACAP. From Father McNab to Father Gibney, Derby, August 1885.

10. ACAP. Father McNab to Father Gibney, 27/6/85. 'Knife' not mentioned by name in this letter, identified to author by Bard people at Lombadina, mission Aborigines Dougal, Benedict and George. He died at Watchelum mission about 1945.

11. ACAP. Father McNab to Bishop Griver from Derby, 1/3/85.

12. ACAP. Father McNab to Father Gibney, 27/6/85.

13. ACAP. Father McNab to Father Gibney, 3/8/85.

14. ACAP. Reference 11.

15. *The West Australians*, 29/5/85.

16. ACAP. Reference 11.

17. ibid.

18 ACAP. Father McNab to Father Gibney, Derby, 4/10/85.

19. Letter, *W.A. Catholic Record,* 15/5/87.

20. ibid.

21. ACAP. Father McNab to Bishop Griver, Derby, 1/3/85.

22. Mark, iv, 27, 28. The quotations from Holy Scripture used in the text are taken from *The Jerusalem Bible*, London, 1966.

23. *The Advocate*, Melbourne, 19/9/96. Obit. Father D. McNab with account of his Requiem and funeral.

CHAPTER FOUR

1. Article in *L'Union Cistercienne*, September 1895 (in French).

2. ibid.

3. ACAP. Letters of negotiation between Bishop Gibney, Cardinal Moran and the Abbot of Sept Fons, France.

4. Thomas Merton, *The Waters of Silence*.

5. Reilly, Report of Bishop Gibney on foundation of a Trappist mission in Dampierland, p. 498.

6. ibid.

7. William Dampier, *New Voyage Round The World,* 1697.

8. Bishop Gibney, Report (Reference 5).

9. ACAP. Bishop Gibney to Daisy Bates, 13/10/10.

10. Reference 5.

11. Reference 5.

CHAPTER FIVE

1. Reilly, Report of Father James Duff for the *Catholic Record*, 1890, pp. 501–505.

2. ibid, p. 503.

3. ACAP. Father Sebastian Wyart, Abbot and Vicar-General, Sept Fons, to Bishop Gibney of Perth, 1890.

4. The Aborigines Protection Board, established 1886, responsible directly to the British Government, was a body of five honorary members and a secretary set up to report on the condition of the natives, to distribute rations and blankets and to subsidise missions from an annual income, stipulated as 1% of the revenue or a minimum of £5,000.

5. ACAP. Abbot Ambrose Janny, Beagle Bay, to Bishop Gibney, Perth. Undated (probably late 1890).

6. ADB. Father A. Bourke, Vicar General, Perth (for Bishop Gibney), to Abbot Ambrose, Beagle Bay, 30/1/91.

7. ACAP. Father Alphonse Tachon, Beagle Bay, to Bishop Gibney, Perth. Probably June 1891.

8. ibid.

9. ibid.

10. Daisy Bates, *The Passing of the Aborigines*, Heinemann, 1966.

11. Reference *1*.

12. Reference 7.

13. Report of Father James Duff for the *Catholic Record,* 1901.

14. Reference 7.

15. ACAP. Father Alphonse, Beagle Bay, to Bishop Gibney, Perth, 27/7/91.

16. Reference 5.

17. Reference 5.

18. ACAP. Father A. Bourke, Vicar General, Perth, on behalf of Bishop Gibney, to Abbot Ambrose, Broome, 30/1/91.

19. ACAP. Father Alphonse Tachon, Beagle Bay, to Bishop Gibney, Perth, 27/7/91.

CHAPTER SIX

1. Thomas Merton in *The Waters of Silence* tells how the successful foundation in Natal eventually abandoned the Cistercian rule and became a separate missionary organization.

2. ACAP. Dom Ambrose Janny to Bishop Gibney, from Sept Fons, 24/7/91.

3. Father Worms quotes (*Anthropos* 54, 1959): 'Französische Forscher unter M. F. Peron entdeckten sie am 5 Aug. 1801. Er schreibt in seiner *Voyage of Discovery to the Southern Hemisphere performed by Order of the Emperor Napoleon during*

*the years 1801–1804*, translated from French, London, 1809:
"On the 5th we discovered another group of small sandy
islands, but nevertheless covered with some verdure, which we
called Lascepede Isles, according to M. de Lascepede, this
learned naturalist." '

4. Lombadina sometimes said to have been named by the
French monks as meaning 'Little Lombardy' actually bore the
name when taken up as a pearling base by Hunter and Hadley
during the 1880s. On evidence of local Aborigines is a place
name of the Bard tribe. The root *lomba,* also applied to other
nearby sites Lombadaitchen and Lombagun (the latter now
usually spelt Lumbingun), is a Bard word meaning 'open', or
'open to'.

5. The schooner *Jessie*, originally owned by a pearler named
Jack Shepherd had already had a colourful career. Mr. C. W.
Coppin of Yarrie Station gave information for a Historical
Society paper (see Extracts from W.A. Historical Society –
*Journals and Proceedings* – III) of how she came through the
big blow of 1887.

6. Information of Cistercian historian Father Joseph O'Dea,
Monte Cistello, Rome, from records at Sept Fons, France.

7. Saying handed down to present-day missionaries at Beagle
Bay.

8. Ephesians, v, 11.

9. ACAP. Sundry reports from Beagle Bay to Bishop Gibney,
1892.

10. ACAP. John Cornelius Daly, Beagle Bay, to Bishop Gibney,
1892.

11. ibid., April 1892.

12. ACAP. John Cornelius Daly, Beagle Bay, to Bishop Gibney,
24/4/93.

13. Bishop Gibney re pearling. Letter to *The West Australian*
22/10/92, Reilly, p. 318.

14. Unmarked grave of Brother Francois d'Assise, pointed out
to author by old Aborigines at Beagle Bay, 1961.

15. *L'Union Cistercienne*, a periodical started at the union of
the Order in 1892 and continued for some years.

CHAPTER SEVEN

1. Report of a meeting held in the Geraldton district, 14/10/92,
in *The West Australian* and quoted in Reilly, pp. 378–391.

2. Correspondence to *The West Australian*, September to October 1892. Reilly, pp. 312–368.

3. A. R. Richardson to *The West Australian*, October 1892. Reilly, p. 355.

4. Bishop Gibney to Governor Robinson. Reilly, pp. 418–429.

5. Bishop Gibney to the Marquis of Ripon, Secretary of State for the Colonies, January 1894. Reilly, pp. 431–442.

6. The Secretary of State for the Colonies to Governor Robinson, Perth, 1894. Reilly, pp. 443–444.

7. ACAP. Report of Mr. Saville Kent, Commissioner of Fisheries, 1894.

8. Information to author from Father Joseph O'Dea from records at Sept Fons, France.

9. The spirit hero Djamar of the Bard tribe. See 'Djamar and His Relation to Other Culture Heroes', E. A. Worms, *Anthropos*, Vol. 47, May–August, 1952, p. 539.

10. ACAP. Father M. Sebastian – Abbot O.C.R., Rome, to Bishop Gibney, Perth, 27/8/93.

11. ACAP. Cardinal Moran, Sydney, to Abbot Sebastian Wyart, Rome, 15/1/94.

12. In 1882 three Jesuit priests and a Jesuit brother attempted to develop a mission at Rapid Creek, seven miles from Darwin, and later at Daly River, and continued there for some years but were compelled to leave owing to lack of finance, remoteness from civilization, and lack of any promising signs of progress.

13. *L'Union Cistercienne*, September 1895, quoting Abbot Sebastian Wyart in his farewell address to the religious leaving for Australia.

14. ibid.

15. Father Nicholas Emo.

16. ACAP. Father Alphonse Tachon, Beagle Bay, to Bishop Gibney, Perth, 20/4/94.

17. ibid.


CHAPTER EIGHT

1. Father Marie Joseph in *L'Union Cistercienne*, September 1895.

2. References to the feet of the missionaries in this song are echoes of Isaiah, iii, 7. 'How beautiful on the mountains are the feet of one who brings good news, who heralds peace, brings happiness, proclaims salvation . . .'

3. Reference 1.

4. ibid.

5. ibid.

6. ibid.
7. ibid.
8. ibid.
9. ibid.
10. ACAP. Bishop Gibney, Perth, to Abbot Ambrose Janny, Beagle Bay, May 1885.
11. ACAP. From Abbot Ambrose Janny, Broome, to Bishop Gibney, Perth, 6/6/85.
12. Information supplied by Father Joseph O'Dea from records in Sept Fons.
13. ibid.


CHAPTER NINE
1. Evidence of old Aborigines at Beagle Bay to the author, including the brothers Remi and Gabriel Balgalai, Gerard Malgan and Manuel Tummunarra.
2. E. A. Worms, 'Djamar and His Relation to Other Culture Heroes', *Anthropos*, Vol. 47, May–August 1952, pp. 539–560. This legend retold to the author by Benedict Jewarr, Dougal Djulegar and George Warb, members of the Bard tribe, at Lombadina, May 1965. N.B. The insistence on monogamy and disapproval of magical practices in the law of Galalang suggest to the author the possibility that this hero was not a spirit of mythical tradition but some shipwrecked mariner of missionary bent whose story, in the passage of time, assumed the characteristics of native legend. Wrecks on this coast were many throughout the centuries. Numbers of survivors were known to have reached the shore but their fate remains a mystery.
3. ACAP. Brother Xavier Daly, Beagle Bay, to Bishop Gibney, Perth, 11/10/96.
4. ACAP. Father Alphonse Tachon, Beagle Bay, to Bishop Gibney, Perth, 10/8/96.
5. ACAP. Brother Xavier Daly, Beagle Bay, to Bishop Gibney, Perth, 9/2/97.
6. Abbot Ambrose Janny did not die until 25/5/12, in a temporary Trappist refuge at Blitterswijk, Holland.
7. Thomas Merton, *The Waters of Silence*, p. 170.
8. Notes to the author from Father Joseph O'Dea, Monte Cistello, Rome, 2/12/61.
9. *The West Australian*, 1892. Reilly, p. 511.
10. Paul Hasluck, *Black Australians*, p. 203.

11. ACAP. Prior Anselm, Beagle Bay, to Bishop Gibney, 29/4/99.
12. ibid.
13. ACAP. Prior Anselm, Beagle Bay, to Bishop Gibney, Perth, 3/12/99.


CHAPTER TEN
1. Notes supplied to author by Father Joseph O'Dea from records of the Cistercian Abbey, Sept Fons. Quoted from letter to Dom Baptiste Chautard, Abbot, May 1900.
2. Father Nicholas, Broome, to Rev. Father A. Bourke, Vicar General, Perth, 8/5/1900 (in Spanish).
3. ACAP. Letter to the Aborigines Protection Board with twenty-seven signatures, August 1897.
4. ACAP. Corporal Thomas, Broome, to Aborigines Protection Board, Perth, July 1897.
5. ACAP. Father A. Bourke, Vicar-General, Perth, to Father Nicholas Emo, Broome, 9/11/98.
6. Report, Royal Commission on the Condition of the Natives, W. E. Roth, B.A., M.R.C.S. Eng. etc., 1905. Evidence of Father Nicholas Maria Emo, 6/10/04, p. 61.
7. ibid.
8. ADB. Notes of Father Nicholas Emo.
9. ibid.
10. ACAP. Father W. B. Kelly, from Wyndham, to Bishop Gibney, Perth, 4/4/97.
11. In notes supplied to author by Father Joseph O'Dea, 2/12/61, taken from records of the Cistercian Order, Sept Fons, France.


CHAPTER ELEVEN
1. ACAP. Father A Bourke, Vicar-General, Perth, to Father Dwyer, Trappist, Beagle Bay, 30/4/1900
2. ACAP Father A. Bourke, Perth, to the Rt. Rev. Bishop Salvado, Rome, 25/7/1900.
3. ACAP. Report of Bishop Gibney on the state of the mission, 1900.
4. ACAP. Father Nicholas Emo, Broome, to Bishop Gibney, Perth, 9/3/1900.
5. Father Alphonse Tachon died at the Cistercian monastery in Latroun, Palestine, in February 1928 where he was noted for his 'remarkable sanctity'. See article *Australian Catholic Digest,*

1/7/1954: Father James Murtagh, 'Trappist Link between Australia and the Holy Land'.

6. This would have been Montague Sydney Hadley who established an Anglican mission on Sunday Island at this time.

7. ACAP. Father Nicholas Emo, Broome, to Father A. Bourke, Vicar-General, Perth, 8/5/1900 (in Spanish).

8. F. K. Crowley, *Australia's Western Third*, London, 1960, pp. 143, 144. 'The improved financial standing of the various churches was obvious by the mid-'nineties, and the government decided that the time was opportune for the separation of Church and State by ending the annual grants made to the principal denominations. It was hoped that this would stop religious controversy and sectarian bitterness in politics associated with the distribution of the annual grant, and with the extent to which religious teaching should be allowed in the colony's schools. It was also thought it would be better for the churches to depend on their own adherents rather than on any subsidy from the State.' The sum of £35,430 was set aside as compensation to the various churches to be divided according to their representation in the population. From 1899 education was free to children between the ages of six and fourteen in all government schools.

9. ACAP. Father A. Bourke, Vicar-General, Perth, to Cardinal Moran, Sydney, 27/8/1900.

10. Chippendall and his partner Haynes died forty-three years apart, one in north-west Australia, the other in England, but they were buried together in the pioneer cemetery, Broome. Inscriptions on their tombstones read:

Edward Cockayne Chippendall, R.N.
Aged 34 years
2nd son of the Rev. John Chippendall
of Cheetham Hill, Manchester, England.
Died at sea 22nd May 1886 and was
interred at this spot.
'Be ye also ready for at such an hour
As ye think not the Son of Man cometh.'

Thomas Henry Haynes
who died at East Preston, Sussex,
May 4, 1929, aged 76.
For many years resident in this colony.
These ashes laid beside his friend and partner . . x

350

11. Daisy Bates, *The Passing Of The Aborigines*, p. 4.
12. ibid., p. 5.
13. ibid., p. 6.
14. ibid., p. 6.
15. ibid., p. 13.
16. ibid, pp. 15–17.
17. Daisy Bates, *Report on the Trappist Mission*, Reilly, p. 534.
18. Daisy Bates, *The Passing Of The Aborigines*, p. 18.
19. Daisy Bates, *Report on the Trappist Mission*, Reilly, p. 529.
20. ibid., p. 526.
21. Daisy Bates, *The Australasian*, 17/8/29.

CHAPTER TWELVE
1. Father W. Whitmee, Rome, to Father Walter, Frankfurt, 13/6/1900.
2. George Walter, *Australien, Land, Leute Mission*; Limburg, 1928.
3. ibid.
4. ADB. Bishop Kelly, Geraldton, to Father Walter, Beagle Bay, 1901.
5. ADB. Father Marie Bernard (for the Abbot of Sept Fons, France) to Father Walter, Beagle Bay, 16/12/1904 (in French).
6. ACAP. Bishop Gibney, Perth, to Mr. H. C. Princep, Chief Protector of Aborigines, Perth, 18/12/1900.
7. Father Walter, Beagle Bay, to the Pallottine Superior, Limburg, 1901. Quoted in J. S. Needham, *White and Black in Australia*.
8. ACAP. Father Walter, Beagle Bay, to Bishop Gibney, Perth, 1901.
9. Dr. J. P. Lauterer was Vice President of the Anthropological Section of The Association for the Advancement of Science in Australia and New Zealand.
10. Report of Mr. G. S. Olivey, Inspector of Native Reserves and Chief Protector of Aborigines, May 1901.

CHAPTER THIRTEEN
1. Information to author by pioneer missionary Sisters of the Order of St. John of God, Broome.
2. ACAP. Brother Xavier Daly, Beagle Bay, to Bishop Gibney, Perth, August 1901.

3. ADB. Father Marie Bernard, Secretary to the Abbot of Sept Fons, to Father Walter, Beagle Bay, 16/12/04.

4. ADB. Abbé Jean Baptiste Chautard, Sept Fons, to Father Walter, Beagle Bay, 28/2/02.

5. Thomas Merton, *The Waters of Silence*, pp. 184, 185.

6. ACAP. Bishop Kelly, Geraldton, to Father Walter, Beagle Bay, 12/3/01.

7. ACAP. Father Walter, Beagle Bay, to Bishop Gibney, Perth (undated, probably January 1902).

8. ACAP. Bishop Kelly, Geraldton, to Father Walter, Beagle Bay, 14/4/02.

9. J. S. Needham, *Black and White in Australia*, quoting information obtained from Pallottine sources.

10. Information to author from the Aboriginal Paddy Djiagween who was taken as a boy from Broome to be educated at Beagle Bay.

11. ADB. Abbot Jean Baptiste Chautard, Sept Fons, to Father Walter, Beagle Bay, 26/5/02.

12. ADB. Abbot Jean Baptiste Chautard, Sept Fons, to Father Walter, Beagle Bay, 2/6/02.

13. ACAP. Bishop Gibney, Perth, to Father Walter, Beagle Bay, 24/4/02.

14. ACAP. Father Walter, Broome, to Bishop Gibney, Perth, 17/5/02. (Probably a reference to a tobacco growing project begun in 1903.)

15. ADB. Father White, Beagle Bay, to Father Walter, Limburg, 1902.

16. Bishop Gibney, Perth, to Sir John Forrest, Perth, 1901. Quoted by P. McCarthy in 'The Foundations of Catholicism in Western Australia 1829–1911', *University Studies in History and Economics*, 1956, p. 61.

17. ACAP. Bishop Gibney, Perth, to Father Walter, Limburg, 27/10/02.

CHAPTER FOURTEEN

1. ADB. Father Jean Marie Janny, Disaster Bay, to Father Walter, Beagle Bay, October 1902 (in French).

2. Evidence of Aboriginal Christopher Parambor of Derby, son of Johnnie Parambor and brother of Marie.

3. ADB. Father Jean Marie Janny, Disaster Bay to Father Walter, Beagle Bay, 1/6/01.

4. Beagle Bay records. Liber Defunctorum of the Mission of

the Annunciation, Disaster Bay, from 1897 to 1905. Report of the death of Juanna Maggado, 16/3/02 (in French).

5. Evidence of Robin Hunter of Broome, half-caste son of Harry Hunter, Syd Hadley's one-time partner. 'Old Syd made them put him through the law. They did it properly and gave him his tribal relations.' See also S. R. Marks, 'Mission Policy in Western Australia 1846–1959', *University Studies in Western Australian History*, 1960.

6. S. R. Marks (reference 5).

7. ACAP. Brother Xavier Daly, Lombadina Station, to Bishop Gibney, Perth, 2/2/92.

8. ADB. Harry Hunter, Leveque Station, Cape Leveque, to 'The Father in Charge, Mission Station, Beagle Bay', 10/10/03.

9. Note (unsigned) at foot of above letter, evidently from lawyer consulted.

10. ADB. Father Jean Marie Janny, Disaster Bay to Father Walter, Beagle Bay, 30/10/04 (in French).

11. ADB. Last entry in the marriage register of Disaster Bay mission between Ambrose Pablbergh and Lucia Peringar, 22/7/04.

12. Information supplied by Father Joseph O'Dea from records at Sept Fons gives the date of his departure from Sept Fons to Maristella monastery, Brazil, as 21/9/1906.

13. Admission of weakness in the betrayal of Galalang, quoted by E. A. Worms in 'Djamar the Creator, A Myth of the Bad (West Kimberley, Australia)', *Anthropos*, Vol. 45.


CHAPTER FIFTEEN

1. ADB. Secretary Father General, Rome, to Father Walter, Beagle Bay, 29/7/04.

2. ADB. Secretary Father General, Rome, to Father Walter, Beagle Bay, 26/10/04.

3. ADB. Secretary Father General, Rome, to Father Walter, Beagle Bay, 15/2/04.

4. ADB. Secretary Father General, Rome, to Father Walter, Beagle Bay, 3/1/04.

5. Royal Commission on the Condition of the Natives Report 1905. Evidence of Father Walter to Dr. Walter Edmund Roth, September 1904.

6. ibid.

7. ADB. Bishop Kelly, Geraldton, to Father Walter, Beagle Bay, 1/4/03.

8. ADB. Bishop Kelly, Geraldton, to Father Walter, Beagle Bay, 30/12/03.
9. Roth Report. Evidence of Father Walter, Beagle Bay, September 1904.
10. ADB. Father W. Whitmee, Vicar-General, Rome, to Father Walter, Beagle Bay, 9/7/01.
11. Correspondence from 1895 to 1907, re expected arrival of Sisters at Beagle Bay.
12. ADB. Daisy Bates, Perth, to Father Walter, Beagle Bay, 3/4/04.
13. ADB. Father W. Whitmee, Rome, to Father Walter, Beagle Bay, 9/6/04.
14. ADB. Father W. Whitmee, Rome, to Father Walter, Beagle Bay, 12/6/05.
15. ADB. Father White, Perth, to Father Walter, Beagle Bay, 24/6/04.
16. ADB. Father W. Whitmee, Rome, to Father Walter, 12/6/05.
17. J. S. Needham, *Black and White in Australia.* Information from Pallottine sources.
18. ADB. Father W. Whitmee, Rome, to Father Walter, Beagle Bay, 9/6/04.

CHAPTER SIXTEEN
1. ACAP. Bishop Gibney, Perth, to Father Walter, Beagle Bay, 4/6/04. See also ACAP letter from Walter James, Premier, to Bishop Gibney, 21/5/04.
2. ADB. Bishop Kelly, Geraldton, to Father Walter, Beagle Bay, 9/9/04.
3. Roth Report. Evidence of Father Walter, Beagle Bay, September 1904, pp. 56, 58.
4. Information to author from the Aboriginal Paddy Djiagween of Broome is that he was one of these. He and two other boys had become homesick for their people and had tried to make back overland to the port. They were tracked, brought back in an exhausted state and punished but later thanked the missionaries for having exercised a firm and stabilizing influence.
5. Roth Report. Evidence of Father Walter, Beagle Bay, p. 58, item 601.
6. ibid. Item 611.
7. Roth Report. Evidence of Montague Sydney Hadley, in

charge of Sunday Island Mission, November 1904, pp.
106–108.
8. Roth Report. Evidence of Father Nicholas Emo, Parish
Priest, Broome, October 1904, pp. 61–63.
9. ibid. Item 711.
10. Roth Report. Recommendations. Beagle Bay, pp. 29–30.
11. ibid. Sunday Island. p. 30.
12. ibid. Broome. p. 30.
13. Roth Report. Evidence of John Byrne, Sergeant of Police,
Broome, October 1904, pp. 58–61.
14. John Byrne, Sergeant of Police, Broome, to Father Walter,
Beagle Bay, 24/3/05.
15. ibid.
16. See P. Biscup, 'Native Administration and Welfare in Western Australia 1965' (unpublished thesis, University of Western
Australia).
17. ADB. Copies of letters from Father Walter to State and
Church authorities, 1905–1906.
18. Actually both priests were wrong as the time of the appointment had been late 1899.
19. He had been, of course, until the return of Father Jean
Marie Janny.
20. Report of Bishop Gibney, quoted by Reilly, p. 515.
21. ADB. Father Nicholas Emo, Broome, to Father Walter,
Beagle Bay, 1905 (in French).
22. ADB. Bishop W. Kelly, Geraldton, to Father Walter,
Beagle Bay, 13/4/05.
23. ADB. Father W. Whitmee, Rome, to Father Walter, Beagle
Bay, 12/6/05.
24. ADB. Telegram to Father Walter re result of vote, 20/10/05,
signed [Father] Drayne.
25. ADB. Agreement signed by Father Nicholas Emo and
Father George Walter, October 1905.
26. ADB. To Father Nicholas Emo, March 1906, *Dispensatio
Votorum Simplicium*, signed by J. Augustius Marre for the
Abbot-General.
27. ADB. Father Walter, Beagle Bay, to Mr. Princep, Chief
Protector of Aborigines, Perth, September 1906:

... During the years 1901–5 our annual grant was only £250
while our annual expenditure was at least £1,500. Even with
the increased grant, the paid up arrears for 1904/6 and the

355

grant for the invalids we received only £2,333 in four years and have to spend £7,500. . . . This left us to cover a balance of £5,167. . . . Given the necessary assistance to develop the property and improve our natural resources I am confident of the success and the credit of the mission to the colony and the whole of the British Empire. . . .

28. Information to the author by pioneer Sisters of the Order of St. John of God, from the account of Father Nicholas.

CHAPTER SEVENTEEN

1. The Sisters of St. John of God was an Order established in County Wexford, Ireland, in 1871, its founders being Dr. Furlong, Bishop of Ferns, and Miss Brigid Clancy (late Mother Visitation). The members of the congregation gave themselves to nursing, teaching, visiting the sick poor and other works of charity. Their first venture abroad followed the acceptance, by four nursing and four teaching sisters under the leadership of Sister M. Antonio O'Brien, of the invitation of Bishop Gibney to work in his diocese in Western Australia.

2. ACAP. Sister M. Assumpta, St. John of God, Subiaco, Western Australia, to Bishop Gibney, Perth, 10/1/06.

3. ibid.

4. ACAP. Sister M. Antonio O'Brien, Wexford, to Bishop Gibney, Perth, 1/1/07.

5. Two applicants must have dropped out and one, later Sister Mary Immaculate Leahy, remained to complete her nursing training before rejoining the Broome community in 1910.

6. Evidence of pioneer St. John of God nuns in Broome.

7. ACAP. Sister Mary Bernardine Greene, Subiaco, to Bishop Gibney, Perth, 7/1/06.

8. ADB. Father Walter, Sydney, to Father Bischoffs, Beagle Bay, 9/4/07 (in German).

9. ADB. Father Walter, Sydney, to Father Bischoffs, Beagle Bay, 16/4/04 (in German).

10. Personal communication from pioneer Sister and later Provincial Mother M. Margaret Carmody.

11. ACAP. Mother M. Antonio O'Brien, Beagle Bay, to Bishop Gibney, Perth, June 1907.

12. Information from Beagle-Bay-educated Aboriginal Paddy Djiagween of Broome.

13. This habit has been modified of recent years to be more in keeping with the climate.

14. The Christian Brothers' Education Record, 1928, contains a biography of Brother Joseph O'Brien who died the previous year. In this it is recorded: 'Reared by a saintly Irish mother, who gave her five sons and two daughters to Holy Religion, he was cradled in piety, and from his infancy imbibed that natural goodness of heart in which vice finds no dwelling.... His Brothers in Religion generally regard him as a man of eminent sanctity and extraordinary virtue....'

15. ADB. Father J. Bischoffs (Protector of Aborigines), Beagle Bay, to Bishop Kelly, Geraldton, August 1907.

16. Father J. Bischoffs, Beagle Bay, to Mr. J. Isdell, Protector and Travelling Inspector for Aborigines, Derby, July 1908.

17. From Bishop Gibney, Perth, to Sir John Forrest, Perth, 1901. Quoted by P. McCarthy in 'The Foundations of Catholicism in Western Australia 1829–1911', *University Studies in History and Economics*, 1956, p. 61.

18. ADB. Father J. Bischoffs, Beagle Bay, to Mr. J. Isdell, Derby, August 1908.

19. 'Die Njol Njol, ein Eingelornestamm in Nordwest Australien', *Anthropos*, 3, pp. 32–40, 1908.

20. These included 'Churinga und Totems in Nord-West Australien', *Anthropos*, 1909, and grammar and vocabulary of the Njol Njol language, Beagle Bay, which he sent to Professor W. Schmidt of Vienna.

21. ACAP. Father Walter, Sydney, to Bishop Gibney, Perth, 24/3/07.

22. C. F. Gale, an ex-pastoralist, who in 1907 took over from H. C. Princep as Chief Protector of Aborigines.

23. ADB. Father Walter, Germany, to Father Thomas Bachmair, Beagle Bay, 12/8/08.

24. Georg Walter: *Australien: Land, Leute Mission*, 1928.

CHAPTER EIGHTEEN

1. ADB. Report of Father J. Bischoffs, Protector of Aborigines, Beagle Bay, to Mr. J. Isdell, Protector and Travelling Inspector of Aborigines, Derby, July 1908. Father Bischoffs commends the 'energetic work' of Mr. Isdell and the co-operation of Mr. McCarthy of Derby and Corporal Stuart of Broome in bringing children to the mission. Also letters (ibid.) from fathers of half-caste children inquiring about terms and advising of the departure of the children by ship from Wyndham or Derby in charge of a police officer.

2. Information from pioneer nuns in Broome.

3. This was not necessarily an indication of cannibalism. The Aborigines frequently carried the bones of their dead, wrapped in bark, over long periods. See R. M. and C. H. Berndt, *The World Of The First Australians*, p. 410.

4. Sister Mary Gabriel Greene (younger sister of Sr. M. Bernardine and Sr. M. Gertrude).

5. Notes made on request by Sister M. Margaret Carmody.

6. ACAP. Bishop Kelly, Cue, to Bishop Gibney, Perth, October 1908: '... impediments, entanglements, misconceptions and misrepresentations seemed to spring out of the very soil and thwart my priests at every step. It will be a relief therefore to be rid of it.' Abbot Torres took over from Bishop Kelly as Apostolic Administrator of the Kimberleys in 1910, He was consecrated bishop in Rome in May of that year. He died in 1914. The Italian Salesian priest Father Ernest Coppo was consecrated first Vicar-Apostolic of Kimberley in 1922.

7. ACAP. Bishop Kelly, Cue, to Bishop Gibney, Perth, 23/10/08.

8. ibid.

9. Information of Sister Mary Margaret Carmody, to whom the watch was given.

10. The Adelaide Steamship Company's vessel *Koombana* disappeared during a cyclone off Port Hedland in April 1912 with crew and 135 passengers.

11. Monument in the Broome cemetery inscribed: 'Erected by the Japanese of Broome, in grateful memory of Sister Mary Immaculate Leahy. Died 12th January, 1912. R.I.P.'

12. Sister Mary Michael Power.

CHAPTER NINETEEN

1. From the journal of Abbot Torres, quoted in the booklet *Kulumburu*, published by the Benedictines, New Norcia, W.A.

2. ibid.

3. F. S. Brockman, *Report on Exploration of North-West Kimberley, 1901*, Perth, 1902.

4. Chamberlain's Well, named after the son of the Fremantle ship-builder, Chamberlain of 'Sunny-side' who had helped deliver many luggers and schooners produced in his father's workshops, to purchasers in the north-west. This well, near the charred stumps of Father Nicholas's chapel on Cygnet Bay, was still in good repair when seen by the author in 1965.

5. ACAP. Telegram from Father Nicholas, Derby, to Bishop Gibney, 9/9/07.

6. ADB. Records show a steady population of ninety-seven natives at Cygnet Bay at that time.

7. ACAP. Father Nicholas, on board the *San Salvador*, to Bishop Gibney, Perth, 28/6/08.

8. J. B. Wylie, Yule River, Roebourne, to *The West Australian*, 28/11/92. Quoted Reilly, p. 364.

9. From the journal of Abbot Torres, June 1908, quoted in *Kulumburu*.

10. ACAP. Father Nicholas, Drysdale River Mission, to Bishop Gibney, Perth, 7/11/08.

11. Among the various accounts of these cave paintings of supernatural fertility beings Wandjina and Unur are those made by J. R. B. Love, A. P. Elkin, A. Capell, the Frobenius Expedition of 1938, R. M. and C. H. Berndt and E. A. Worms. Father Worms, interested by the descriptions of Father Nicholas, dated 1905, visited the site and described the figures in detail in his illustrated paper: 'Contemporary and Prehistoric Rock Paintings in Central and Northern Kimberley', *Anthropos*, Vol. 50, 1955.

12. In a letter to Mr. Gale, Chief Protector of Aborigines, Perth, 16/4/11, Father Nicholas, enclosing copies of the cave paintings (Reference 11) wrote: 'The replicas of native cave paintings . . . I got in caves about fifteen miles from the mission (Drysdale). To make full cover would need three men (with guns!) to remain for two or three days and this I could not obtain.'

13. The letter quoted (Reference 12), accompanying a parcel of 'curios', gives some idea of the various articles collected:

According to my promise I have sent for the Department: With the Inspector Sellenger, the skull of a half aged wild native, and *his brain* in a phial . . .'

(This specimen was probably intended for Professor Hermann Klaatsch, M.D., who had visited Dampierland in 1906 and the missions. He studied the Aborigines of north Australia for three years with particular attention to skull measurements and brain structure. Some of his observations are to be found in the Report of the 11th Meeting of the Australian Association on Scientific Travel among the Black Population of Tropical Australia, 1904, 1905, 1906. The specimen referred to was most likely obtained from the Dampierland area about 1911.)

... Recently sent care of Corporal Stuart of Broome, 4 big parcels containing 2 small canoes, 6 long spears, a cradle of 'pingen', 3 iron tomahawks, a collection of stone tomahawks and stone spears, 2 phials of green powder, a big 'Wakeboor' or 'Coddor', 2 'Gnaolos' with the native blood, 2 parcels of sticks for making fire, collection of sticks called 'Paren' they continually use for *kill louses* one to the other, a collection of their daily food, also sticks found in their camps.

The two phials of green powder from leaves found in possession of a wild woman who carried all her things in a piece of my cut sails. The powder was carefully enveloped in fine paperbark also in phials. I would like a chemical analysis to discover the properties for the importance the natives attach to this powder and careful manner enveloped and carried made me convinced it is a medicine or nourishing food as is the Coak in the Bolivian Republic of S. America where the native Indians use it when in voyages, taking a pinch two or three times a day to give them vigour and strength.

The small canoes for children were hidden in a tree between Vansittart Bay and Napier Broome Bay.

You may think perhaps I have sent you too much *rubbish*!! but considering I have selected all the stones etc. in peculiar places amongst perhaps more than 200 camps, they were to me of special value. I have sent the whole collection on and nothing remains to me.

14. ACAP. Father John Creagh (Redemptorist), Broome, to the Archbishop's Secretary, Perth, 15/7/18. Also ADB. Father John Creagh, Broome, to Father Thomas Bachmair, Lombadina, 15/5/18.
15. The Departments of Aborigines and Fisheries were amalgamated under one official in 1909.
16. P. Biscup, unpublished thesis, 'Native Administration and Welfare in Western Australia', 1965.
17. ibid.
18. Evidence of the Aboriginal Monty Inganboor, taken by author in 1965, at Cygnet Bay, on site of Father Nicholas's mission. This native had gone to Drysdale River with Father Nicholas in 1908 and returned with him to the Dampierland peninsula in 1910.

CHAPTER TWENTY

1. ADB. First Lombadina register of births, marriages and deaths, kept by Father Nicholas Emo, 1911/1915.

2. Lombadina register. Notes of Father John Herold, 1948.

3. Evidence of pioneer St. John of God nuns, Broome and Beagle Bay.

4. ibid.

5. Sibasado, Joseph Martin, born Marble Bar, 1893. He was brought to Broome from Cossack by Captain Owen in 1900 and taken by Father Nicholas to Beagle Bay in 1901. He joined Father Nicholas at Lombadina in 1913 and was married there to Eriberta Idon, of Disaster Bay, in February 1915.

6. News of these attacks led to the government's requesting Bishop Torres to abandon the so far fruitless mission. This the abbot refused to do and the community persevered until the natives, evidently surprised to find that the missionaries were not interested in reprisals, eventually accepted them.

7. *Liber Defunctorum*, Lombadina mission.

8. Story as related by missionaries and people at Lombadina mission also told to the author by the late Captain James MacKenzie.

9. James Theodore Cluitt MacKenzie later entered into a pearling partnership with Maurice Lyons. Generally known as 'Long Mac' he was a much loved and respected resident of the Broome district to the time of his death in December 1957. He is buried in the Broome pioneer cemetery.

10. See letter from Father Nicholas Emo to Bishop Gibney, 1900, quoted in Chapter 11.


CHAPTER TWENTY-ONE

1. J. S. Needham, *Black and White in Australia*, quoting Pallottine sources.

2. ADB. Report of Father J. Bischoffs, Beagle Bay, to Mr. J. Isdell, Derby, July 1908.

3. Evidence of north-west pioneer missionaries and Aborigines.

4. Roth Report. Evidence of Father Walter, p. 58, item 601.

5. Archbishop P. J. Clune, D.D., born County Clare, Ireland, 1864, Redemptorist, consecrated Bishop of Perth 1911, became first Catholic Archbishop of Perth 1913. He was senior chaplain for W.A. Catholic troops during World War I and was a celebrated preacher.

6. Pender Bay Station, then owned by Streeter and Male and managed by David Bell, who died and was buried there in 1917.

7. Father Droste, Beagle Bay, to the Pallottine house, Lamburg, 1915. Quoted by S. J. Needham in *Black and White Australia*.

8. ADB. Father J. Creagh, Broome, to Father Thomas Bachmair, Lombadina, April 1918: '... Thomas is now under the influence of Parks and is, I am told, going to sell the place to Parks if the agreement between Freney and Parks can't be carried out ...'

9. Mr. A. O. Neville, formerly Secretary to the Immigration Department, appointed Chief Protector of Aborigines 7/5/15. See Chapter 22, move to close missions on Dampierland peninsula.

10. ACAP. Father J. Creagh, Broome, probably to Bishop Kelly, Geraldton, 15/7/18.

11. ADB. Father J. Creagh, Broome, to Father Thomas Bachmair, Lombadina, April 1918.

12. ADB. Father J. Creagh, Broome, to Father T. Bachmair, Lombadina, July 1918.

13. ADB. Father J. Creagh, Broome, to Father T. Bachmair, Lombadina, 15/5/18.

14. The original ceiling of the Beagle Bay church was demolished in a hurricane some years later.

CHAPTER TWENTY-TWO
1. ACAP.

2. Moseley Report. Evidence of Mr. A. O. Neville, Chief Protector of Aborigines.

3. Dr. W. Ramsay Smith (1858–1937), anthropologist, doctor of medicine, permanent head of Department of Health, South Australia. *Official Year Book of the Commonwealth of Australia*, No. 3, 1910.

4. Daisy Bates, *The Passing Of The Aborigines*, p. 243.

5. A. O. Neville, *Australia's Coloured Minority*.

6. Although many theories have been advanced there is still an element of mystery in the decrease of the full-blood Aborigines over this period. J. S. Needham in *Black and White in Australia* quotes one owner-manager of a station where there were 300 natives in 1913 as saying in the 1930s: 'None have been shot, none have been poisoned, none have been driven off, yet the numbers are now only 30.' This rate of decline was typical of all outback properties.

7. Battye Library, Perth, N.WT. 58/1920.

8. Underwood, Rufus H., Member for the Pilbarra district 1906/24, appointed Minister for the North-West, without portfolio, 1914/17, 1917/19.

9. A. O. Neville, *Australia's Coloured Minority*, 1947, p. 98.

10. Statement of A. O. Neville to the author, 1931: 'More human problems are dealt with by this Department than anyone could imagine.'

11. Paddy Djiagween, well known and respected in Broome.


CHAPTER TWENTY-THREE

1. Fathers Siara, Setaro, Gullino, Lopez and Rosetti, Brothers Acerni and Asseli.

2. The missionary branch of the Sisters of St. John of God in Kimberley was not amalgamated with their Order in Ireland until 1928.

3. Mother Antonio O'Brien and Mother Bernardine Greene both died in February 1923 and are buried in the Broome cemetery.

4. P. McCarthy, 'The Foundation of Catholicism in Western Australia, *University Studies in History and Economics*, August 1956, p. 275.

5. At the end of 1921 a hookworm campaign, organized by the Commonwealth Government was carried out in Kimberley. It was found that this disease, introduced by indentured labour, was endemic to the whole of the Dampierland peninsula with a 91.9% incidence at Beagle Bay. See A. H. Baldsin and L. F. Cooling, *An Investigation into Hookworm Disease, Malaria and Filaria in Western Australia*, Melbourne 1922.

6. Dr. Cecil Cook, Chief Commonwealth Medical Officer for the Northern Territory, following the discovery of cases of leprosy in Derby in 1922, made an inspection of Kimberley in 1924. See Chapter 24.

7. Recalled by Broome residents at a farewell to Lord Montague Sydney Hadley in 1923. He had at last succeeded in getting external support for Sunday Island, which he left in the hands of the fundamentalist United Aborigines Mission.

8. ACAP. Each sister then in Kimberley was asked officially to write privately whether she accepted amalgamation with the mother-house or wished the missionary branch to join the new congregation of Our Lady Help of Christians. They voted in favour of continuing with their own Order.

In 1924 when the Sisters of St. John of God in Ireland and

England united under the rule of a Mother General in County Wexford the Australian branches founded from Subiaco (with the exception of the Kimberley mission) came under the same jurisdiction. Several attempts to unite the Kimberley congregation with the other branches were made without success but in 1928 this congregation was reunited with the rest of the Order under the same Mother General.

9. Excluding their surrounding Kalumburu mission, which was administered by the Benedictine Abbot of New Norcia.

10. J. C. de Lancourt, *The Western Mail*, 12/11/25.

11. 'Broomite', *The Western Mail*, 4/3/26.

12. The late M. P. Durack, the author's father, is quoted here.

CHAPTER TWENTY-FOUR

1. Professor S. D. Porteous, *The Psychology Of A Primitive People*, Arnold, London, 1931.

2. Father E. A. Worms, Pallottine House, Addison Road, Manly, to the author, 30/5/61.

3. In putting forward his case to the Catholic community (*The Advocate*, 28/3/30) Father Raible continued:

> We spent over £900 in the first year for this purpose, but owing to heavy drought the first harvest was bad. . . . To cut it short last year's expenses consumed all returns of cattle sale [from Beagle Bay] – £1,248, sale of vegetables – £500, subsidy of Association of Propagation of the Faith – £400, Government subsidy – £250, donations £1,000. We were left with a debt of about £1,450. We suffered also the loss of about 600 head of cattle on Beagle Bay owing to the excessively dry summer. Two weeks ago we shipped 107 head . . . the returns will be about £500. . . .

4. This occurred in April 1935 during the absence of Bishop Raible in Europe. In an interview for the *Catholic Record*, Father Worms, then parish priest in Broome, described how, with the help of several half-caste boys, he had cleared the track of broken scrub and uprooted trees, got a car through to within ten miles of the mission and walked the rest. 'The children saw my white topee in the scrub and ran to tell me the worst – the noviciate destroyed, the tamarind tree, the children's dormitory, the roof of the church at Lombadina, one of the new mission luggers sunk. Father Benedict approached slowly, bent by his pioneer years and this last disaster. On all sides were pieces of

364

twisted sheet iron and paperbark. The church tower was hanging and many buildings roofless, the windmill in shreds. It looked like a village destroyed by shell fire, even the foliage blown from the trees. In all the cyclones of the years never was so much damage done, but no lives were lost, except for one old leper who died when the storm was at its height. . . .'

5. Dr. Cecil Cook, in his *Epidemiology Of Leprosy In Australia* observes that the disease was not known and could not logically be supposed to have been endemic among the Aborigines at the time of colonization.

6. Records of the Department of Public Health. J. J. Holmes, quoted in Report on *Leprosy and the Treatment of the Aborigines*, 11/6/36.

7. ibid.

8. Ibid., A. O. Neville to Chairman of the Road Board, Broome, October 1924.

9. ibid.

10. P. Biscup, unpublished thesis, 'Native Administration and Welfare in Western Australia', 1965.

11. Records of the Department of Public Health. Instruction to station managers to send leper suspects to Beagle Bay.

12. Records of the Department of Public Health. Report of Dr. A. J. King, D.M.O., Wyndham, July 1937.

13. Captain Henry Scott, F.R.G.S., previously Fisheries Inspector, Broome. He was later found to have himself contracted leprosy.

14. The lugger had to turn back to Broome from where G. Howard, one of the patients, despatched a letter (ADB) to the parish priest, Father Worms. This read:

Dear Rev. Father Worms. P.S.M. . . . We just came in last night. Dear Father had to turn back from Swan Point where we lost anchors and sailed to Boolaman creek got two old anchores. I would like that you came an see in what way we are packed we haven't got the list of room to move about an the worst part the boat deck is leaking like a bucket. Its two nights that we slept with water all our stuff is wet. Were ever we have to move we must walk over each other. I want if you can see about this we are not to be treated by the depat. in this way when they can provide a better and bigger lugger. If this things happen in the beginning what will be when we be in that long trip we will have to pass on heaving seas. I know

365

those parts I have been on the boat working before. Lord
knows how will be. Its now four days and the women are
lying with wet wet blankets an even they can move about on
the deck. Its only a small place that we have. So dear Father
if you can do anything I'll thank you so many hearty thanks.
Yours sincerely Gregory Howard.

Father Worms wired the Minister for Health asking that the
patients be allowed to remain in Broome until a better lugger
was provided, but orders were issued that the *Rolland* must
proceed without delay. Mr. Munsie, Minister for Health, replying to criticism in *The West Australian*, stated that the Manager of Harbour and Lights and a Native Welfare officer had
reported that the boat was quite satisfactory.

15. Report of the Royal Commission, 1935.
16. ibid. Evidence of A. O. Neville, Chief Protector of Aborigines.
17. ibid.
18. Notably, Professor A. P. Elkin, T. G. H. Strehlow, the Rev.
J. R. B. Love, the Reverend Professor H. Nekes and Father E.
A. Worms.
19. Ernest Charles Mitchell, formerly Inspector of Aborigines.
20. These missions were: Beagle Bay, Lombadina and
Kalumburu (Catholic); Forrest River (C. of E.); Kunmunya
(Presbyterian); Sunday Island (United Aborigines). These
missions were then supporting between them 700 natives by
their own means and 180 with the aid of government subsidy,
providing schools for over 200 children and sheltering several
hundred half-castes.

   P. Hasluck states in *The West Australian*, 6/9/34: 'The efforts
of these private bodies has relieved the State of a good deal of
cost – always assuming the State would have done as much –
and has taken over a good deal of its worry. The State owes
them a debt of gratitude and respect for their opinions.'
21. ibid.
22. ibid.
23. Records of the Public Health Department. Letter from J. J.
Holmes (Member for the Kimberley district) protesting that
Bishop Raible's offers were rejected but no satisfactory alternative measures taken. 11/6/36.
24. In August 1937 the Beagle Bay mission chronicle records the
grief of the community at the departure of Dr. Betz and 'his

noble wife', after twenty months' hard work, during which they got the mission 'thoroughly cleaned up', leaving only a few suspect cases. Leprosy cases had been sent to Derby and other complaints treated locally. Dr. Betz died in Germany not long afterwards.

25. Records of the Public Health Department. Report of Dr. Davis, D.M.O. Derby, 1936.

26. Evidence of Mother M. Gertrude Greene.

CHAPTER TWENTY-FIVE

1. Bernard Everett Bardwell, ex-pearler and conchologist, who died in 1955 and is buried in the pioneer cemetery, Broome.

2. Ruth M. Underhill, *Red Man's America*, University of Chicago Press, 1953.

3. Father E. A. Worms, Manly, N.S.W., to the author, 1/9/58.

4. A. E. Worms, S.A.C., 'Djjamar and His Relation to Other Culture Heroes,' *Anthropos*, Vol. 47, 1952.

5. ADB. Statement of Father Worms for the use of missionary teachers.

6. ADB. In notes left for the use of his fellow missionaries Father Worms wrote:

> The often harmful practice of subincision of the lower urethra was introduced into Kimberley soon after circumcision from a radiating centre probably situated west of the Aranda provinces in historic times. The arrival of the white man at the beginning of the 19th century arrested the conquest of the entire continent by these mutilating ceremonies, leaving a more or less broad circle along the West, South and East coast of Australia untouched by this practice. Both operations (circumcisions and subincision) can be replaced by baptism and sacramental consecrations, but slowly and with much consideration where our north-west missions are concerned. The deep scarification of chest, back and legs (and the removal of front teeth) has disappeared from coastal tribes, but I have had to dissuade the drinking of human blood at the beginning of initiation ceremonies, especially on account of the frequent appearance of Hansen's disease and hookworm. . . .

7. W. E. H. Stanner, 'On Aboriginal Religion', *Oceania*, Vol. XXX, No. 2, 1959.

8. A. P. Elkin, *The Australian Aborigines*, p. 211.

9. E. A. Worms, s.a.c., 'Place Names in Kimberley, Western Australia', *Oceania*, Vol. XIV, No. 4, 1944.

10. ibid.

In a later article ('The Poetry of the Yaoro and the Bard, North-West Australia', *Annali Lateranesi*, Vol. XXI) Father Worms remarks: 'The surprising similarity between the poetic technique used in West Kimberley and that found in Central Australia, more than 1,500 miles distant, gives a new indication of uniform intellectual forces at work in the souls of the natives scattered over the Australian continent. . . .'

11. A. E. Worms, *The Aboriginal Concept of the Soul*, 1959.

12. This work still in ms. form at the time of this writing.

13. At the conclusion of his essay *The Aboriginal Concept of the Soul,* Father Worms made the following note:

While this article was already in the printers' hands a rather sensational discussion about the probable sacrificial character operating in the Karwadi (Mother of All) initiations of the tribes in the north-western parts of the Northern Territory was published by W. E. H. Stanner, 'On Aboriginal Religion', in *Oceania*, Sydney, 1959, Vol. III, pp. 108–127. It contains such a striking comparison with the partitions of the Sacrifice of Mass: 'Participation – Consecration – Immolation – Destruction – Transformation – Return', that it presents a challenge to the theologian and to the student of comparative religion.'

In the following year Professor Stanner published another article on this theme: 'Sacramentalism, Rite and Myth', *Oceania*, Vol. XXX, June, 1960, No. 4.

14. T. G. H. Strehlow, quoted by E. A. Worms in *The Aboriginal Concept of the Soul*.

15. T. G. H. Strehlow, *Aranda Traditions*, Melbourne University Press, 1947.

16. Professor Herman Neke, s.a.c., and E. A. Worms, s.a.c., 'Australian Languages, Grammar and Comparative Dictionaries', Micro-Bibliotheca, *Anthropos*, Fribourg, Switzerland, 1953.

17. ibid.

18. E. A. Worms, 'Contemporary and Prehistoric Rock Paintings in Central and North Kimberley', *Anthropos*, Vol. 50, 1955.

19. Balgo Hills Mission records. A chronicle of Rockhole was

kept by Father Francis Huegel and later by Father John Herold. It is there stated that Rockhole was purchased from Francis P. Castles for £1,400.

20. The surveying of this route is described in *The Beckoning West* by Eleanor Smith, 1966. The route was discontinued after World War II.

21. Records of the Aboriginal Welfare Department, Perth.

22. R. Coverley.

23. ACAP. Bishop Otto Raible, Rockold Station, Hall's Creek, to Archbishop Prendiville, Perth, 2/9/39.

24. ACAP. Archbishop Prendiville, Perth, to Bishop Raible, Broome, 7/9/39.

25. ACAP. Bishop Raible, Broome, to Archbishop Prendiville, Perth, September 1939.


CHAPTER TWENTY-SIX

1. ACAP. Bishop Raible, Beagle Bay, to Archbishop Redmond Prendiville, Perth, 1/12/38. Archbishop Prendiville succeeded Archbishop Clune who died in 1935.

2. ibid.

3. *Hansard*, 1938. The Hon. C. H. Wittenoom.

4. A letter from Bishop Otto Raible to the author from Limburg, 9/4/64, tells something of his attachment to the country and to his old friends. He writes:

... It is just five years today that I sailed from Fremantle harbour on my way to Europe. And I can still picture you standing on the wharf with Julie and John waving farewell to a good friend, and I may say, your spiritual father. The last minute before sailing Fr. Luemen managed to bring your farewell gifts on board ... for which I am still thankful, for it used to cheer me up whenever pains of homesickness for sunny Australia made my heart heavy.

I am sure you still remember the song we made together at your old home: 'You ask why I love it, this house on the plain ... so far from the world that is gay ...' – dear old Argyle with the rolling plains and hills that break on the sky.* It was

* Bishop Raible wrote a charming melody to the sentimental ballad of which one verse ran:

If you hear not the song of these wide-sweeping plains,
Of these ranges that break on the sky,
No words can convey the strange magic they hold
And only my heart can reply.

369

there in the early thirties where I discovered the heart of the Kimberleys. . . . Those were happy carefree days for all of you children. . . .

I am now living at our provincial house, where I had made my studies, was ordained and consecrated bishop twenty-nine years ago. There are a few old Fathers here with whom I had been associated during my first few years as a missionary in Cameroon, W. Africa. My health is gradually declining, my feet are often on strike and my eyes are getting dim. Yet what else can you expect at seventy-six! Before long the time will come when Our Lord takes me out of circulation, as he did with our dear friend Fr. Worms last year. His last work 'Die Religion der australischen Ureingeborenen' is in the press. . . .

5. From the Beagle Bay mission chronicle, then kept by Father Francis Huegel, 22/10/40.
6. ACAP. Report of Bishop Raible, from Kew, Melbourne, 17/6/41.
7. The remains of the Dutch refugees were returned to relatives in Holland after the war.
8. Anne Robertson Coupar, *The Smirnoff Story*, Jarrolds, London, 1960.
9. ibid., p. 181.
10. As told to the author by Paddy Djiagween, Broome.
11. Father John McGuire, *The Record*, 31/12/59.
12. ibid.
13. Balgo Mission records. The Rockhole chronicle.

CHAPTER TWENTY-SEVEN
1. The Native Citizen Rights Act of September 1944.
2. H. D. Moseley, Report of the Royal Commission, 1935.
3. F. E. A. Bateman, Report of the Royal Commission, 1948.
4. ibid.
5. A graphic account of this well organized rising is to be found in D. R. Stuart's novel, *Yandy*.
6. P. Biscup, 'Native Administration and Welfare in Western Australia', 1965 (unpublished thesis).
7. ibid.

CHAPTER TWENTY-EIGHT
1. H. B. Hawthorn, C. S. Belshaw and S. M. Jamieson, *The Indians Of British Colombia: A Study of Contemporary Social Adjustment*, Californian University Press, 1958.

Some Indians, also some whites for various reasons advocate some sort of return to the past. . . . But acculturation is irreversible. There is no point in working to turn the clock back or to hold the line where it is *now*. . . . Within careful limits the goal of policy should be an adaption to present and to future needs, but a sharp distinction should be maintained between trying to force assimilation and allowing for continuing change, with careful attention to timing and initiative at any particular time the specific goals of this policy should even appear to lead in a direction opposite to that of assimilation. Such apparently backward steps might include continuing or implementing special welfare, educational and corrective services for the Indians – distinct and separate from the general provincial ones. . . .

2. Mr. F. Wilmington, later manager of Lissadell Station, East Kimberley.
3. The town orphanage was closed and orphan or neglected children removed to Beagle Bay in 1965.
4. F. E. A. Bateman, Report of the Royal Commission, 1948.
5. Mother Mary Gertrude Greene was killed in a motor accident in Broome in 1965.
6. See Roth Report 1905 and Moseley Report 1935.
7. The vicariate of Kimberley was raised to the status of the Diocese of Broome in 1966.
8. The Most Rev. Otto Raible, D.D., S.A.C., Vicar-Apostolic of the Kimberley Vicariate (now the Diocese of Broome) died in June 1966 at the age of 79, at his birthplace, Stuttgart, Germany.

EPILOGUE
1. David W. Potter, *People of Plenty, Economic Abundance And The American Character*, University of Chicago Press.
2. The Official Year Book of 1968/69 gives the Catholic population of Kimberley (including Aborigines) as 2,250. Children in Catholic schools 675. Priests 13, Brothers 7, Nuns 45, Lay Missionaries 24.
3. Elizabeth Durack, *Sydney Morning Herald*, 11/5/63.
4. From *The Advocate*, Melbourne, Victoria, 27/1/66.

When Father Silvester, Vice-Provincial of the Pallottine Fathers in Australia, met the late Holy Father in private audience about a year before his death, Pope John said to him: 'How is it going Father?' F. Silvester replied: 'Your Holiness, if you are asking me as a human being, I would answer, I can't go on, but as a priest ...' With tears in his eyes the Holy Father interrupted him: 'Carissimo Padre,' he said, 'if you and your brothers don't look after these poor children of ours in the wilds of Western Australia who then will?'

5. The present population of Beagle Bay mission is 165 under 16 years, 108 over 16 years. The annual report for 1966 of the Commissioner of Native Welfare states:

Probably the most exciting project during the coming year will be the erection of a secondary school on the mission, thus providing academic, technical and domestic education up to this standard.

6. Lombadina population for 1966, 67 under 16 years, 75 over 16 years.

7. In 1966 seventeen boys and girls living at the Riverton hostel and attending nearby secondary schools gained the Junior Public Certificate and one boy obtained the Leaving Certificate with a Commonwealth Scholarship for University studies. Three boys obtained the Trade Ticket after five years' apprenticeship in carpentry, boilermaking and welding. Five ex-student girls are nursing, six are junior clerks and one is a receptionist at a government city office. Nine ex-student boys are apprenticed to various trades, and one is a junior clerk in the General Post Office in Perth.

8. The population of La Grange is listed as 94 under 16 years, 82 over 16 years. The official report states:

Excellent co-operation and assistance has been received from the mission in regard to acceptance of committal cases and delinquents. A rehabilitation programme has been carried out with these cases with apparent success. Fringe area natives continue to arrive at the mission and wherever possible these natives are employed or housed at the mission.

9. The population of Balgo Hills mission for 1966 is 143 under 16 years, 105 over 16 years.

10. ADB. Statement of Father E. A. Worms, 1962.

11. T. G. H. Strehlow, *Assimilation Problems, the Aboriginal Viewpoint*, University of Adelaide, S.A., 1961.

Professor A. P. Elkin estimates the Aboriginal population of the Dampierland peninsula at the beginning of white settlement as about 1,500. Today the number is given as 844, not counting approximately 50 Dampierland natives working in other parts of the north. Few areas in Australia show a smaller overall rate of decline, while in the same time full-blood Aborigines have completely disappeared from many parts of the continent.

12. *Aboriginal Advancement*, a pamphlet prepared under the authority of the Minister for Territories, July 1967, states:

> Aborigines are Australian citizens. They have equal rights with others in social service benefits and in voting for all Commonwealth, State and Territory elections. . . . All Australian Governments have adopted as policy – That all persons of Aboriginal descent will choose to attain a similar manner and standard of living to that of other Australians and live as members of a single Australian community – enjoying the same rights and privileges, accepting the same responsibilities and influenced by the same hopes and loyalties as other Australians. Any special measures taken are regarded as temporary measures, not based on race, but intended to meet their need for special care and assistance and to make the transition from one stage to another in such a way as will be favourable to their social, economic and political advancement.
>
> The word 'choose' is possibly the most significant word in the definition. The Aborigines themselves are deciding the extent and rate of change from their traditional way of life. . . . As a result of a referendum in May 1967 . . . Aborigines will be counted in all future censuses.

In 1966 of the estimated 130,000 Aborigines and part-Aborigines in Australia about 9,500 were attending special primary schools, between 10,000 and 15,000 were attending public primary schools and more than 2,500 were students at secondary schools. Exact figures cannot be tabulated since many part-Aboriginal families have merged into the general community.

13. Report of the Commission on Education in New Zealand (under the chairmanship of Sir George Currie), 1962, pp. 415–416. Quoted in Watts-Gallacher Report.

> Although there is no retreat from the belief that the Maori child must be equipped to take his place on terms of equality as a New Zealand citizen, there is a belief now that, in addition, the dignity and pride of race which are his heritage must be safeguarded to him. The Maori child like the Maori

adult well may share the dominant idea of the New Zealand community that we are all New Zealanders ... but he must also be able to feel that such an idea does not imply an attempt to eliminate what is characteristically Maori any more than we should wish in our mixed racial community to eradicate the residual culture inheritance of the Scottish, Welsh, Dutch and other racial groups in our midst, even if it were possible. ...

14. An important recent work of this nature is by B. H. Watts, Lecturer in Education, University of Queensland, and J. D. Gallacher, Inspector of Schools Welfare Branch, N.T. Administration: *Report on an Investigation into the Curriculum and Teaching Methods used in Aboriginal Schools in the Northern Territory, 1964/66.* The writers list the major differences between European and Aboriginal outlook as being concepts relating to future-orientation, time, saving, work, competition and methods of learning. They point out that the Aboriginal was interested in 'being' not 'becoming'. Time, as divided into small segments, was of little significance to him and his way of life was co-operative rather than competitive. For the Aboriginal work 'was a part of the on-going and unified activity of living, not ... an activity occurring within a separate and rigorously defined portion of the day'. Aboriginal children were not encouraged to question, to explore ideas and to seek understanding. 'The pattern had already been determined and they were taught to accept this pattern.' They learned by rote, observation and imitation rather than by inductive/deductive thinking. Their white teachers are therefore faced with many basic problems in equipping them to understand and to cope with the wider world they are now entering.

See also, *Maori Policy in New Zealand*, by J. W. Warburton, 1967, in which the author compares and contrasts the problems of Maori and Aboriginal integration: 'The New Zealand experience suggests that the best way to help tribal people to live with a more advanced culture is not to destroy their links with the past. They need the sense of significance that can never be felt by those who participate in an alien dominant culture. If this sense of significance can be created by living in their own communities until they have the confidence to move out, then this would certainly seem to be the method to employ.'

374

# INDEX

Aborigines, 21, 22, 23, 36, 38, 39; assimilation and integration, 25, 34, 328, 371, 373; Neville policy on, 249, 252, 253; concept of authority, 144–5, 328; of death, 287; of God, 288; of sin, 85–6; of time, 21, 374; of virginity, 86, 288; of work, 261, 374; early development, 22–3; kinship system, 23, 283–4; racial preservation, 196; white man's view of, 24–6, 294–6, 336–8; see also population data

Aborigines Department, 256, 265, 276, 294; relations with missions, 314; see also Bray, F. I.; Middleton, S. G.; Neville, A. O.

Aborigines Protection Board (Queensland), 35

Aborigines Protection Board (Western Australia), 64, 66, 83, 108, 117, 345

Aborigines Protection Society, London, 30

aircraft crash and diamonds cargo, 303–5

air raids on Broome, 302, 305

Alcade, Father Inigo, 215, 217, 230

alcoholic priests, 171, 182

*Alice* (schooner), wreck of, 231

Alkaleno, Sebastian, 131

allotment scheme, 118, 179

Alphonse, Father; *see* Tachon, Father Alphonse

Ambrose (Aboriginal), 165, 166

Ambrose, Dom; *see* Janny, Dom Ambrose

Anabia, Caprio, 117

anthropological studies, 162, 194, 197, 220, 281–9, 334–6

Antonio, Mother; *see* O'Brien, Mother Antonio

assimilation policy, 249–51, 311, 317

atrocities against Aborigines, 29–30, 33, 48, 81–2; allegations concerning missions, 294

authority, Aboriginal view of, 144, 328

Bachmair, Father Thomas, 193, 200, 205, 237–8, 242, 245

Balgalai, Gabriel and Remigius, 237

Balgo Hills mission, 306, 322, 334, 372

*Balleli* (initiation rites), 104–5

ballot of Broome Catholics, 183

Bard people, 46, 104, 161, 178, 221

Bateman report, 309, 315, 322

Bates, Daisy, 138, 248; visit to Beagle Bay, 131, 131–5

Beagle Bay chosen for mission site, 56–7, 59; churches at, 237–8, 245, 362; conditions in 1890, 62–3; in 1895, 95–6; in 1904, 167; in 1906, 191; in 1908, 202; in 1918, 246–7; in 1928, 266; in 1966, 372; freehold

convict labour, 113, 341
Cook, Dr. Cecil, 271, 363, 365
co-operatives, 310, 333
Coppo, Bishop Ernest, 256–60, 262, 358
Cormar (William), 66
Cossack, 29, 42, 112
Courtney, Sister Mary Benedict, 189, 204
Cox, David, 255
Creagh, Father John, 241–4, 246, 256
Creagh, Monckton, 243
culture pearls, 326
curios, 155, 359–60
cyclones, 28, 148, 202, 213, 269, 358, 364
Cygnet Bay, 44, 48; mission at, 212–14, 358

Daly, John Cornelius (Brother Xavier), offers as postulant 57; pioneer journey, 57, 60, 62, 63; protectorship, 65–6; service at mission, 76, 78, 84, 121, 131; recall, 133, 140; illness and death, 145, 146
Daly, Sister Alphonsus, 278, 303, 323
Dampier, William, quoted, 58
D'Antoine, 'Frenchy', 161
Darwin, leprosy in, 270, 272
death, Aboriginal concept of, 287
demonic ceremonies, 283–4
Derby, 42, 56, 333; leprosy, 271, 277, 363; hospital for, 322, 333; nursing home for, 333; novitiate in, 331
*Diamant* (schooner), 146, 168
diamonds, lost in air crash, 304–5
dictionary of Njul Njul language, 170, 197
Disaster Bay mission, established, 72, 103; Trappist withdrawal, 121; bishop's visit, 133; Father Janny at, 146, 150–51, 157–61;

decline and closure, 164–5
discipline of children, 194; of Aboriginals, 141, 235
diver's paralysis, 207–8
Djiagween, Paddy, 191, 352, 354, 363
dormitory for women's protection, 106, 107, 131
'dreaming', 21, 24, 220, 282, 283, 285, 287
Drostë, Father William: arrives at mission, 233–4; present at Father Emo's death, 230, 238; practical advice, 238; journey to Beagle Bay, 239; and trained workers, 252, 253; anti-German sentiment, 256; and M. S. Hadley, 262; tours district, 264–5; death, 265
drovers, Aboriginal, 318
Drysdale River mission, 213, 214–23, 229, 290
Duff, Father James, 67
Dutch aircraft crash, 303–4
Dwyer, Father, leaves Trappist Order, 122

education, 149, 195–7; adult, 320; secondary, 333–4, 372; policies for, 247, 318, 337, 341; problems of, 51; *see also* evening classes; schools
Emo, Father Nicholas, begins mission, 114; in Broome, 98, 107, 112, 114, 140, 209, 270; in charge of Trappist withdrawal, 112, 120, 121, 124, 178; bishop's visit, 130, 131, 135; disputes with Pallottines, 138–9, 139, 144, 149, 155; Roth Commission, 176, 178, 181–4; leaves Trappist Order, 184; at Cygnet Bay, 212–15; takes families to Beagle Bay, 201, 215; at Drysdale River, 213, 214–20; at Lombadina, 222, 224–8; as

378